The Sense
of an Audience

Janice Carlisle

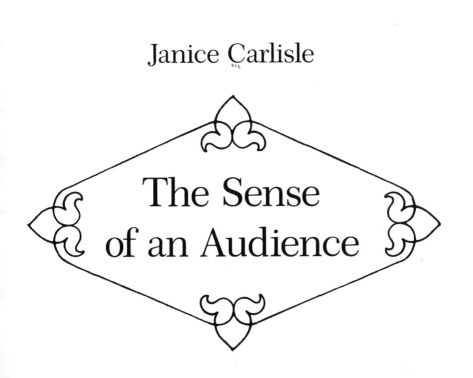

The Sense of an Audience

Dickens,
Thackeray, and George Eliot
at Mid-Century

The University of Georgia Press
Athens, Georgia

Set in 10 on 13 point Primer type
Printed in the United States of America
Design by Martyn Hitchcock

The ornaments in the chapter-openings are taken from
Florid Victorian Ornament by Charles Klimsch (New
York: Dover Publications).

The illustration on page 39 is from *Thackeray: The Uses
of Adversity* by Gordon N. Ray. Copyright © 1955 McGraw-
Hill Book Company. Used with permission of McGraw-Hill
Book Company.

Library of Congress Cataloging in Publication Data

Carlisle, Janice.
    The sense of an audience.

    Includes bibliographical references and index.

    1. English fiction—19th century—History and crit-
icism.   2. Literature and morals.   3. Dickens, Charles,
1812–1870—Criticism and interpretation.   4. Thackeray, William Makepeace, 1811–1863—Criticism and
interpretation.   5. Eliot, George, pseud., i.e. Marian
Evans, afterwards Cross, 1819–1880—Criticism and
interpretation.   I. Title.

PR878.M67C37   823'.8'09   81-435
ISBN 0–8203–0559–6   AACRI

To Joe

Contents

Illustrations

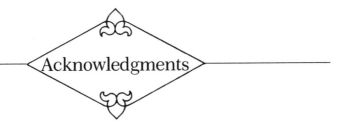

Acknowledgments

I wish to thank the University of Virginia for two summer research grants and for a fellowship from its Center for Advanced Studies. The editors of *Studies in the Novel* and *The Journal of Narrative Technique* kindly gave me permission to reprint portions of essays that originally appeared in their journals. The drawings from *Dombey and Son* have been reproduced courtesy of the Rare Book Department of the Olin Research Library, Cornell University; those from *Vanity Fair* and *Punch*, courtesy of the Rare Book Department of the University of Virginia Library.

Many teachers, colleagues, and friends have contributed to this study, and I will be able to mention only the chief among them. Jean Sudrann of Mount Holyoke College first introduced me to the diversity of Victorian fiction and its pleasures. Edgar Rosenberg, Francis Mineka, and Daniel Schwarz, all of Cornell University, advised me during my first attempt to deal with this subject. Edgar F. Shannon, Jr., of the University of Virginia, read several drafts and offered timely advice. To Anthony Winner and David Levin, also of the University of Virginia, I am particularly indebted, not only for reading the manuscript at various stages, but for many acts of friendship. I am also grateful to those graduate students at Virginia whose lively conversations have stimulated my thinking on this and other subjects. Elizabeth Mansfield offered her good cheer as well as her aid in the reproduction of the *Dombey and Son* illustrations. My work was also expedited by the unfailing cooperation of the librarians at the Mary Helen Cochran Library at Sweet Briar College, specifically Mary Hartman, John Jaffe, and Christopher Bean. For her willingness to share so many of her vacations with this project, affectionate thanks go to my stepdaughter, Adrianne. Finally, my husband, Joseph R. Roach, gave generously of his time to read and reread, advise and encourage; for all his efforts on my behalf, I owe a debt that the most elaborate of dedications could not repay.

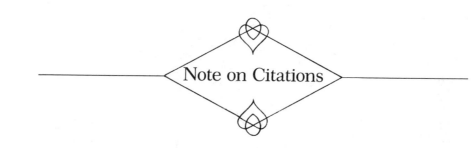

Note on Citations

The following editions have been cited in the text.

Carlyle

The Works of Thomas Carlyle. Edited by H. D. Traill. Centenary Edition. 30 vols. London: Chapman and Hall, 1896–99. *Critical and Miscellaneous Essays*, vols. 1–5, cited as C M E.

Dickens

Dombey and Son. Edited by Alan Horsman. Clarendon Dickens. Oxford: Clarendon, 1974.

The Letters of Charles Dickens. Edited by Madeline House, Graham Storey, and Kathleen Tillotson. Pilgrim Edition. 4 vols. Oxford: Clarendon, 1965–77. Cited as Pilgrim *Letters.*

The Letters of Charles Dickens. Edited by Walter Dexter. Nonesuch Dickens. 3 vols. Bloomsbury: Nonesuch Press, 1938.

Little Dorrit. Edited by Harvey Peter Sucksmith. Clarendon Dickens. Oxford: Clarendon, 1979.

The New Oxford Illustrated Dickens. London: Oxford University Press, 1951–59.

Oliver Twist. Edited by Kathleen Tillotson. Clarendon Dickens. Oxford: Clarendon, 1966.

The Speeches of Charles Dickens. Edited by K. J. Fielding. Oxford: Clarendon, 1960.

George Eliot

Essays of George Eliot. Edited by Thomas Pinney. London: Routledge and Kegan Paul, 1963.

The George Eliot Letters. Edited by Gordon S. Haight. 9 vols. New Haven: Yale University Press, 1954–78.

Middlemarch. Edited by Bert G. Hornback. Norton Critical Edition. New York: W. W. Norton, 1977.

The Mill on the Floss. Edited by Gordon S. Haight. Clarendon Edition. Oxford: Clarendon, 1980.

The Works of George Eliot. Cabinet Edition. 24 vols. Edinburgh: Blackwood and Sons, 1878–85.

Scott

Waverley Novels. Dryburgh Edition (reissue). 25 vols. Edinburgh: A. and C. Black, 1899. Cited by chapter and page.

Thackeray

The Letters and Private Papers of William Makepeace Thackeray. Edited by Gordon N. Ray. 4 vols. Cambridge: Harvard University Press, 1946.

The Oxford Thackeray. Edited by George Saintsbury. 17 vols. London: Oxford University Press, 1908.

Vanity Fair. Edited by Geoffrey Tillotson and Kathleen Tillotson. Boston: Houghton Mifflin, 1963.

Wordsworth

Lyrical Ballads 1798. Edited by W. J. B. Owen. London: Oxford University Press, 1967.

The Poetical Works of William Wordsworth. Edited by Ernest de Selincourt. 5 vols. Oxford: Clarendon, 1940–49.

The Prelude (1850). Edited by Ernest de Selincourt. Revised by Helen Darbishire. Oxford: Clarendon, 1959.

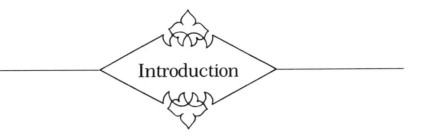

Introduction

Critical theorists have repeatedly warned us that every act of interpretation is determined by its often unacknowledged perspectives or
assumptions. This study of narrative technique has its origins in a
context that is unabashedly historical. Victorian fiction seen from the
vantage points offered by Freud or Marx would necessarily be a phenomenon unlike the one I describe here, for the authority whose perspective I have adopted is the Victorian novelist himself. After visiting
the Britannia Theatre in Hoxton, Dickens praised its proprietor in
terms which exactly convey his own aesthetic concerns and their relation to mid-Victorian culture; the owner's "sense of the responsibility
upon him to make the best of his audience, and to do his best for them,
is a highly agreeable sign of these times." Speaking as he was in 1860,
Dickens could have been summing up the work in which he and his
fellow-novelists had been engaged for the last two decades. The "sense
of an audience"—as Virginia Woolf would later call this characteristic
of Victorian fiction—did indeed determine the way in which the novelist saw both his art and his public role. This concern imbues works as
diverse and otherwise incomparable as *Hard Times* and *The Tenant of
Wildfell Hall.* Dissimilar though they were in temperament and training, writers like Dickens and Anne Brontë defined the purpose and
value of their work in relation to the needs of their readers. Even at this
distance in time, each Victorian novel is essentially, if not primarily,
an appeal, a gesture in the direction of the reader and his imaginative
capacity for assent and participation. Writers from G. M. Young to
Jerome Buckley, Walter Houghton, Kathleen Tillotson, and Richard
Altick have given us illuminating studies of the climate which encouraged the "moral aesthetic" and its influence on Victorian letters.
Taking this context as the framework for my critical inquiries, I have

attempted to answer a single question: how did the novelist's sense of moral responsibility to his audience affect the narrative form of his art?

To answer this question I have examined the fiction written by Dickens, Thackeray, and George Eliot during the central decades of the century, and I have chosen to discuss at length seven novels which demonstrate the range of their responses to the moral demands they made on their art. The reason for focusing on the mid-century is obvious. Although the form of the novel might be said to have arisen out of the moral debate between Richardson and Fielding, although the genre may be, as Lionel Trilling has claimed, the primary vehicle of the "moral imagination," at no other time in its history were its moral intentions and their implications so insistently at the forefront of its aesthetic. Earlier in the nineteenth century the escapist fiction of Newgate and the silver fork had been preeminent; later on, the achievement of more self-sufficient and purely formal excellences would become the chief desideratum. At mid-century, however, it would seem natural for a woman trying to overcome the death of her only son to turn to the writing of a novel about the greater suffering of the Manchester poor. No less typical was the "conversion" of a slightly raffish newspaper writer who had previously boasted of the strictly mercenary motives which impelled him to choose literature as a career. Gaskell's writing of *Mary Barton* and Thackeray's advocacy of Fun, Truth, and Love in the *Snob* papers are, like Dickens's response to the Hoxton theater, signs of the mid-century. During these years Dickens himself was at the height of his powers. Growing steadily more assured of his craft and gaining control over his extraordinary imaginative energy, he turned from the specific social issues that had concerned him in *Oliver Twist* and *Nicholas Nickleby* to more general and therefore more comprehensive moral issues. In *Little Dorrit*, for instance, he attacks the defunct institution of the debtor's prison so that he can embody his earlier reforming instincts as well as transcend their limitations. During the same period George Eliot was articulating her aesthetic principles in her *Westminster Review* essays; the late 1850s saw her both exploring her narrative gifts and establishing her hold on the public's attention before she turned to the more private and esoteric worlds of *The Mill on the Floss* and *Romola*. With the success of *Vanity Fair* and its Satirical-Moralist, Thackeray emerged into popularity after long years of relative obscurity. The mid-century offered him the satisfactions of a public art before he retreated into the solipsistic world of self-repetition, doubt, and disinclination that had always threatened to undermine his work. Novels like *Dombey and Son*, *The Newcomes*, and *Adam Bede* are the products of what Leslie Stephen nostalgically described as a "flowering time of genius," a time when individual talent could find sustenance and strength in the challenges set by its cultural context.

The novelist at mid-century lived in a world rife with divisions. Widespread commercial competition, religious controversy, political dissension, and class distinctions all provoked a commentator like Carlyle to declare divorce the keynote of contemporary society. To counter such tendencies, the novelist turned for his definition of morality to those principles of charity and common humanity that had constituted the central moral impulse of romanticism. He asked his readers to recognize, as Wordsworth puts it in "The Old Cumberland Beggar," that "we have all of us one human heart." The term *moral* did not mean for the Victorian novelist what the reader of Trollope's *Autobiography* might take it to imply—the "pure" and therefore safe treatment of unchallenging material. Rather it meant—as it did for the man who wrote *Can You Forgive Her?* and *The Vicar of Bullhampton*—all those considerations that allow men not only to tolerate life together, but to create out of the inescapable fact of their communal nature a life that is humane and responsible, a life that might even be, in rare moments, a genuine communion. For Dickens and Thackeray and George Eliot that ideal was and remained the central moral bearing of their art. It may seem facile to reduce the impressive range and diversity of their work, let alone of their minds and psyches, to the confines of one aesthetic orientation. Yet the fact that Victorian fiction at its best seems to transcend the simplicity of the moral aesthetic on which it depends is itself a result of the advantages which that aesthetic offered the novelist, not a contradiction of its assumptions or a proof of its irrelevance. The mid-century conception of moral life encouraged variety even as it invited the recognition of similarity. Its very simplicity offered the novelist the opportunity for subtle and widely differentiated elaborations of its basic tenets. Its cogency proffered reassurance at a time when the novel was still a slightly suspect form. If this aesthetic served as a common basis for the fiction of these three writers, its very generality granted them the freedom of their individual differences. Their first readers responded to their work by isolating and defining their distinctive imaginative modes, their diverse subjects, and their individualizing attitudes. It will be the business of later chapters to distinguish among their various approaches to the morality of narrative form. But even then we would do well not to overlook the mutuality of their concerns.

Because the starting-point of this study has been the intentions and aims which the novelists themselves articulated—though I hope its insights are not strictly limited to the confines of those intentions—I have often turned for evidence to the comments on their art in their letters, essays, or speeches. The best evidence for such intentions is, however, found in the texts of the novels themselves, and my method has been to locate the distinguishing narrative techniques of a novel and to explore the kinds of moral demands which such techniques presume to satisfy or the response which they presume to elicit. When the narrator of *Vanity Fair* turns to speak to the supercilious mock-reader he calls "JONES, who reads this book at his Club," we are witnessing his fear that his description of Amelia's schooldays will be dismissed as silly. When the author embellishes his text with a woodcut depicting this hostile reader even before he offers a drawing of Amelia herself, we are witnessing a preoccupation with his audience that might be termed obsessive. That it has both a place and function within the text, however, is clear. The comment is directed not at Jones, but at the reader who is not Jones, who is not at his club. By admitting that Jones would find his details "foolish, trivial, twaddling, and ultra-sentimental," the narrator is asking for quite other responses—perhaps that the reader find such details amusingly apposite, telling in their very triviality. The Victorian novelist's appeals to his reader may either be as explicit and direct as this dismissal of a mock-reader or as subtle and indirect as the handling of the pace of a narrative or its use of figurative language. In general, however, mid-century fiction developed a coherent tradition of narrative techniques that all bear witness to the novelist's moral concerns. They range from direct address to the reader and passages of obvious commentary to present-tense narration and the widespread use of the narrator as a mediating presence. Although many of these conventions were adopted from earlier writers, they were elaborated with an energy and used to achieve ends that are, again, distinctive signs of the times. Behind each of these conventions is the desire to establish morally effective relations between the fictive life of the novel and its reader.

It is a commonplace of literary history that Victorian novelists inherited the romantic belief in the power of the sympathetic imagination. Their confidence in their ability to affect their audience rests on their faith in the reader's innate capacity to feel with and for the characters in their stories. What has not been adequately recognized is how that process was supposed to work, how a particular narrative technique might be expected to achieve a particular effect. My first chapter, therefore, treats this issue by examining the ways in which

"JONES, who reads this book at his Club," chapter I, *Vanity Fair*

Dickens, Thackeray, and George Eliot conceived of the relation between a story and its audience, as well as some of the principal ways in
which they felt they could encourage and strengthen their readers'
imaginative capacities. These issues are, logically enough, most explicitly addressed in the fiction written early in their separate attempts
to accommodate their individual talents to the interests of a wide public audience—in works like *A Christmas Carol*, the *Scenes of Clerical
Life*, and, the culmination of Thackeray's long journalistic apprentice-
ship, *Vanity Fair*. Later chapters treat narrative technique in the wider
context of larger issues such as a novel's plot, style, genre, or topicality.
As varied as these discussions may be, however, they all seek to answer the same central question: how does technique attempt to create
and determine the reader's relation to the text? Although Victorian
novelists were not always certain that reading is an enlightening activity, their work rests on the conviction that George Eliot articulated:
"Art is the nearest thing to life; it is a mode of amplifying experience
and extending our contact with our fellowmen beyond the bounds of
our personal lot."

If the Victorian novelist's sense of his audience was responsible for
the narrative relations that he strove to create between the reader and
his work, it extended to his recognition of the literary culture which he
shared with his audience. Indeed, one of the clearest indications of the
impact of the novelist's moral intentions on his art is his handling of
the narrative models offered by other writers or by other times. George
Eliot's late entry into the profession of novel writing meant that she
had not only to satisfy the demands which her audience made on her
art, but also to establish her individuality in response to a well-defined
body of conventions which her contemporaries had already created;
my full-length treatment of the *Scenes* is the story of that dual purpose.
Yet an even more telling context for a discussion of Victorian fiction
and its moral forms is that offered by certain key figures of an earlier
generation. In his well-known essay on Scott, Walter Bagehot explained that neither the works of one's peers nor the literary monu-
ments of a distant age have the kind of profound impact that the
achievements of the previous generation are capable of exerting: "The
generation which is really most influenced by a work of genius is com-
monly that which is still young when the first controversy respecting

its merits arises; with the eagerness of youth they read and re-read; their vanity is not unwilling to adjudicate: in the process their imagination is formed; the creations of the author range themselves in the memory; they become part of the substance of the very mind." I have repeatedly focused on three such figures of artistic authority and accomplishment—Wordsworth, Scott, and Carlyle—because their work illuminates, either by comparison or contrast, the distinctive qualities of Victorian narrative technique. Like the Wizard of the North, the poet and the social critic were writers who had tales to tell, and it was precisely in their roles as storytellers that the later novelists found in all three what Harold Bloom would call artistic "fathers," precursors who were not, however, sources of anxiety, but occasions for creative appropriation. Commenting specifically on one of these figures, George Eliot had said, "There is hardly a superior or active mind of this generation that has not been modified by Carlyle's writings." "The reading of *Sartor Resartus*," she continued, was an "epoch" in the mental "history" of even those who disagreed with his ideas. Carlyle's relation to works such as *Dombey and Son* and even *The Newcomes* often pertains less to matters of social or moral philosophy than to formal considerations. Accordingly, my first chapter begins with an examination of *Sartor Resartus*, that odd amalgamation of novel, tract, autobiography, and fantasy which in the 1830s foretold the central assumptions of mid-century narrative technique.

Although there is no doubt that the potential for narrative relations between the reader and the text underlies the Victorian novelist's moral definition of his art, this assumption raises some daunting, if not insurmountable problems. It depends, quite clearly, on a conjunction of morality and aesthetics that is in itself an eminently Victorian quality. Most modern readers, however, are suspicious of such thinking. They tend to agree with Henry James that "questions of art are questions . . . of execution; questions of morality are quite another affair." Yet if the Victorian novelist and his original audience complicated those issues by combining them, they viewed neither questions of art nor questions of morality in any simpleminded fashion. The novelist could never be certain that his work would have the kind of effect which he desired. Readers and reviewers were constantly offering examples of intentions mistaken or ignored—as the picture of Jones in the first chapter of *Vanity Fair* attests. Except in the case of *The Virginians*, the exception by which I hope to prove the rule, these novelists continued to write as if there were a direct and vital relation between a novel and its reader's moral life. For the novelist at mid-century the moral aesthetic was clearly a kind of faith. He acted as if his potential impact were a verifiable phenomenon; he hoped, by acting as if it were real, that he might have a chance to make it real. In discussing the effect of three novelists' moral ideals on the narrative form of their fiction, I have often adopted their viewpoint by writing as if such moral relations between reader and text are indisputable, but I have no wish to suggest that there are timeless and universal verities that make such an assumption the authentic way either to read or to write fiction. That question, of course, is left for each reader to prove upon his own pulses. Even if a belief in the moral power of art is a fiction, however, it is nonetheless the premise on which the novelist based his art. For the professional novelist at mid-century, duty to one's audience and its needs was as profound a certainty as he might be able to discover. Faith in one's readers was inextricably linked to faith in one's art and in one's world. Keeping an eye on his readers (as the novelist's concern with his audience is sometimes crudely described) distracted him less often than it provided him with a more sharply defined sense of his proper subject. The bond between novelist and public was as complex as it was pervasive. This marriage was not always a happy one—not without its risks and strain and cost, not without its failures and ruptures. But it was the union that made creation possible.

The Victorian identification of morality and aesthetics rests, in turn, on an even more comprehensive and significant assumption about the relation between art and life. Although the novelist was always careful not to proclaim that the two have the same ontological status—he would explain that art should "seem like" life or approximate its textures—he was clearly gratified by the responses of precisely those readers who reacted to his work as if it were reality itself. Yet simple generalizations on this issue are particularly misleading. The same public which demanded mimetic art also preferred to set the most minutely detailed of realistic paintings—and even their mirrors and photographs—in the most elaborately ornate of frames. Clearly the relation between art and life for the Victorian was no simple matter of coextension or duplication. Indeed, in the following chapters I have repeatedly found myself describing a highly sophisticated narrative frame that contributes in sometimes complex or even paradoxical ways to the "reality" of the picture it contains. Modern readers, once again, often find something either charmingly or dangerously naive about Victorian assumptions. U. C. Knoepflmacher begins his study of nineteenth-century fiction by claiming that a novel is a "feigned reality," not to be confused with "fact." Ever since his work on Dickens, J. Hillis Miller has insisted that a novel is a "verbal copy of a reality [which] presupposes the distancing for the readers of the reality copied." His recent deconstructionist tendencies have simply intensified his conviction on this point. In a recent article on narrative, he has reversed George Eliot's dictum: "Story-telling, the putting into language of man's 'experience' of his life, is in its writing or reading a hiatus in that experience." I have no doubt that in his darkest moments the Victorian novelist would have recognized the force of that statement. He might have looked at his career, as Scott did in a passage of his diary, and wondered about the effects of "this wielding of the unreal trowel," but such musings would have been a denial of the principles which were in large part the source of his creative energies. Although he could often sustain the correlation between life and art only by admitting how inconclusive, uncertain, and unsatisfying both are, the novelist wrote as if his art were intimately connected to life both in its mimetic capacities and in its potential effect on his reader. Throughout this study, I have accepted that assumption so that I might gauge its formative effect on narrative technique. In this respect I have followed the practice of critics like Juliet McMaster and W. J. Harvey, readers who have chosen to chart the relations between life and art hypothesized in Victorian fiction rather than deny their possibility.

From this perspective Victorian fiction emerges as an art of mediation; its form is literally a *via media* whose goal is reconciliation. The identification of morality and art is the primary integration from which others necessarily follow. Both Mill and Carlyle pointed out that the reconciliation of opposites is the end and aim of human life, and the novel imitates that process at both its most difficult and most successful junctures. For Thackeray, such reconciliations are typically a precarious balance; for George Eliot, a comprehensive and holistic vision; for Dickens, an interpenetration wrought by dizzying imaginative flights and conjunctions. In some cases, the mediations sought are threatened as soon as achieved; in others, they are ideals never to be substantiated. Nevertheless, they remain a motive for creative activity. If the Victorians had lost a clear view of providential design, the order of the universe mirrored by a union at the end of a novel, they still believed that they could forge, by force of will and imagination, a marriage of opposing tendencies. To a surprising extent, the novelist managed to bring together, if only temporarily or tentatively, forces that have often seemed stubbornly irreconcilable: the individual and the community, society and nature, the imaginatively true and the empirically real. The form of the novel allowed its creator to explore private anguish—the blacking factory, the indifference of Isaac Evans or Mrs. Brookfield—in a manner relevant to a reading public that could have no sense of its source. The novelist could reconcile past patterns of cultural integrity with the pressures of the present, man's longings and his inevitably limited or defeated attempts at fulfillment. Frequently, too, the expansive form of the Victorian novel moved beyond the limits of narrative itself. The novelist focused on what Dickens called the "marked stop in the whirling wheel of life." The story is allowed to "pause a little," and contemplation and vision are conjoined to process and action. To its contemporary readers, the novel offered a social mediation. One reviewer called *Vanity Fair* a "common friend," an imaginative meeting-ground on which men, isolated from each other, could be united. The pressing need for such communal expressions of emotion explains, for instance, the enthusiasm with which a "whole nation" fell to weeping over the death of Paul Dombey. To Tolstoy a Dickens character seemed a "bond of union between man in America and man in Petersburg." Now that St. Petersburg has become Leningrad, we might question the ability of a Victorian novel to accomplish such stunning feats of mediation, but Tolstoy's claim is an accurate although exaggerated statement of its reach, if not its grasp. By a paradox that reflects the satisfying complexity and achievement of its form, the Victorian novel, in striving to fulfill the moral requirements imposed upon it, attains the end that Coleridge attributes to the "synthetic and magical power" of the imagination: "the balance or reconciliation of opposite or discordant qualities."

Wordsworth had spoken for his literary generation when he compared the new world conceived by the romantic poet to a wedding of the mind with nature: "A balance, an ennobling interchange / Of action from without and from within; / The excellence, pure function, and best power / Both of the object seen, and eye that sees." The Victorian novelist desired a more modest consummation of the marriage between the artist and his public, but the terms of both unions are much the same. The reading of a novel would be an "ennobling interchange of action" that would elicit the best qualities of both the reader and the narrative persona of the novelist. As Dickens put it in his characteristically more humble fashion, he would do his "best" to make "the best" of his reader. A later novelist like James might speak of the "dead wall" between life and the "house of fiction," but the generation of novelists who preceded him strove to bring their readers into that house without causing them to lose sight of the "spreading field, the human scene" beyond it. For the novelist at mid-century, narrative forms were, at least potentially, "hinged doors opening straight upon life."

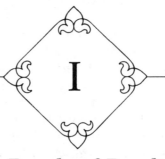

The Bonds of Reading
Mid-Century Aims and Ideals

"Yes, Friends," elsewhere observes the Professor, "not our Logical, Mensurative faculty, but our Imaginative one is King over us. . . . The Understanding is indeed thy window . . . but Fantasy is thy eye."

—Carlyle, *Sartor Resartus*

When Diogenes Teufelsdröckh declared the imagination king, he defined its sovereign power in a fashion particularly useful to the generation of novelists who came after him. Although Carlyle's allegiance to a transcendent reality is always clear, his recognition of time and space as its vesture lends a consistently social orientation to his thinking. In less abstract and more specifically personal terms than either Coleridge or the German transcendentalists whom both he and Coleridge read, Carlyle views the "synthetic power" of the imagination as a capacity which reveals the hitherto unacknowledged correspondences between subject and object. The human eye sees in the physical world the facts of human life. Individuals who stand at the furthest reaches of time and space, history and geography, are not "detached, separated" (p. 56). Time is the weaver of a great garment in which each man becomes part of a "living indivisible whole" (pp. 194–96). Teufelsdröckh's first outcry as he emerges from the Center of Indifference bespeaks this new, holistic vision: "With other eyes, too, could I now look upon my fellow man. . . . O my Brother, my Brother" (pp. 150–

51). Teufelsdröckh learns that language is a vast construct of metaphors; all communication, a matter of articulating similarities and continuities. Life itself is a "bottomless, shoreless flood of Action," a process of "perpetual metamorphoses" (p. 56) which attest to the organic interrelation of apparently disparate elements. Imagination is the eye capable of perceiving the relations that constitute the whole. Although the Victorian novelist would have little reason to adopt the grand scale on which Carlyle proclaimed such exalted insights, he based his art on precisely such a conception of the imagination.

This fact, if not its implications, was often attested to by the novelist and his contemporary readers. Thackeray's fascination with mirrors and their frequent appearance in *Vanity Fair* bespeak his interest in an art which identifies the perceiver and the object of his perception. Similarly, John Forster's defense of Dickens's "humour" recalls the more lofty terminology of *Sartor Resartus*: "To perceive relations in things which are not apparent generally, is one of those exquisite properties of humour . . . which bring us all upon the level of a common humanity."[1] E. S. Dallas, reviewing *Adam Bede* (1859) for the *Times*, made much the same point when he explained that Thackeray and George Eliot differ from all previous novelists because they ask the reader to recognize either their own strengths or their own weaknesses in the characters they portray. Their works declare, along with Teufelsdröckh, "O my Brother, my Brother." George Eliot offered the fullest explanation of the connections generated by the imagination when she commented on the moral dimensions of art in "The Natural History of German Life": "The greatest benefit we owe to the artist, whether painter, poet, or novelist, is the extension of our sympathies. Appeals founded on generalizations and statistics require a sympathy ready-made, a moral sentiment already in activity; but a picture of human life such as a great artist can give, surprises even the trivial and the selfish into that attention to what is apart from themselves, which may be called the raw material of moral sentiment" (*Essays*, p. 270). Even as the century advanced and earlier aesthetic theories were called into doubt, this ideal would continue to exert its force. Indeed, chapter 80 of *Middlemarch* (1871–72) contains the most moving, even ecstatic example of such imaginative powers. When Dorothea looks from her window at dawn toward the light on the horizon, she sees not only the world of human activity, not only the man with a burden on his back, but also her relation to the figures in that world. The "bending sky" and "pearly light" join in a wedding of heaven and earth that mirrors the communion of human beings (p. 544). Like a rising sun, Dorothea's sympathetic imagination bestows this new light, and the dream vision of Bunyan's pilgrim has become the waking reality of Dorothea's life. The great garment that Teufelsdröckh envisions is now George Eliot's web. To perceive the bonds which constitute its texture is the province of imagination.

As the visionary quality of this image suggests, such a definition of the imagination is part of the romantic heritage which the older Carlyle shared with a younger generation of novelists, but it was a legacy significantly modified to meet the moral demands that the Victorian writer made on both his life and his art. In the passage from the "Defence of Poetry" which George Eliot's well-known definition echoes, Shelley had justified calling the imagination "the great instrument of moral good" by explaining that it encourages "a going out of our own nature, and an identification of ourselves with the beautiful which exists in thought, action, or person, not our own. A man, to be greatly good, must imagine intensely and comprehensively; he must put himself in the place of another and of many others." If we were to replace Shelley's choice of the beautiful as the object of perception with an emphasis on the real, the ordinary, and the commonplace, the passage would outline the moral basis both of Carlyle's grudging respect for the "poor, miserable, hampered, despicable Actual" (s r, p. 156) and of the novelist's insistence on the mimetic authenticity of his art. Yet these writers expanded the purview of romantic ideals in another, even more distinctive fashion. Hazlitt had conceived of the imagination as the "intuitive perception of the hidden analogies of things," and Keats had written of the bonds which imagination creates between the disparate realms of the human observer and a sparrow, but for both writers this power resided either in the work of art itself or in the man of unusual sensibility. Yet Carlyle and the Victorian novelist insisted that such capacities belong equally to the artist and his audience. What had been the exclusive preserve of genius became the responsibility of every common reader. What Teufelsdröckh sees, theoretically at least, is a vision available to everyone who will simply look.[2]

In *Sartor Resartus* the demand that the reader open his eyes is the moral imperative motivating Carlyle's eccentric narrative techniques. Although the Editor hopes to create "a firm Bridge for British travellers," a bridge that will span the gap between their own experience and the alien world of the Professor's wisdom, he knows that it will stand only if it is built with his reader's help. It can bind together a "little band of Friends," it can transcend the abyss of chaos, only if each reader is willing to journey across it. Without such collaboration, the six paper bags containing notes on Teufelsdröckh's life cannot yield even the "sketchy, shadowy fugitive likeness of him [that] may, by unheard-of efforts, partly of intellect, partly of imagination, on the side of Editor and of Reader, rise up between them" (p. 62). The almost comic complexity of the Editor's syntax suggests the difficulty and originality of his task. Although he knows that his wayward motions and tortuous logic may create an audience of bewildered, even irritated readers, he confers on the reader's imagination a primacy and significance that would become the keynote of Victorian narrative form. Feeble as he admits his own attempts to be, the Editor asks, "May not our own poor rope-and-raft Bridge, in your passings and repassings, be mended in many a point, till it grows quite firm, passable even for the halt?" The reader's perception, not the Editor's pathetic diligence, constructs firmer, more certain connections among the Editor, his potential audience, and the "new promised country," the "far region of Poetic Creation and Palingenesia" which they seek to discover (pp. 213–14). The creative role of the writer is, therefore, only part of a more extensive process in which the audience's imagination is an equally indispensable agent.

Novelists as diversely gifted as Dickens, Thackeray, and George Eliot—as well as others, such as Trollope, Gaskell, Kingsley, and Charlotte Brontë—all adopted this focus on the reader as an essential aesthetic principle. Like the reader of *Sartor Resartus*, the reader of *Vanity Fair* or *Little Dorrit* ultimately bears the burden of perceiving the connections that will grant fiction its status as a moral art. Narration, according to these novelists, is a mutual activity, including both author and reader, a process which reveals new grounds of comparison and coordination as it invites the reader to experience what Shelley had called a "going out of [his] own nature." The predominant subject of Victorian fiction—community, man in his social relation to other men—is simply, then, the thematic equivalent of its formal characteristics. The lesson of sympathy and common humanity that the novelist professed is, necessarily, a means as well as an end; it can be a goal only if it is also the process by which the reader apprehends and actually experiences its validity. Reading, as Teufelsdröckh says of language, is a matter of metaphor. It demands the fulfillment of a simple and irreducible requirement: it must be a process in which the reader sees the analogy between himself and what he reads. In actual practice this ideal might prove as elusive as it was essential. But unless the reader puts "himself in the place of another and of many others," his reading has neither moral relevance nor moral power.

Although no Victorian novelist ever formulated this principle or its ramifications in any theoretical or abstract fashion, its centrality as an unspoken assumption and its power as a source of moral justification are evident whenever the novelist depicts the storyteller in action. Three specific and otherwise dissimilar episodes from their fiction speak to this point. Whether the incident involves Mrs. Pipchin lecturing Paul in *Dombey and Son* (1846–48), or Janet Dempster listening to Tryan's confession in "Janet's Repentance" (1858), or Beatrix reading a counterfeit *Spectator* paper in *Henry Esmond* (1852), the moral value of the story depends on the same analogical process. In these episodes the storytellers achieve varying degrees of success, yet in all three instances characters serve as "readers" to demonstrate what their creators believe to be the essential, unvarying criteria by which any act of narration is to be judged.

A comic contretemps early in *Dombey and Son* depicts exactly those moralistic shortcomings which Dickens's own work seeks to avoid even as it presents a model of the process which all storytelling entails. The frail Paul Dombey has been sent to Brighton so that he can benefit from Mrs. Pipchin's "child-quelling," a system meant to foster by denial. Paul is not a tractable child, and one of his more delightful confrontations with this Gorgon occurs when she tries, quite unsuccessfully, to tame his wayward impulses. Like Pip after him, Paul asks too many questions. When he wants to know what a "bold-faced hussy" is, Mrs. Pipchin responds, "Never you mind, Sir."

"Remember the story of the little boy that was gored to death by a mad bull for asking questions."

"If the bull was mad," said Paul, "how did *he* know that the boy had asked questions? Nobody can go and whisper secrets to a mad bull. I don't believe that story."

"You don't believe it, Sir?" repeated Mrs. Pipchin, amazed.

"No," said Paul.

"Not if it should happen to have been a tame bull, you little Infidel?" said Mrs. Pipchin.

As Paul had not considered the subject in that light, and had founded his conclusions on the alleged lunacy of the bull, he allowed himself to be put down for the present. But he sat turning it over in his mind, with such an obvious intention of fixing Mrs. Pipchin presently, that even that hardy old lady deemed it prudent to retreat until he should have forgotten the subject. (p. 104)

Mrs. Pipchin's story is, of course, a fine example of how not to point a moral or adorn a tale.

Here Dickens clearly comments on the limitations of Evangelical modes of sugaring the pill. Throughout the first half of the nineteenth century, Evangelical writers had inveighed against the dangers of reading novels even as they had used the weapon of narrative in the battle for the true faith. Dickens, of course, was well aware of the ubiquity of the "moral" tracts written by Hannah More and her Victorian successors.[3] As he punningly points out, Mrs. Pipchin is an "exemplary dragon" because she is continually recounting exemplary tales or reciting "early readings" which prove, among other nonsensical doctrines, that a sniffing child is surely on his way to hell (pp. 110, 103). Dickens's depiction of her discomfort in this instance, like numerous direct statements by Thackeray and George Eliot, is an obvious attack on stories told to elucidate a specific lesson or propagate religion based on the Old Testament emphasis on law. The moral drawn by Mrs. Pipchin exaggerates the inherent weaknesses of all such Evangelical lessons. "Do Not Ask Questions" is a rule set down for the comfort of teachers and parents rather than the mental or spiritual development of the child, and Evangelical tales were notorious for treating the poor or the young, their presumed audiences, in precisely this self-serving fashion. Yet the shortcomings of this cautionary anecdote go beyond its moralizing. It has no mimetic authenticity; in real life no one would dare whisper secrets to a mad bull. Paul can see no relation between himself and the boy in the tale; he cannot put "himself in the place of" this stereotypical little sinner. The story forces him into a posture of distrust. Not at all reformed, he actually becomes a "little Infidel," an unbeliever. In short, Mrs. Pipchin is gored by her own cock-and-bull story. The exemplary tale meant to discourage Paul's questioning simply leads to further and more imponderable questions.

Thackeray, surprisingly enough, offers a more optimistic, if typically circumscribed instance of storytelling. In one of his futile attempts to force Beatrix to denounce her marital ambitions and recognize his claims on her heart, Henry composes a counterfeit *Spectator* essay and places it on her breakfast table. In it she finds a fictionalized version of one of her own earlier embarrassments, an amusing anecdote about Saccharissa, a "heartless worldly jilt" who cannot remember the name of one of her more ostentatiously eligible and attentive suitors (13:347). Beatrix reads the paper, sees herself and her experience in the tale, but refuses to change her ways. She becomes, finally, not Henry Esmond's humble and loving wife, but the Pretender's mistress. Considering Thackeray's denial of any but the most limited of moral developments—"we alter very little," as he says in *Pendennis* (12:766)—we would not expect the *Spectator* essay to effect any grand reformation. Yet Beatrix is not untouched by her reading of this anecdote. At first angered and outraged by Henry's trick, she eventually becomes chastened by his vision of herself. The argument she has with Henry leads, finally, to one of the few moments of tenderness they share. With her usual defenses at least partially overcome, she can admit that she feels with Henry the loneliness and dissatisfaction that he sees as the curse of the Castlewood family. Like the reader of one of Thackeray's novels, she experiences the common humanity that she shares with the man who has told her a story. The *Spectator* paper does for her exactly what Mrs. Pipchin's ridiculous tale of the mad bull cannot do for Paul.

Exactly the same analogical process, in a more complete and reassuring form, takes place in the last of George Eliot's *Scenes of Clerical Life*. By the latter half of the 1850s the assumptions with which the Victorian novelist justified the moral value of his work had been repeatedly propounded and illustrated. George Eliot's own *Westminster Review* essays had strenuously defended the seriousness of a popular art. Significantly, however, she felt compelled in her first collection of tales to examine the process on which such values depend and to present it as an ideal capable of incarnation in even the most mundane of domestic situations. Indeed, "Janet's Repentance" might stand as an emblem of the distinctive moral orientation of the novel at mid-century. Like a Victorian version of Scheherazade, its main character is quite literally saved by a story—not because she creates such a life-giving tale, but because she listens to one. If George Eliot could never be certain that her own novels would have the same effect, at least here she could embody the ideal to which they continually aspired.

Janet Dempster is a character much in need of moral reform. Her complacency has been eroded by squalid marital disputes which are aggravated by both her husband's drinking and her own recourse to the bottle. George Eliot does not disregard the unattractive qualities of her basically sympathetic heroine. Janet's endless whining complaints are the result of a debilitating egoism, and her addiction to alcohol is an attempt to deny her relationship to others by blotting out consciousness. Finally there is the inevitable crisis; late one night, Janet's drunken husband locks her out of the house. Taking shelter at a neighbor's, she seeks the aid of the Rev. Mr. Tryan, the Evangelical cleric whose piety she has earlier scorned and ridiculed. Now she looks forward to the luxury of unburdening herself to a kindred soul. Significantly, though, confession offers Janet little comfort. She requests words of wisdom or counsel from Tryan—"I thought you could tell me something that would help me" (2:222)—but he makes a veiled and unimpressive reference to his own "evil passions," and then offers God as the answer to her difficulties. Janet rejects God as literally too remote: "I can feel no trust in God. He seems always to have left me to myself" (2:225). The two characters have reached an impasse. Conventional religion cannot provide Janet with the solace she seeks, and her attempt to alter the downward course of her life by admitting her faults has led only to a new accession of self-pity and despair.

At this point, however, Tryan chooses to put aside the role of counselor and assume the role of storyteller. His pity for Janet forces him to renounce the impersonal or elevated stance of the priest. Instead of listening to a confession, he offers one himself. Because "sympathy is but a living again through our own past in a new form" (2:226), Tryan hesitatingly accepts the painful duty of recounting to Janet the story of his earlier sins and subsequent conversion. The story is a luridly melodramatic tale about a young man who seduces an innocent girl and, years later, finds her dead and prostituted body on a London street. Yet Tryan's evident sincerity, the emotion he conveys in his attitude and voice, convince Janet of the story's authenticity. Like the image of Teufelsdröckh conjured up by Carlyle's Editor and Reader, Tryan's tale is an idea, a "poor ghost . . . made flesh" (2:236), and its impact on Janet is profound. Instead of hearing "mere vague words" of wisdom, she apprehends the "facts" of Tryan's suffering and the source of his faith (2:227). With this new knowledge she can begin the slow process of her own similar redemption.[4] The excessive conventionality of Tryan's story, an obvious characteristic that both Lewes and Blackwood deplored, suggests perhaps that George Eliot conceived of it as a recognizable fiction-within-a-fiction. Its form and function parallel those of Mrs. Pipchin's anecdote and Henry's forged essay, tales which both clearly have their source in recognizably literary traditions. In its effect on its audience, Tryan's tale, furthermore, might be taken as a paradigm for the Victorian novel. What Tryan does for Janet, the novelist would do for his readers, though it is distinctly a result of George Eliot's background and personal concerns that the religious context of this act of narration is as palpable as it is.

As these three episodes demonstrate, any act of narration is motivated by the same moral impulse: to set all three of its agents, reader and narrator and character, in analogical relation to each other, to formulate correspondences that the reader's imagination is encouraged to perceive and re-create as he reads. Unless the "narrator"—Mrs. Pipchin, Tryan, or Henry—can persuade the "reader"—Paul, Janet, or Beatrix—to see his or her connection with the character depicted, the story can have no meaning. Narration reveals this connection in precisely the fashion that Trollope described when he noted that a novel can "teach" most effectively "by representing to [its] readers characters like themselves,—or to which they *might liken* themselves."[5] Reading, then, is a process in which the subject is invited to identify through sympathy with the object of his perception. Thackeray heads the *Spectator* paper in *Henry Esmond* with a motto from Horace which makes exactly this point: *Mutato nomine de te Fabula narratur* (p. 344). The ambiguity of the seventeenth-century translation which he gives along with the original—"thyself the moral of the Fable see"— is even more telling: the reader both sees and is what he perceives. The novelist, of course, does not indiscriminately invite the reader to recognize his own story in those of all the characters he depicts. On the contrary, he tests the reader's moral capacities and encourages their development by inviting him to take this particular kind of interest in one character rather than another, just as Janet is encouraged to identify with the younger Tryan rather than with the conventionally melodramatic figure of his prostituted sweetheart. Yet the bond established between reader and character is only one of the essential analogies that must be created if narration is to fulfill its potential for moral relevance. If the reader perceives the correspondence between himself and at least one other agent in the narration, be it either one of the characters or the narrator, that analogy will inevitably lead to the creation of yet further connections. Janet Dempster is, at least in part, convinced of her similarity to the young Tryan because she has previously felt that a bond of suffering identifies her with the man who tells her about him. Conversely, Mrs. Pipchin's story fails because Paul knows that she is his adversary in a debate, rather than his fellow sinner or fellow sufferer; her authoritarian badgering marks her distance from him. Beatrix's experience reveals yet a third possibility. Because she immediately sees herself in the character depicted to her, she comes to recognize her relation to Henry, the "narrator." Naturally such correspondences can rarely exist when the story opens. They are, rather, the conditions that develop as the story is being told. Typically, the novelist begins by assuming a lack of sympathy between character, reader, and narrator; they are strangers, ignorant of one another, presumably even indifferent to each other. By the end of the story, however, new bonds have been formed. The "perpetual metamorphoses" of narration, as Teufelsdröckh might call them, create "organic filaments" which define an imaginative community composed of the storyteller, his audience, and his subject. The bonds of reading are, therefore, not unlike the bonds of matrimony. Indeed, as the following discussion of *Little Dorrit* suggests, marriage, the Victorian novelist's favorite image of community, becomes an eloquent metaphor for narration in his fiction.

Although such a description of this process and its goal of inter-linked analogies may seem too schematic to express the subtlety and richness of novels like *Vanity Fair* and *Bleak House*, it does convey the Victorian novelist's uniquely holistic ideal of the morality of his art. Even the often elaborate and sophisticated narrative forms discussed in these chapters can be attributed to this relatively simple conception. Yet if this ideal and its embodiment in a work like "Janet's Repentance" are both fairly straightforward and simple matters, the examples of Mrs. Pipchin and Henry Esmond and Carlyle's Editor all suggest the difficulty of attaining such bonds and their tenuousness once attained. To the novelist their theoretical desirability might be one thing, their practical achievement quite another. For this reason novels like *Little Dorrit* and *Henry Esmond* typically test as often as they uphold this ideal by measuring it against the rigorous demands of the life they por-tray. Just as egoism, the principal moral disease of Victorian fiction, tests and qualifies the romantic virtue of sympathy, the characteristic narrative techniques of these novels frequently restrict as well as af-firm the functions of the analogizing powers of the imagination. The Victorian novelist, as he emerges from the following studies of his nar-rative technique, often resembles the melancholy figure of Henry Es-mond, the man who courts failure in his attempts to do good and who achieves only severely limited satisfaction for his pains. Yet if we are to understand why this configuration of narrative agents, though so often compromised, was a central premise of Victorian fiction, we need to examine some of its more fundamental implications.

This circle of linked analogies was essential for one simple reason. It proposed a potential resolution of the duality that persistently threat-ened the moral relevance of the novelist's work, the age-old opposition of life and art. Carlyle's early attacks on the froth and trickery of the fashionable novel, fulminating versions of Plato's more temperate ar-gument, had claimed that the distinction between art and life wholly invalidates fiction. Because art is not life, because fiction is not real, it is necessarily false: "Fiction, while the feigner of it knows that he is feigning, partakes, more than we suspect, of the nature of *lying*." The competition between life and art which Carlyle describes necessarily puts art at a disadvantage: "Let any one bethink him how impressive the smallest historical *fact* may become, as contrasted with the grandest *fictitious event*; what an incalculable force lies for us in this consideration: The Thing which I here hold imaged in my mind did actually occur . . . is not a dream, but a reality!" ("Biography," C M E, 3: 49, 54). This objection to fiction was, of course, not limited to minds as strictly puritanical as Carlyle's; even that old worldling Major Pendennis self-righteously dismisses his nephew's craft by blithely declaring, "Novels ain't true" (p. 566). The fact that fiction is false was the principal source of its disfavor with both Evangelical and utilitarian schools of thought. The Victorian novelist, unlike his successors, was not content simply to accept this fact, and he chose to affirm and justify his art on precisely those grounds which made it susceptible to attack. Mimesis was certainly one way to subvert such objections. Thackeray uses this justification to counter Goethe's declaration that "Art is called Art . . . precisely because it is *not* Nature." On the contrary, Thackeray explains, "the Art of Novels *is* to represent Nature: to convey as strongly as possible the sentiment of reality" (*Letters*, 2 : 772). But this protest does not reconcile the perdurable distinction between life and art; Thackeray can attribute to fiction only the feeling of reality, not reality itself. The duality is not to be eliminated by simple assertion. Even when George Eliot makes her classic statement—"Art is the nearest thing to life; it is a mode of amplifying experience" (*Essays*, p. 271)— she avoids the more radical claims that her fiction would like to suggest: that art is experience, that aesthetic apprehension is coterminous with life.

The eighteenth-century novel had demonstrated one way in which such conclusions might be reached, but, like other Victorian uses of the past, this earlier formulation had to be reenvisioned before it could be of any use. The tradition of the genre from *The Pilgrim's Progress* through the mid-eighteenth century had based its claims for moral value on a simple yet compelling assumption of the inherent relation between art and life. Christian, Tom Jones, Clarissa, and even Moll Flanders are presented as the embodiments of virtues which the reader is asked both to recognize and to practice. Richardson explicitly defines the exemplary function of narrative at the beginning of *Clarissa* when Anna Howe begs her "perfect" friend to tell the "whole" of her story: "Every eye, in short, is upon you with the expectation of an example." Art, which imitates life, is to be imitated in the reader's life. This circle of imitative influence, like the Victorian conception of a sympathetic imagination, was a premise, an ideal considerably modified by actual practice. Samuel Johnson, for one, was worried about the possibility of confusing vice and virtue, of choosing the wrong example for imitation, and Jane Austen offers a wonderfully comic instance of this possibility when Sir Edward Denham patterns himself after Lovelace, whose seduction of Clarissa he sees as the epitome of all manly valor. Yet such early objections or instances of misuse simply point to the power and predominance of this imitative aesthetic.

By the Victorian mid-century the Evangelicals' adoption of the exemplary mode had severely limited its moral relevance by identifying it with narrow doctrinal interests. Nor were they alone in this prescriptive use of narrative. From the late 1830s on, other religious groups tried to popularize their ideas in such series as the Tractarian Englishman's Library and Cardinal Wiseman's Catholic Popular Library.[6] Still other, more secularly inclined writers exploited the propagandistic potential of the exemplary mode. Charles Kingsley's *Alton Locke* and Disraeli's *Sybil* demonstrate how a specific social or political message can compromise both the moral scope and the mimetic capacities of the novel, and Gaskell's first fictional sketches, published for the benefit of the working-class reader, suggest that even the most humanitarian of purposes can be vitiated by the desire to exemplify the proper path to virtue. Significantly, the novelists whom we have come to consider as the major figures of the period refused to constrain their works within such limitations, and they replaced the earlier aesthetic with their version of the romantic imagination and its circle of analogical bonds, thereby reconstituting the relation between the reader and the tale. The exemplary formula might be the avowed aesthetic of an early work like *Oliver Twist*—echoing Fielding's description of Tom Jones, Dickens noted in the 1841 preface that the parish-boy represents "the principle of Good surviving through every adverse circumstance" (p. lxii)—but Dickens reduced none of his later novels to such simple equations. In novels like *Bleak House* and *Little Dorrit*, the heroines' conventionally "good" qualities, their penchant for meaningless self-sacrifice, are precisely those which threaten to compromise their moral stature. Even when a character in a Victorian novel seems to embody his creator's values and therefore partakes of the earlier tradition of exemplification, as do characters like Dobbin and Dinah Morris and Florence Dombey, the novelist is sure also to qualify that status by elaborating on the character's shortcomings and by implying that the character's use as an "example" is secondary to the larger "extension of our sympathies" which reading his story entails. Moral distinctions are not only less important to this aesthetic than they had been in earlier fiction, they actually tend to subvert it. As George Eliot explained in her review of *Wilhelm Meister*, "The line between the virtuous and vicious, so far from being a necessary safeguard to morality, is itself an immoral fiction" (*Essays*, p. 147). *Sartor Resartus* again forecasts this development in the Victorian novel; Teufelsdröckh is only "hieroglyphically" human (p. 161), and the elusive quality of his actions defeats both imitation and categorization. Because Victorian fiction defines the reader as one of the three essential agents in the analogical process that constitutes storytelling, the act of reading—not the reader's behavior after he has finished reading—is the link between life and art. Narration is a process comparable to life itself. Theophrastus Such speaks for a generation of writers when he says that "powerful imagination" is a "creative energy constantly fed by susceptibility to the veriest minutiae of experience, which it reproduces and constructs in fresh and fresh wholes" (p. 197). Because the reader's imagination is the agency by which art achieves its ever "fresh and fresh wholes," the distinction between life and art has, at least provisionally, disappeared. If the reader is able to enter into the circle of analogous relations offered by the narration, the novelist has reason to believe that his own imaginative apprehension of experience can actually become the reader's experience.

Although creating the context for such imaginative bonds was clearly the task that the Victorian novelist set himself, the relationship between this intention and the exigencies of narrative technique is another, more complex problem. Yet to begin to appreciate its ramifications, one has only to consider the putative source of narrative technique in any novel, the narrator himself. The importance of his moral stature in Victorian fiction goes without saying. Beatrix and Janet can assent to the validity of the stories told them because they can believe in the integrity of men like Henry and Tryan. Paul distrusts Mrs. Pipchin's tale because he distrusts its teller; he is simply too wise to credit anything he hears from a woman whose only values consist of mutton chops and toast, served "hot and hot." J. Hillis Miller has claimed that the "omniscient narrator is the most important constitutive convention for the form of Victorian fiction, . . . the one requiring the most analysis and explanation"; [7] and when the effect of the novelist's moral concerns on the form of his art is at issue, that claim should be extended to include first-person narrators like Pendennis and David Copperfield as well. The subtlety and self-consciousness with which narrative voice is handled in novels like *Vanity Fair* and *Adam Bede*, or the polyphonic freedoms exercised by Dickens in *Dombey and Son* and *Bleak House*, all stem from the novelist's desire to establish a bond between his narrator and his reader, presumably the first in a linked chain of morally forceful relations.

This gesture toward the reader is, however, only one of the ways in which the novelist revealed his continuing allegiance to his audience; the various identities of the Victorian narrator, the analogies and roles and metaphors by which he was defined, are based on the novelist's response to his public and his hopes about his potential relation to it. In adopting the values of his culture—in agreeing that fiction must be both useful and morally responsible—the novelist undertook to create a narrative version of himself which his public would respect. The terms he used to define this public self, often outlined in his letters and essays as well as in his fiction, became, naturally and inevitably, the basis of his narrator's relation to his reader. Although this influence is sometimes indirect in the case of a novelist like Dickens—the public role defined in his newspaper ventures or in his occasional tales satisfied needs which the narrator of his major fiction was then free to ignore—the dependence of the narrator's identity on the novelist's sense of his public self again suggests the fluid boundaries between art and life typical of the mid-century novel. The definition of the narrator in a timeless artifact like *Adam Bede*, for instance, was clearly determined by the personal and historical context in which the novel was conceived. We need to examine how Dickens, Thackeray, and George Eliot viewed their relation to their contemporary audience (particularly in the early stages of their careers, when they were trying to win or strengthen their hold on popularity) if we are to understand either the extent of the moral demands they typically placed on their narrators or one of the chief ways in which those demands were to be satisfied.

In this matter the Victorian novelist could find little guidance from the precedents set by either the eighteenth-century novelist or the romantic poet. Unlike the founding fathers of his genre, Defoe and Richardson and Fielding, he avoided analogies drawn from other literary realms. The titles of editor, historian, biographer, all convey the author's relation to his subject, but ignore the novelist's sense of his more crucial relation to his audience. Even the one exception proves this rule. Motivated perhaps by his allegiance to the eighteenth century as well as by his admiration for Scott, Thackeray did adopt such traditional roles in novels like *Pendennis* and *The Virginians*, but in the mid-century work which won him his initial popularity, *Vanity Fair*, he playfully modulated the role of the historian against an identity which has a social rather than literary source. Moreover, in his later works the central function of the narrating historian or biographer is to correlate his subject and the world of his readers, not to prove the factual authenticity of his account of events. To all three novelists the traditional romantic metaphors for the artist's identity were more suspect still. The poet had imaged his artistic function in impersonal terms such as the Aeolian harp or the fading coal, or in the figures of solitaries like Alastor or Kubla Khan, but such definitions could only exacerbate the Victorian distrust of the artist. Indeed, like the polemicist's misuse of exemplary narratives, they forced the novelist to adopt new modes of conceiving his identity if he was to establish himself in a productive relation to his readers.

George Eliot's treatment of artistic sensibility in "The Lifted Veil" (1859) reveals both the shortcomings of such earlier models and the principal requirement that the Victorian writer made of any model which might supplant them. Latimer, the narrator and main character, is an Ancient Mariner whose isolation is made more intolerable and more ironic by the social context of marriage in which George Eliot sets him. His diseased gifts of foresight and insight identify him as a novelist manqué.[8] He tells us that he has a "poet's sensibility," but he reveals his distinctively Victorian perspective (he is writing his story, appropriately enough, in the fall of 1850) when he explains that such capacities are a curse if the poet has no faith in a responsive audience:

A poet pours forth his song and *believes* in the listening ear and answering soul, to which his song will be floated sooner or later. But the poet's sensibility without his voice—the poet's sensibility that finds no vent but in silent tears on the sunny bank, when the noonday light sparkles on the water, or in an inward shudder at the sound of harsh human tones, the sight of a cold human eye—this dumb passion brings with it a fatal solitude of soul in the society of one's fellow-men. (p. 284)

Here George Eliot revises another point in Shelley's "Defence of Poetry": her nightingale is not content to sit in the darkness and sing "unseen" to an audience that may or may not be listening. Without the "voice" that will evoke the listener's "answering soul," the poet is merely a passive exile from the human community. All the Gothic grotesquerie of this tale merely highlights its significance as yet another Victorian fable of community and the artist's proper place in that context. Latimer is a more extreme version of Dickens's Henry Gowan or Thackeray's depiction of Áddison in *Henry Esmond*; the isolation or cold indifference of the artist negates both his art and his humanity. Particularly at the beginning of their careers, therefore, Dickens, Thackeray, and George Eliot created versions of their artistic selves that mediate directly between the novelist and the community of his readers. Once again all three authors share the same assumptions and ideals as they strive to fulfill their requirements in uniquely individual ways.

The Victorian novelist often turned to contemporary models to satisfy contemporary demands, and the institution which offered the most productive source of metaphors for his role as an artist was religion. The Church may seem an odd frame of reference for the secular writer who was also a freethinker, skeptical Christian, or atheist, but he discovered in its offices and functions a number of congenial analogies for his own duties. Although the Evangelicals consistently taught that sympathy subverts morality by breaking down the distinction between good and evil, the revival of latitudinarianism that began during the late 1840s again allowed the Church to represent an ideal of moral responsibility based on the value of charity and fellow feeling. In part as a measure of self-defense against the suspicions of a basically conventional and Christian audience, the novelists who most thoroughly rejected traditional forms of belief found in the Church the most obvious source of self-definition; it affected the narrative identity of George Eliot more than that of Thackeray, and Thackeray's more than that of Dickens. Thackeray told John Chapman that his "religious views are perfectly *free*, but he does not mean to lessen his popularity by fully avowing them." He refused to "martyrize himself for the sake of his views,"[9] and he retained the title of secular preacher precisely so that he could conceal his skepticism from his audience. There is certainly no more effective way to assert one's responsibility than by claiming the sanction that religion bestows on those employed in its service, as long as that sanction implies no specific doctrinal or even spiritual orientation. Carlyle had given currency to the basic analogy in his 1841 lectures, *Heroes and Hero-Worship*, when he proposed that the true writer is a "Preacher preaching not to this parish or that, on this day or that, but to all men in all times and places" (p. 159). As George Eliot's paradigmatic treatment of Tryan suggests, the identification of pastor and novelist was, at the outset of her career, a sufficient statement of her role—though, significantly, hers was a distinctly traditional conception of a contemporary model. For Dickens, the identification was often a matter of implication rather than direct assertion. For Thackeray, a point-blank statement of the novelist's identity as a preacher became an important form of comic self-deprecation. Moreover, both Dickens and Thackeray evolved other roles that are more vital or equally telling embodiments of their moral aims. Yet in each case, the novelist saw himself as preacher, pastor, or minister so that he could express, not his distance from his congregation of readers, but his equality and intimacy with each of its members.

In the late 1850s George Eliot adopted this clerical mode as the essential and single sanction for her work. She was able to rely on it rather than on the variety of roles that typify the self-definitions of her two colleagues, simply, I think, because hers was the last of the three identities to develop. The earlier work of Dickens and Thackeray as well as that of Gaskell and Charlotte Brontë had created a context in which George Eliot's more severe conceptions of realism and her more consistently earnest moral aims would find a receptive audience. That was, of course, not the way she viewed her potential reading public. In the *Scenes of Clerical Life* and *Adam Bede*, the works written before she achieved widespread recognition, she adhered to the role of the parish priest as a way of appealing to her readers on their own terms. Yet her earliest extant letters tell us how deeply this role was engrained in her sense of self. Already at the age of twenty, she wishes she were a "well instructed scribe" so that her letters might offer spiritual comfort, "something worth reading" (1 : 32, 42). Like Ruskin's, George Eliot's "deconversion" from Evangelicalism set the stage for a "reconversion" to art. Her religious training provided the language that would later define her fiction. Imagination, in such a scheme, takes on all the sanctity of grace. A contemporary review of *Adam Bede* focused on the result of this process—the novel is a "religious utterance which somehow differs a good deal from the general tone of the pulpit utterances we have been used to." [10] The novel partakes of religion without evoking the image of the pulpit because the narrator is not a preacher looking down at his flock. His relation to his audience is considerably more familiar.

Fiction, for George Eliot, is the source of a bond between novelist and public comparable only to the relationship that the pastor and his parishioner establish in times of suffering and moral crisis. They know each other with an intimacy and immediacy that social forms rarely allow. George Eliot took very seriously the concept of a "fellowship in suffering," as she calls it in "Janet's Repentance" (2 : 181). Even in her later novels, suffering has the capacity to reveal the reality of human experience that Wordsworth attributes to rural life and Meredith would later locate in the manners of the drawing room. The intimacy effected by suffering transcends even the bonds of kinship. As George Eliot says in the case of Janet and Tryan, "In our moments of spiritual need, the man to whom we have no tie but our common nature, seems nearer to us than mother, brother, or friend" (2 : 214). Jane Carlyle's exuberant letter of thanks for a copy of the *Scenes* is a telling comment on George Eliot's unique conception of her role and its implications. The book had been a "*consolation*" when she was suffering from sleeplessness, fever, and a sore throat: "It helped me through that dreary night, as well—better than the most sympathetic helpful friend watching by my bedside could have done!" (*Letters*, 2: 425). Reading the tales is "better" than being watched over precisely because the novelist, like the pastor, tries to be a source of relief and strength, and he can do so more effectively than even the "most sympathetic" friend.

Although George Eliot rejected the manner in which Keats or Shelley defined the arist's role, her conception of the novelist revived and reaffirmed Wordsworth's definition of the role of the parish priest. Her choice of an epigraph for *Adam Bede* points to this derivation. The lines are from *The Excursion*; they explain the Pastor's intention to recount stories about his parishioners so that he can evoke "something more / Than brotherly forgiveness" for his subjects (vol. 5, bk. 6, ll. 651-58). These events have taken place in a remote village like Hayslope. One tale in particular, that of the "weeping Magdalene," Ellen (bk. 6, l. 814), probably provided suggestions for George Eliot's conception of Hetty Sorrel. Ellen believes herself guilty of child-murder; she recognizes, as Hetty eventually does, that her chief fault is the "stony region in [her] heart" (bk. 6, l. 918). Ellen has confessed her sins to the Pastor; he performs, in her story, the function of Dinah Morris in the account of Hetty's experience. His relationship to his present audience—the Poet, the Wanderer, and the Solitary—is a model for what George Eliot hopes to accomplish in her fiction. The three friends have been discussing questions of conduct, a central issue in *Adam Bede*. The Solitary is perplexed by the contrast between abstract ideals and the contingencies of earthly experience, "the prospect of the soul" and "man's substantial life." He claims that if the inhabitants of the graveyard in which they are standing could speak, "we should recoil, stricken with sorrow and shame" when the dead revealed how little their acts have accorded with the dictates of reason and conscience (bk. 5, ll. 248–57). The Wanderer then asks for the light of the Pastor's guidance. The Pastor dismisses speculative thought as proper only to the angels and states his conviction that life is not a matter simply of pain and defeat. The Wanderer responds to these convictions in precisely the terms that George Eliot uses in *Adam Bede*: "The mind's repose / On evidence is not to be ensured / By act of naked reason. Moral truth / Is no mechanic structure, built by rule" (bk. 5, ll. 560–63). The Solitary asks the Pastor:

> May I entreat
> Your further help? The mine of real life
> Dig for us. . . .
> There lies
> Around us a domain where you have long

Watched both the outward course and inner heart:
Give us, for our abstractions, solid facts;
For our disputes, plain pictures. . . .
So, by your records, may our doubts be solved.
                    (bk. 5, ll. 629–54)

In response to this request, the Pastor proceeds to tell the stories about the lives of those now lying in the graveyard. He provides "solid facts" and "plain pictures" in place of abstractions and disputes. In this context, he tells Ellen's story. In essence, the Pastor has become a narrator who embodies George Eliot's conception of the novelist's role. He tells stories gathered from his close observation of the "real life" around him, and the act of narration constitutes a specific response to his audience's spiritual needs and moral confusions. Wordsworth's Pastor, like Edgar Tryan after him, has become a storyteller. In George Eliot's case, however, the reverse is true; for her, the novelist has become the parish priest.

As her career progressed, George Eliot became less dependent upon this self-consciously conceived role. Yet even in her last work, the indirectly autobiographical sketches of *Theophrastus Such*, the speaker announces that his father was a country parson, a contemporary of Scott and Wordsworth. For George Eliot that statement is the figurative if not the literal truth. Like Ruskin, she cherished a Tory past. In the *Scenes of Clerical Life* and *Adam Bede*, she tried to return to those roots. Like Theophrastus Such, she valued the provincial clergyman because his office, more than any other, allows him to be familiar with all classes and sorts of men. George Eliot began her career by identifying herself with a tradition that is, in two senses, genuinely pastoral. Her work, not surprisingly, recalled to contemporary minds *The Vicar of Wakefield* rather than the Evangelical narratives she set out to invalidate. She began by treating clerical subjects so that she could correct the failings and supply the shortcomings of religion as she maintained its traditional forms and modes. In this sense she was, with many other Victorians, a radical conservative. The *Scenes of Clerical Life* are, like Trollope's *Barchester Towers*, an embodiment of the sometimes ironic but always constructive relation between Victorian narrative and religion; and no analysis of the form of these early tales is complete unless it recognizes that fact. As early as *The Mill on the*

Floss (1860), George Eliot was ready to criticize more openly the tradition in which her earlier works were nurtured. Maggie reads Thomas à Kempis and pathetically, like Jude Fawley after her, thinks she has the "key" to this "hard, real life" (p. 250). But, as George Eliot knows, no key is furnished in or for this life, and perhaps she came to realize that even the most liberally conceived and humanized form of a clerical role implies that there is an answer to our perplexity. The very idea of a lesson or a rule—even if it is the rule of renunciation—implies a stasis which cannot respond to the changing conditions that constitute human life. Powerful as the monk and his lesson are, they will fail when tested against the pressures of desire. Only imagination, sympathy with others, and the memory that binds one to them can serve as moral guides, and even these, as *The Mill* demonstrates, are not always proof against the conflict between familial and erotic love. But the discovery of such private truths would await George Eliot's establishment of herself in her public role as an approved and popular novelist—a goal that the metaphor of the pastor helped her to attain. By beginning in the *Scenes* with clerics at the center of her fiction, George Eliot could later move them to its periphery. By making the role of the pastor the source of her novelistic identity and the intimacy of her voice, she gained the freedom to transcend its inherent limitations.

If George Eliot's clerical role allowed her readers to enjoy the illusion of her comforting presence, Dickens and Thackeray created equally familiar, if sometimes less reassuring presences. They did so by combining the roles inspired by religion with others that stress the pleasing as well as the useful facets of their art. In 1853 when he delivered a speech entitled "Charity and Humour," Thackeray unabashedly defined the popular entertainment of comic fiction as a form of religious observance. The comic writer is a "gay and kind weekday preacher," and "his audiences are [now] enormous; every week or month his happy congregations flock to him; they never tire of such sermons" (10: 614, 625). Thackeray used his definition of the charitable nature of comedy to link the eighteenth-century tradition of Steele, Fielding, and Goldsmith to their mid-century counterparts—Dickens, the *Punch* staff, Jerrold, and himself. Late in his career, Dickens made a speech in which his role as the entertainer, the purveyor of a "fancy," is given a similar religious mission. Recalling a passage from the

Psalms in which the word of God is compared to "silver tried in a furnace of earth, purified seven times" (12: 6), Dickens proclaimed, "As
the gold is said to be doubly and trebly refined which has seven times
passed the furnace, so a fancy may be said to become more and more
refined each time it passes through the human heart." Here his audience punctuated the speech with a rousing response of loud ap-
plause. Then Dickens continued, "You have, and you know you have,
brought to the consideration of me that quality in yourselves without
which I should have beaten the air. Your earnestness has stimulated
mine, your laughter has made me laugh, and your tears have over-
flowed my eyes" (*Speeches*, pp. 387–88). The novelist's basically the-
atrical stance as performer or entertainer, combined with his ability to
take over the function of traditional religion, creates an almost incon-
ceivably literal sense of intimacy; the reader's tears fill the author's
eyes, their laughter amuses him. The bonds wrought by imagination
could be no stronger, reciprocity could go no farther. The audience actually transmutes the author's work by responding to it.

Although Thackeray never achieved the sense of profound intimacy with his readers that was the hallmark of at least the first half of
Dickens's career, his insistence on the comic and popular orientation
of his role was an attempt to adapt himself to the attitudes of an audience which he found fundamentally alien. Even Thackeray's most
earnest statements about his profession and its value are tinged with a
cavalier mockery which betrays his uneasiness—with himself, with
the novel as an art, perhaps with his century. His long, hard climb to
popularity and public acceptance may partially explain such feelings,
but he often betrayed, as did Sir Walter Scott before him, a need to remain hidden from his public, a need that seems temperamental in origin. His famous comparison of the novelist to the Manager of the
Performance in *Vanity Fair* recalls a comment made by Peter Pattieson, one of Scott's many authorial alter egos, at the beginning of *The
Bride of Lammermoor*: instead of public recognition, "I confess that
. . . I should more enjoy the thought of remaining behind the curtain
unseen, like the ingenious manager of Punch and his wife Joan, and
enjoying the astonishment and conjectures of my audience." In Thackeray's case, the manager came out before the curtain and took his
place as one of the performers, but the continuing critical debate about

Thackeray's "real" views of himself and his art suggests that to some extent he maintained the privacy of his beliefs.[11] The narrative form to which he reverted in both *The Newcomes* and *The Virginians* attests to this urge for anonymity. Throughout his career, Thackeray's self-portraits, like those of the narrator of *Vanity Fair*, are changing facets of a sometimes elusive identity. Yet at mid-century Thackeray was able to adopt a combination of narrative roles that seemed to satisfy both himself and his audience.

The clown, Thackeray's most distinctive metaphor for his novelistic identity, is modeled on another amusing chameleon, the Punch figure of the *London Charivari*.[12] The attribution is doubly appropriate. Like Thackeray himself, the puppet in *Punch* is an impersonator and quick-change artist; according to the demands of the occasion, he appears as a tourist, Byronic poet, police magistrate, noble Roman, and king. Secondly, Punch, like Thackeray, had managed to overcome his own inauspicious beginnings as a Bohemian. Converted to socially responsible authorship, both the grotesque little puppet and the man who wrote for him were able to win respectability and status. Early in the eighteenth century Steele had characterized Punch as a "prophane leud Jester" (*Tatler*, no. 44). The traditional Punch and Judy shows are indeed genuinely "low" art. The extravagant and often brutal violence of their plots satisfies primitive asocial longings; every limitation on Punch's aggressively male energy—wife and family, magistrate, hangman, and finally the devil himself—is destroyed by his lawless will. Mark Lemon, *Punch*'s first editor, knew he had to reform this image if the paper was to succeed at a time when Regency values were clearly giving way to a new order. In 1841, in his opening editorial, he repudiated many of Punch's traditional actions; "merry Master PUNCH" was to be a "teacher of no mean pretensions." As a member of the *Punch* staff, Thackeray was well aware of the precedent set by the puppet; in both his articles for the paper and his private correspondence, he often adopted Punch's identity and spoke from behind this mask. In *Vanity Fair* Thackeray would assume an antic disposition, but only if he, like Punch, could be "our motley teacher." The role of the clown was not altogether respectable—here Carlyle's contemptuous reference to the novelist as a "mountebank Juggler" should be recalled (CME, 3:60)—but at least it was a role that the public could

Initial drawings,
chapters 18, 37, and 40,
Vanity Fair

understand and accept. Like the clumsy puppet who entertains the crowds in the street, the novelist makes his audience laugh.

The puppets of *Punch*, then, became the clowns of *Vanity Fair*, and no one who has seen only a modern reprint of the novel would imagine how often their highjinks enliven Thackeray's chapter initials. Just as George Eliot freed the role of the novelist-as-pastor from its specific religious implications, Thackeray took the image of *Punch* and generalized it in *Vanity Fair*, thereby obscuring its origin in his work for a newspaper with a specific social and political orientation. In *The Snobs of England*, Punch-as-author had contemplated his own visage in the mirror of his art; the clown on the title page of *Vanity Fair* is similarly engaged. Although Thackeray continued privately to think of himself as a slightly ridiculous Punch-figure, the public persona which he created was now that of the clown, as the well-known tailpiece to chapter 9—the drawing of his woebegone face above the jester's suit—would suggest. To this image he added the role of the cleric, and the narrator of *Vanity Fair* became the motley preacher. His narrative commentary assumes the pattern of the traditional sermon: "O brother wearers of motley!" he cries out to his audience (p. 180). Unlike George Eliot's pastor, however, Thackeray's preacher is raised above his auditors; as the drawing on the serial title-page shows, the narrator, dressed as a clown, stands on a barrel so that he can look down on his listeners and exhort them as fellow clowns. No companionable sitting at the sickbed for the Thackerayan narrator—what he shares with his audience is a fellowship in sin rather than suffering. As Thackeray noted in one of his letters, "We must lift up our voices about these [weaknesses] and howl to a congregation of fools." But the novelist and his narrator belittle the audience because they see in each of its members their "own weaknesses wickednesses lusts follies shortcomings" (*Letters*, 2:424). Neither character nor narrator is allowed to maintain the grand moral pretensions to which he lays claim. If Dobbin must come to know that he has been the dupe of an unworthy woman's selfishness, the narrator must learn that every time he starts to preach he will end up by calling attention to his cap and bells. The preacher is a jester; more importantly, like the rest of us, he is a bit of a fool.

In the novels he wrote after *Vanity Fair*, Thackeray was to discard

From Puppet to Clown: (above) initial drawing, chapter 16, "on Literary Snobs." *The Snobs of England, by One of Themselves* (*Punch*, 1846); (right) detail, title page, *Vanity Fair* (1848)

the role of the preaching clown and develop, as the characteristic mark of his fiction, the more sedate role of the biographer and historian. Yet again he found a way of defining himself that his audience would recognize and respect;[13] as Carlyle stated in 1832, history is "the most honoured" form of composition (CME, 3:46). That assertion would have been even more accurate at mid-century, after the publication of works like *The French Revolution*, and Thackeray found ways to make this rather conventional role perform rather unconventional moral functions in novels such as *The Newcomes* and *Henry Esmond*. Yet even his later narrators retain something of the quality of the voice in *Vanity Fair*. Thackeray himself confessed in one of his last *Round-*

Roles of the Author, Private and Public: (left) "With the author's compliments," drawing in a presentation copy of *Vanity Fair*; (below) tailpiece to chapter 9, *Vanity Fair*

about Papers, "De Finibus" (August 1862), that "perhaps of all the novel-spinners now extant, the present speaker is the most addicted to preaching." With characteristic self-mockery, he admits that this preaching, this "sin of grandiloquence," is the "sin of schoolmasters, governesses, critics, sermoners, and instructors of young or old people." He claims that he wants to reform, to write a novel without any preaching, with "an incident in every other page, a villain, a battle, a mystery in every chapter" (17:596). Thackeray, however, could no more give up preaching than he could give up writing. His one attempt at a novel written without the narrative "sin" of moral commentary, the unfinished *Denis Duval* (1864), is a dismal failure, a storybook for children. No matter how indirect, the role of the preacher, a voice expounding on our fallen human nature, is central to Thackeray's fiction.

For Dickens, organized religion was less the source of an analogy for a novelist's role than a frame of reference in opposition to which he could define his unique belief in his artistic integrity. More boldly than either Thackeray or George Eliot, Dickens set the novelist-as-entertainer in direct competition with every form of church and chapel. This rivalry is implicit in his adoption of the voice of the preacher in novels like *Dombey and Son* and *Bleak House*. The discourse delivered over Nemo's dead body is a vitriolic parody of Christian conceptions of brotherhood. *Hard Times* (1854), however, embodies most fully one of Dickens's consistent beliefs: the novelist could do the work of religion, not by adopting its modes, but by insisting on the traditional functions and the moral relevance of entertainment. Elizabeth Gaskell had used the pseudonym of Cotton Mather Mills to reconcile her preacherly instincts to the industrial world of Manchester, but Dickens was convinced that religion, particularly the joyless rigor of Low Church and Dissent, was one of the more dehumanizing institutions in an increasingly drab, dull world of cranks and cogwheels. His "key-note" description of Coketown tells us that the eighteen denominations which have chosen to establish themselves there have erected "pious warehouse[s] of red brick" that are almost indistinguishable from the factories (p. 23). These churches contribute to "the triumph of fact" by denying the worker the exercise of his fancy. Opposed to the suppression of the imagination practiced in Coketown by religion, education, and industrialism is, of course, Sleary's Horse-riding. The message that the narrator articulates and that Sleary lispingly repeats is simple. People must be amused. By lodging the circus performers at a public house called the Pegasus's Arms, Dickens suggests that the Horse-riding stands for the value of all popular art, and it is repeatedly equated to the books in the Coketown library or to the fairy tales that Gradgrind has denied his children. At times Dickens's comments on his art suggest that he was obsessed by the image of a lower-class audience whose only entertainments were gin and hangings. His treatment of the Horse-riding in the context of the social criticism of *Hard Times* suggests the relationship between this sense of his audience and his role as a reformer. His art is a response both to an imaginatively impoverished audience and to the conditions which foster its deprivation. Like Thackeray's clown, Sleary's crew is very much down at the heels, common indeed, perhaps more than a bit vulgar, but precisely by placing themselves on the same level with their audience, they offer what other more elevated institutions deny. Dickens could embody the role of his art in this humble form only because he was convinced that its humility was the source of its dignity.

Dickens often seemed to suggest that it was his responsibility as a novelist to humanize, almost singlehandedly, a world that was becoming more intransigently materialistic, mechanistic, and barbaric. For Dickens the novelist—if not for Dickens the private citizen—the home is the source and basis of one's humanity. In *Sartor Resartus*, Carlyle had quoted Goethe to express his conviction that the writer-as-philosopher must "'station himself in the middle. . . . The Philosopher is he to whom the Highest has descended, and the Lowest has mounted up; who is the equal and kindly brother of all'" (p. 53). Dickens, more than any other Victorian novelist, tried to follow this exhortation and make every reader his brother. Visions of the hearth, evenings by the fire, and warm domestic intimacy pervade his distinctive conception of himelf as the reader's friend and equal. The relationship between Dickens and his public was based, he felt, on shared interests and the common experience of a fictional world; as far as he was concerned, it was firmly established with the publication of *The Old Curiosity Shop*. In a speech he gave during his first trip to Edinburgh, he described the death of Little Nell as the fictional event that bound him to his readers: "I feel as if I stood amongst old friends, whom I have intimately known and highly valued. I feel as if the deaths of the fictitious creatures, in which you have been kind enough to express an interest, had endeared us to each other as real afflictions deepen friendships in actual life; I feel as if they had been real persons, whose fortunes we had pursued together in inseparable connexion, and that I had never known them apart from you" (*Speeches*, p. 9). The comment is an intriguing, if more specifically morbid version of George Eliot's "fellowship in suffering"; the shared memories of the dear departed sanctify a friendship in the present and insure its continuance.

Dickens's original plans for *Household Words* illustrate his need to domesticate nearly every public function he assumed. He first wrote to Forster in June 1845 to announce his idea for a weekly journal called *The Cricket*, "A cheerful creature that chirrups on the Hearth." Dickens himself was to be that cricket; he would "make such a dash at people's fenders and arm-chairs as hasn't been made for many a long day. . . . I would at once sit down upon their very hobs; and take a personal and confidential position with them" (Pilgrim *Letters*, 4:328). Eventually by the end of 1849, *Household Words* was conceived. The list of proposed titles is instructive: *Charles Dickens: Conducted by Himself; The Household Voice; The Household Guest; The Household Face; The Comrade;* and finally *Household Words* (*Letters*, 2:202–3). The implications are clear: Charles Dickens was the Household Voice and Face, the Comrade, the source of Household Words. Although he hoped to achieve financial independence by editing a newspaper, Dickens may also have wished literally to make himself his public's constant companion. Every week he would enter their homes in a new and different form.

Perhaps this need for intimacy, which was displayed by Dickens's public as often as by the novelist himself, explains why he persisted in publishing his Christmas books and the Christmas numbers of his magazines even when they took an immense toll in time and energy. Not until 1868 did he discontinue this almost religious observance, though he had been tempted to do so as early as 1846 when the writing of *The Battle of Life* had interrupted his work on *Dombey and Son*. He was loath to lose more than the profits involved; he could not resist the opportunity to join his readers at their hearths when they expected him to participate in their holiday cheer. Like any more orthodox ritual, the Christmas books every year reenacted and revitalized a crucial aspect of Dickens's creative faith; they reestablished his relationship to his audience as one of comfortable and secure intimacy. In 1852, speaking of the Christmas number of *Household Words*, he explained the principle upon which all these occasional works rest. He does not care if the tales in the number actually refer at all to Christmas; more important is the domesticity suggested in the traditional image of the old wives' tale: "I propose to give the number some fireside name, and to make it consist entirely of short stories supposed to be told by a family sitting round the fire" (*Letters*, 2:422). Significantly, the first of the

Christmas books was conceived immediately after Dickens's unexpected reverses with *Martin Chuzzlewit*, a disappointment which convinced him that he might not always retain his readers' undying
loyalty. In *A Christmas Carol* (1843) the freedom of fantasy, which he
indulges throughout the succeeding Christmas tales, allows him to
use his most intimate tone of voice. The popular mode of the traditional winter's tale creates a conversational atmosphere; each story begins with a chatty dialogue that assumes a lively responsiveness on the
part of the reader. Dickens's evocation of this casual familiarity in his
most self-consciously fanciful stories is significant. Although he was
aware of the difficulty and fragility of such a relationship, he knew it
was the source and function of formidable imaginative energy. As long
as his Christmas books reassured him of his potential for intimate converse with his reader, he was free to explore, in the more demanding
work of full-length novels such as *Little Dorrit*, other more austere
and even scathing tones of voice. Like George Eliot's use of the clerical
role, Dickens's conception of himself as the reader's friend is a premise, a starting point for more elaborate formulations of the morality of
his narrative presence.

In his use of the domestic metaphor, Dickens took a tendency in
the work of his two contemporaries to its logical extreme. He hoped to
be what the *Times* notice of his death eventually called him, "the intimate of every household," because that title could transform a vast and
impersonal public into one's family. The world becomes a hearth, perhaps a more satisfying home than the novelist has known either as a
child or as an adult. Writing becomes an activity in which the novelist
can grant himself the domestic happiness and concord that he bestows
on Florence Dombey, David Copperfield, and Esther Summerson. The
imaginative home that Dickens and his reader come to inhabit is,
therefore, another ideal model of the relation that should obtain between all men, a model created by fiction and sustained, one hopes, in
every reading experience. Thackeray and George Eliot found this
model as profoundly attractive as Dickens did (both of them had been
in a sense dispossessed, one by the insanity of his spouse, the other by
her extramarital union), but neither felt quite the assurance or the
self-confidence that allowed Dickens to appeal openly for his reader's
friendship. Yet their treatment of their narrators embodies such an ap-

peal in less directly personal manners and attests as fully as Dickens does to the importance of such a bond. The popularity that the great Boz still enjoyed at mid-century often allowed him to assume that the tie between his narrator and the reader has been established before each new act of storytelling—although in *Dombey and Son* he attempts both to recognize and avert the reader's potential for hostility. Throughout Thackeray's career and particularly at the beginning of George Eliot's, Dickens's colleagues felt it necessary to re-create their narrative identities for each new narrative occasion, as later discussions of *The Newcomes* and *Adam Bede* will suggest. The responses of their contemporary audience, like the *Times* account of Dickens, prove that such efforts were not in vain. George Eliot became the object of an adulation that was as intensely personal as it was widespread, and Trollope even accused Thackeray of achieving too overwhelming a sense of intimacy with his readers. Yet when Trollope complained that Thackeray's style "causes the reader to be almost too much at home with his author,"[14] he was defining a central mid-century ideal of which there could hardly be, for the novelist at least, "too much."

Despite, then, the considerable differences in their feelings about either themselves or their audiences, these three writers adopted roles that rest on the same assumption. Whether the novelist is entertainer, reformer, or preacher, jester, pastor, or friend, he has presumably established a relation with his reader that both justifies the moral claims he makes for his art and provides the first step toward their realization. The novel he writes is an act of communication, a gift of amusement, wisdom, affection, or experience that has value only as it is accepted by the audience for whom it is intended. Even "The Lifted Veil" attests to these bonds. Awaiting his death by angina pectoris, utterly cut off from all human contact, whether it be with wife or friend or servant, Latimer nonetheless makes a remarkable claim on the reader's fellowship. He explains that he no longer needs to dwell on his "inward experience," as he has done previously, because he can trust the reader to understand his feelings; the narration of his tale has made them "people . . . well known to each other" (p. 320). The "cold human eye," which Latimer has dreaded earlier as the only audience available to him, has now become the "answering soul" of a responsive listener.

Latimer's apparently eccentric responses again reveal a hope shared by all the major mid-century novelists. Once he has found his Wedding Guest or his Janet Dempster, the narrator may be able not only to teach the lesson of community but also to enter into the imaginative communion which his work creates.

The Victorian narrator does not alone bear the burden of establishing the bonds upon which such a communion depends. The figures who exist within the fictive world also inevitably invite the reader to cross the boundaries that usually demarcate art from life. The fictitious Saccharissa who solicits the attention of a reluctant Beatrix is an instance of their power. The Victorian novelist typically located the source of such claims in the universal appeal which fictive characters exert, and he tended to view character as the primary fact of any reader's experience of his work. George Eliot's early letters to her editor John Blackwood repeatedly state her anxious hope that her characters will strike him as she intends, that the unconventionally mundane inhabitants of Shepperton and Milby will win not only his interest, but also his sympathy and respect. Thackeray's creation of Colonel Newcome was calculated to harmonize with his readers' values and to gain, as indeed it did, their full assent. Dickens's handling of Walter Gay's fate reveals the strength of the appeal inherent in even a conventional figure; acquiescing in Forster's advice on the matter, he decided not to send Walter to the devil simply because he knew that it could not be done "without making people angry" (Pilgrim *Letters*, 4:593). In short, the Victorian novelist appreciated a phenomenon too often ignored in modern criticism: the reader's intrinsic interest in characters, in what makes them who they are and in what will happen to them. This interest was of particular value to the novelist concerned with the imaginative bonds created by narration. As Thackeray said of Tiny Tim, "There is not a reader in England but that little creature will be a bond of union between the author and him" (6:416). How the Victorian novelist uses character to generate his uniquely analogical bonds, relations that go beyond his own ties to his audience, is an involved question, one that will dominate the later, more extended discussions of novels like *Dombey and Son* and *Adam Bede*. Before turning to such works, however, it is important to realize that these three novelists, the nature of whose art is so often thought to distinguish them from each other, frequently relied on the same basic techniques when handling the ties between the three agents of narration. If we compare several relatively early works—significantly, again, each was published early in the novelist's bid for popularity—we cannot help but recognize this fact. *Vanity Fair, A Christmas Carol*, and "Janet's Repentance" all deal with change, with an aesthetic or moral transformation; and the change depicted within the story is a model of the imaginative energy which the novelist hopes will be exerted on or by the reader. Moreover, each tale demonstrates the way in which a character, in his relation either to the narrator or to the reader, invariably engenders further analogies. The direction which this process takes may vary, as *Vanity Fair* proves, and it is usually more complicated than these instances suggest, but its final goal remains the same. Ultimately, all three agents are joined in a "bond of union."

A Christmas Carol is central to any understanding of the characteristic moral implications of Dickens's narrative techniques. Its main character would appear to be an exemplary figure drawn from an earlier conception of the reader's imaginative relation to the text, but closer examination reveals that his exemplary status rests on a series of complex analogical bonds. Through explicit definition and direct statement, Dickens identifies the narrator with the Ghosts of Christmas Past, Present, and Yet to Come; simultaneously, he equates the reader with Scrooge himself, and the interplay between these two equations encourages the reader's engagement in the tale. In the preface the author expresses his hope that "this Ghostly little book" will "raise the Ghost of an Idea" and "haunt" the reader's home, for the story is a spirit empowered to reveal both Scrooge and the visions he sees. Within the narration Dickens refines the implications of his basic analogy. The narrator is to the reader what the spirits are to Scrooge. When the first ghost appears at the miser's bedside, the narrator comments that Scrooge "found himself face to face with the unearthly visitor . . . as close to it as I am now to you, and I am standing in the spirit at your elbow" (p. 24). Like the presences in Scrooge's bedchamber, the voice of the story attends the reader "in the spirit." The tie between character and reader springs, therefore, from their similar relation to a narrating presence. To emphasize this analogy, Dickens actually portrays Scrooge's younger self as a reader. One of the visions of himself that the miser sees is of a little boy enthralled by storybook characters. As the boy reads, both he and Scrooge see the characters as presences; Ali Baba and Robinson Crusoe are, like the ghosts, "wonderfully real and distinct to look at" (p. 28). Scrooge's relation to these figures again equates him with the reader. For both of them, fictive character is presumed to take on the immediacy and substantiality of life itself. The process which the miser undergoes, therefore, can become a process which reading his story will invite the reader to experience. The reformation of the crusty old skinflint comes to exemplify, not a pattern of behavior or an Old Testament law, as he would in an Evangelical tract, but a mode of perception. Like Carlyle's Teufelsdröckh or George Eliot's Dorothea, Scrooge acquires a new power of vision, one which the reader is asked to adopt. These interdependent analogies justify the novelist's faith in a number of otherwise simply fanciful transformations. Not only does the *Carol* posit a reconciliation of art and life, but the idealized power of imaginative energy that it presents presumes to transform the facts of life.

In the *Carol* Dickens presents one night of magic as a gradual development with distinct stages. Scrooge's imagination has atrophied in the cold and dark sanctuary of his materialism. The Spirit of Christmas Past begins his reformation simply by introducing a "bright clear jet of light" (p. 25) into Scrooge's house. As he "reads" the visions that the Spirits reveal, Scrooge's imagination gains in strength until, like a child learning to walk, it can stand on its own. Although he tries to extinguish the light of the first ghost, he not only accepts but seeks out the "blaze of ruddy light" (p. 38) emanating from the second ghost. Like the reader enchanted by the humorous fancy of the *Carol* and perhaps even awed by its imaginative flights, Scrooge cannot help but respond to a force too often excluded from his life. The ghosts provide visions so fully realized that Scrooge becomes part of them. At Fezziwig's ball, "his heart and soul were in the scene, and with his former self" (p. 33). Like the narrator, these ghosts only rarely comment upon the visions they create; the scenes themselves present their "latent moral" (p. 60). By following their inherent exhortations to open his eyes, Scrooge encourages his own moral transformation. At the close of Fezziwig's ball, Scrooge, not Christmas Past, explains that gestures of affection outweigh the value of money. After his visit to the Cratch-

its, Scrooge pleads with the Ghost of Christmas Present to say that
Tiny Tim will not die; the ghost quotes Scrooge's previous comment on
surplus population, and Scrooge assumes the attitude of the man to
whom every individual life is precious. This exchange of roles is complete by the time that the third spirit appears. Christmas Yet To Be pro-
jects the future that the unredeemed miser would face, and he, not
Scrooge, is enveloped in darkness. Scrooge reaches out to touch his
hand, but the ghost retreats. Scrooge voices the hope that he will "live
to be another man" (p. 58), but the ghost refuses to speak to him. At
the end of this third visit, Scrooge stands for hope and change and the
values of community; the spirit, like his pupil on the previous day, is
"immovable," silent, and isolated (p. 70). Imaginative energy has been
transferred from the Spirits to Scrooge. As they fade, Scrooge remains
endowed with all their best characteristics. Similarly, the narrator of
the *Carol* may "die" when the story ends—like the Spirit of Christmas
Yet to Be, he becomes silent—but the reader is expected, like Scrooge,
to embody in his continuing experience all the moral life and light that
the narrator has lavished on his storytelling.

The more fanciful qualities of the *Carol* illustrate the faith that
prompts such acts of narration. The Spirits appear to Scrooge because
there is a chance to remedy his blindness, and the narrator addresses
his readers in the hope that his story will change not only the way in
which they will see their world, but the very conditions of life. Dickens
repeatedly stresses the grim realities of the society he is portraying.
The slums, the Cratchits, the children Ignorance and Want are all typical of 1843, the year in which Carlyle announced that "England is dying of inanition" (PP, p. 1). But Scrooge's reformation changes all that.
The bitter fog, darkness, and cold of Christmas eve are replaced by
sunlight, fresh air, and a "Heavenly sky" on Christmas day (p. 72); the
promised land of Teufelsdröckh's Palingenesia has been reached.
Scrooge himself becomes a transfiguring presence. He is so cheerful
that he evokes greetings from the people he passes and finds pleasure
in everything he sees. In good romantic form, he creates the vision he
perceives. When the narrator foretells Scrooge's future, he describes
his place in a world radically different from the one in which the story
opens: "He became as good a friend, as good a master, and as good a
man, as the good old city knew, or any other good old city, town, or bor-

ough, in the good old world" (p. 76). The conventions of the fairy tale have become a statement of fact.

Although there has been some debate recently about whether Scrooge has actually changed his ways,[15] neither Dickens nor his Victorian audience would have been bothered by such doubts. Carlyle's response to the tale, his decision to share a Christmas turkey with friends, bespeaks not only a belief that Scrooge has become a new man but a conviction that reading his story could itself effect equally stunning transformations. Yet modern skepticism about this tale betrays more than a simplistic contrast between the ease of Victorian optimism and the rigor of twentieth-century doubt, even if such a contrast were valid on any occasion. It reveals a refusal to take seriously enough the fanciful mode of the *Carol*. The tale demonstrates what Dickens would have all storytelling achieve if we lived in the best of all possible worlds; its ending suggests that if the action of the story accurately depicted everyday experience, we would indeed be living in a utopia. Thackeray claimed that if the *Carol* had been published two weeks earlier, "all the prize cattle would have been gobbled up in pure love and friendship, Epping denuded of sausages, and not a turkey left in Norfolk" (6:415). His exaggeration of such potential festive excesses mirrors exactly the excesses of hope which the *Carol*'s status as a fairy tale allows it to present. More importantly, for the purposes of this discussion at least, the *Carol* stresses the generative connections that obtain in the ideal between one analogical bond and another. In Dickens's later twenty-number novels, the aesthetic principles would remain the same, though their practical implementation would become considerably more ornate. In both *Dombey and Son* and *Little Dorrit*, the moral force of the narration depends on the correlation of the reader's relation to one character and the narrator's relation to another character. In the "sermonizing" passages of *Dombey and Son*, such connections are hammered home in acts of self-conscious rhetoric; in *Little Dorrit* they are the result of subtle allusion and inference. Like the more explicit definitions of the *Carol*, however, in each case they define the narrative form of the novel.

In spite of George Eliot's famous dismissal of Dickens as a novelist who failed to contribute his gifts "to the awakening of social sympathies" (*Essays*, p. 271), her interests and even some of her methods are surprisingly like his. Although she insisted on the "reality" of Janet Dempster's Milby life, her treatment of moral transformation in the *Scenes* is no less ideal than Dickens's treatment of Scrooge. Both tales are conversion stories; both draw on a traditional pattern of religious experience to illustrate the saving grace of imagination. Both Janet and Scrooge return to the human community by recognizing their relation to the drunken husband and the crippled child who have been too long ignored. When Scrooge awakens from his nightmare of Mammon-worship, he declares, like the orthodox Evangelical experiencing a comic rebirth in Christ, "I'm quite a baby" (p. 72). Dempster's unspoken recognition of Janet's presence as she sits at his bedside is another rebirth: "It was almost like meeting him again on the resurrection morning, after the night of the grave" (2:277). There are, of course, both generic and historical differences between the two works. They stand at opposite ends of what I have been calling a mid-century tradition, and they reflect the atmospheres of their respective decades. When George Eliot expressed her approval of Ruskin's definition of realism and dismissed "vague forms, bred by imagination on the mists of feeling" in favor of "definite, substantial reality," [16] she was dismissing the popular conventions of romance that had fostered the *Carol*. Her methods, however, depend on the same kind of bonds that the *Carol* creates. The analogy between reader and character that generates the moral force of the *Carol* reappears in "Janet's Repentance" as the implicit equation of Janet's experience and the reader's apprehension of and participation in that fictive life.

Like the *Carol*, this tale records a central transformation in order to describe other, more far-reaching changes. The benefit of Tryan's relation to Janet extends beyond her life and transcends the fact of his death much as the Spirits' effect on Scrooge outlasts their disappearance. At the beginning of the tale, the town of Milby is presented as a distastefully mundane provincial backwater. It is a divided town, split between the Tryanites and the anti-Tryanites. The only bond between men, like Carlyle's cash-nexus, is a parody of community. The railroad offers an appropriate image for a world as materialistic as Scrooge's; people join together for reasons of "convenience, that admirable branch system from the main line of self-interest" (2:158). Yet when Janet begins her reformation, the townspeople become united in their pity and respect for her. Through Janet's intervention they are able to accept Tryan and to regret the cruelty which their earlier ignorance had occasioned. The jeering procession of detractors who demonstrate against Tryan at the beginning of the story is replaced by the large group of "mourning friends" who follow him to his grave (2 : 315). The reader is asked to participate in the process which transforms, first, Janet and, through her, the entire town. Indeed, the reader is put in precisely the position of a high-and-dry Milby resident who, like Janet, initially rejects Tryan as both a newcomer and a troublemaker. Late in the tale, Janet confesses, "You know what foolish things I used to say about him, knowing nothing of him all the while" (2 : 240). The reader is encouraged to make the same mistakes that Janet makes, until he learns, by listening to the story, the "only true knowledge of our fellow-man . . . which enables us to feel with him—which gives us a fine ear for the heart-pulses that are beating under the mere clothes of circumstance and opinion" (2 : 166). To achieve this refined imaginative sympathy, the narrator takes an indirect but ultimately instructive route.

Through the first eight chapters of the tale, the narrator feigns an ignorance of Tryan's "heart-pulses," and this pose of feigned ignorance exactly corresponds to the genuine ignorance of both Janet and the reader; as far as Tryan is concerned, they are all—to use a famous phrase from *Middlemarch*—"well wadded with stupidity" (p. 135). The narrator first acquaints the reader, not with Tryan, but with those silly Milby women who take up his Evangelicalism as if it were the latest novel or a new fashion in handicrafts. George Eliot's satiric abilities were well developed by the time she wrote this tale; by placing the reader's first introduction to Tryan in the context of Mrs. Linnet's living room, she destroys any sympathy one might be tempted to feel for him. Although the narrator complains about "that facile psychology which prejudges individuals by means of formulae, and casts them . . . into duly lettered pigeon-holes" (2 : 145), it is at first almost impossible to see Tryan as anything but a stereotype. The reader finds himself forced to accept one of the most popular and crude clichés about Evangelicalism—the latent connection between unsatisfied sexual energies and religious piety. Miss Pratt may write poems addressed to the "young wrestler for the truth," but most of the other women waiting for his arrival entertain romantic fancies about his "very fine cambric

handkerchiefs" and his "breeding." George Eliot even ridicules the
overweight and middle-aged spinster whose heart leaps up as Tryan
enters the room. His appearance on the scene in chapter 3 does nothing to change this initial impression. The narrator draws attention to
his "delicate hands and well-shapen feet." He looks with "beaming
timidity" on the only pretty girl in the room (2:77–91). He is self-
righteously contentious on petty matters of church doctrine. Tryan
reveals no engaging quality that might relieve such unflattering impressions. His self-imposed martyrdom, his insistence on living in un-
healthy lodgings, his refusal to accept the use of a horse when it is
offered, all smack too much of a whited sepulcher.

While the narrator's tone and choice of materials provide the
grounds on which Tryan is initially condemned to such a stereotype,
Janet is the agent who eventually mediates between the reader and
this apparently unappealing character. As soon as Tryan reveals his
past to Janet, the reader is asked to reconsider his earlier conventional
judgments. As soon as Tryan offers the "true knowledge" of himself
that replaces "the mere clothes of circumstance and opinion," both
Janet and the reader begin to hear faint echoes of that complete and
therefore unattainable sympathy which *Middlemarch* defines as "that
roar . . . on the other side of silence" (p. 135). Reader, narrator, and
character are now bound together by their mutual awareness and
understanding. At the end of the story, the narrator can speak of Tryan's last illness as "that sad history which most of us know too well"
(2:312). The reader has come to know the end of the story without
needing to hear it recounted; like Latimer in "The Lifted Veil," the narrator can assume that the reader possesses knowledge previously beyond his reach. After seeing only the first part of the story, Blackwood
wrote to protest against its cold-hearted treatment of Tryan. But *Maga*'s
relatively inexperienced writer knew what she was doing. Blackwood's
response was precisely the one that she hoped to elicit, and she could
calmly reassure him that "Mr. Tryan will carry the reader's sympathy"
(*Letters*, 2:347). In many ways the process at work here foreshadows
George Eliot's treatment of an even more unattractive Evangelical,
Nicholas Bulstrode; in both cases the reader is encouraged to entertain narrowly conventional attitudes toward the character in order to

reject them. The third Clerical Scene is as much the occasion for the reader's repentance as it is the record of Janet's.

The narrative technique which encourages such conclusions is one of the simplest and perhaps most effective ways in which a novelist can create the analogical bond between character and reader. By limiting what the reader knows to what the main character feels and sees, the novelist inevitably equates the act of reading with events that, as the past tense indicates, have already taken place. Narration revivifies the past action in two ways: first by recounting it and then by asking the reader to experience it as it was supposed to have been originally experienced by the character. This process, certainly, is not unique to Victorian fiction. Any reader of first-person narratives from *Moll Flanders* to *The Good Soldier* will recognize its appeal and its implications; anyone who has followed Emma Woodhouse's adventures for the first time knows how artfully the narrator can conceal information to make such a process work in a third-person narrative like "Janet's Repentance." Yet unique to Victorian fiction is the way in which the reader's identification with the main character generates further sympathetic bonds with other characters. To the extent that the reader identifies with Emma, he is encouraged to dismiss the claims of both the egregious Mr. Elton and the pathetic Harriet Smith. To the extent that the reader identifies with Janet Dempster, he will be encouraged to grant the claims of Tryan and even of those Milby spinsters who idolize him. George Eliot's early fiction explores the ways in which character may constitute the prime appeal or challenge to the reader's moral energies, and the character singled out as the object of sympathetic engagement in *Adam Bede* presents much greater potential difficulties than the self-righteous cleric of the *Scenes*. Moreover, these works depend on the same interlinked analogies between reader and character and character and narrator that determine narrative form in Dickens's novels. Dickens, in turn, also uses the simpler method of "Janet's Repentance." In *Dombey and Son* and *Little Dorrit*, he equates the role of his reader with the limited vision of one particular character so that that vision might be expanded both in the course of the events recorded in the novel and in the act of reading about those events.

Such a primary and even primitive mode of identifying the reader
and character is only one of a number of narrative methods which the
Victorian novelist developed so that he could define his fiction, not
simply as a mimetic artifact, but as a mimetic process that mirrors the
conditions of the characters' lives. One of the most striking examples
of this process—striking both in the literal quality of its enactment and
the length to which its creator takes this premise—is *Vanity Fair*.
Thackeray's first major work fully displays his own recent "conversion"
to the mid-century aesthetic as well as his characteristically playful or
even skeptical attitudes toward it. His preaching clown establishes an
often uncomfortable intimacy with the reader, but for Thackeray such
a bond is not itself a sufficient basis for the reader's relation to the text.
Like Scrooge himself, Thackeray's clown must undergo a comic transformation. This aesthetic change is revolutionary. It alters the reader's
relation to the characters, completes the analogical process which his
presumed intimacy with the reader has initiated, and once again
equates the act of reading and the facts of living.[17]

In chapter 62 of *Vanity Fair*, in the middle of the eighteenth
monthly number, the narrator challenges the reader to think of the
true gentlemen he can recall from his "circle" of acquaintances: "Let
us take a little scrap of paper and each make out his list" (p. 601). The
narrator naturally includes himself in this challenge and announces
that his "friend the Major" will figure in his own list. For many hun-
dreds of pages, he has been suggesting a generalized, figurative
friendship between himself and his characters, but this inclusion of
Dobbin in his "circle" is more specific. By the end of the following paragraph, the literal quality of this reference is unexpectedly explained
when the narrator describes an incident from his own biography. He
has been commenting on the mutual happiness of Amelia and Dobbin
during their stay on the Continent. In an offhand way that should alert
us to the importance of the upcoming announcement, he adds, "It was
on this very tour that I, the present writer of a history of which every
word is true, had the pleasure to see them first, and to make their acquaintance" (p. 602). We now learn that the narrator's familiar attitude towards the characters is based on an actual acquaintance with
them. His meeting Amelia at Pumpernickel is significant simply because the narrator is the man "predestined" to write "this particular

lady's memoirs" (p. 603). By the end of the chapter, he has turned himself into an extremely minor character in the novel; he is one of a group of young Englishmen who take their hats off to Amelia, who watch her responses to the opera at the court theater, and who later talk with Jos Sedley about the advantages of an extended stay in Pumpernickel.

Quite early in the novel the narrator has had some fun at the expense of artists and actors who confuse art and life. The Neapolitan storyteller who is enraged by the wicked deeds of characters he has invented and the French performers who refuse to play the roles of villains or foreigners are all taking themselves and their work too seriously. It is indeed surprising, then, to discover that by the end of the novel the narrator himself is capable of the credulity he has earlier mocked. Within the framing device of the preface and the final closing of the puppet-box, the narrator offers a performance in which his art, deftly juggled, becomes life. As he plays with the roles of preacher and jester, he transforms himself from the romancer and novelist to the historian and biographer. *Vanity Fair* may open as a "Novel without a Hero," but it ends as a "Comic History," the "memoirs" and "biography" of the characters. Carlyle had cried out for a "magic rod to turn all that . . . artificial fictitious soap-lather, and mere Lying" of the popular novel into a "faithful study of Reality" ("Biography," C M E, 3 : 59–60). Almost as if in direct response to this appeal to the "mountebank Juggler," Thackeray uses the powers of authorial fiat to reveal the reality of the story that his narrator, like the itinerant Neapolitan, has invented.

Vanity Fair begins on a premise familiar to any reader of the introductions and footnotes in the collected Waverley novels. The story is a fiction, "untrue" and "unreal" in the sense that it is "entirely imaginary," as Sir Walter Scott would say, and not an account of "actual" experience. The narrator openly refers to the subtitle, "this 'Novel without a Hero,' which we are now relating" (p. 58), and he repeatedly draws attention to his omniscience, to his freedom and power, to the scope of his knowledge and understanding: "The novelist, who knows everything, knows this also" (p. 318). The narrator is a "brother of the story-telling trade" (p. 80); he creates the tale the reader hears and, like the reader, he has an existence independent of it. Yet in chapter 62 we discover that he is no more than a gossip. He merely passes on the stories he has overheard. Tom Eaves appears in chapter 64 to tell part of Becky's "biography" (p. 625), and Tapeworm, the English chargé d'affaires at Pumpernickel, narrates the "history" of the Crawley family for Dobbin's benefit in chapter 66. It is here "at that very table years ago that the present writer had the pleasure of hearing the tale" (p. 644). We are asked to believe that the entire novel is the result of Tapeworm's attempt to warn the major against Becky's reputed immorality. The "novelist, who knows everything," has had his creative role usurped by the gossip, the man "who knew everybody" (p. 625), the man who "knew everything and a great deal besides, about all the world" (p. 644). In a baffling way, the novel becomes a self-generating document. It is not the product of one man's fancy; rather, it is the work of the gossips who exist within the story itself. The narrator does not create the fiction; the facts of his characters' lives dictate what he must say next.

By establishing the narrator's essential identity wih figures like Becky, Rawdon, and Amelia, Thackeray inevitably initiates an analogical process that comes to include the reader as well. Early in the novel the characters' status as fictive beings has contributed to the illusion of both the narrator's credibility and his reality. Like the voice of *Tom Jones*, he emphasizes the artificiality of his tale so that, by contrast, he himself will seem less artificial, more substantial than his subject. The reader is encouraged to trust the narrator simply because he does not try to trick him into thinking the fiction true. When the narrator eventually reveals that he too is a character, he implies that his earlier qualities have become the attributes of the other characters; now all three agents in the narration, reader and narrator and character, inhabit a realm in which life and art unequivocally interpenetrate. Thackeray's sleight-of-hand, the narrative magic he displays in the treatment of his storyteller, is one way of persuading the reader to entertain the possibility that the characters are beings whose lives are very much like his own. To reach such a conclusion, however, Thackeray offers some amusing instances of circular logic. Even the narrator's credibility takes on a self-reflexive quality. Carlyle was fond of quoting words from Novalis that Thackeray would have found appropriate and that Conrad would later use in *Lord Jim*, "It is certain, my Belief gains quite *infinitely* the moment I can convince another mind thereof" (SR, 171). In *Vanity Fair* we find the narrator convincing himself of his own belief. With more success and audacity than the Marlow who addresses the listeners on the verandah, Thackeray's narrator asserts that his perception of fact is no fiction. He can say, as Carlyle has said in "Biography," "The Thing which I here hold imaged in my mind did actually occur . . . is not a dream, but a reality!" Thackeray has proven the persuasiveness of his fiction. Even the narrator, who creates the story, is finally convinced of its reality. How does he know that it is true? Simply because, as he tells us, he himself has met the participants at Pumpernickel.

Thackeray turns what might seem a concession to his readers' preference for fact rather than fiction into a rigorous challenge to their conventional conceptions of morality. If George Eliot disarms the reader's prejudices by allowing him to entertain attitudes he must eventually relinquish, Thackeray triumphs over such prejudices by seeming to acquiesce in them. He was indeed troubled by the infamous though exaggerated prudery of the mid-Victorian audience. In his fiction, more frequently than in that of Dickens and George Eliot, morality means, specifically, one's attitudes toward sexual behavior, as the weaknesses of *The Virginians* quite sadly attest. Thackeray often responded to his readers' squeamishness by using a familiar rhetorical ploy: in order to say what he has on his mind, he begins by stating what he is not going to say. Yet Thackeray issues a more effective declaration of freedom when he identifies his narrator as a gossip and transforms the narration itself into an instance of tale-telling. Significantly, the narrator does not give up his claim to the authorship of the novel until Becky shows up in Pumpernickel as Madame de Raudon. Her "sad, sad reputation" (p. 619) has followed her across Europe from Boulogne to Dieppe, then to Caen and Tours; she is now the "perfect Bohemian" (p. 625). In previous chapters she has soared above the narrator's level in society. Now she has plunged so far below the reader's presumed moral and social status that the narrator feels he must disavow responsibility for this nasty turn of events. The recorder of a "true" history is at the mercy of his characters' actions. It can hardly be his fault if Becky's behavior offends the reader.

More importantly, however, Thackeray's deft handling of this potentially hazardous development implicates the reader in the process which keeps such nasty tales in circulation while it questions their reliability. When Tom Eaves stands before Gaunt House and tells salacious stories about the Marchioness of Steyne, we begin to understand that scandal, both as gossip and immoral behavior, is not a matter of simple truth or fiction; we also learn that the scandalmonger is both a toady and a bit of a voyeur. Yet if the narrator of *Vanity Fair* is a gossip, the reader is the one who offers the willing ear that occasions his narrative sins. In a new and startling fashion, Thackeray has reestablished the link between reading novels and immorality that the Evangelicals had proposed. Instead of demanding that we declare our moral superiority to such activities, Thackeray suggests that we can scarcely avoid them. The form of *Vanity Fair*, as it is defined by its source in gossip, proves that both the reader and the narrator are more like Tom Eaves than they would like to think. And if the comfortable illusion of that distinction no longer obtains, we might be asked to admit our fundamental identity with even that unrepentant reprobate Becky Sharp.

Thackeray's narrative technique extends the possibility for such bonds. Reading *Vanity Fair* is an act of participation in the social forms of the world it depicts because he so cleverly equates reading with the most prominent form of communication in that world, taletelling. Becky is declared innocent or guilty according to the credulity with which the other characters listen to the stories told about her. Dobbin and Sir Pitt disassociate themselves from her specifically because of the rumors that Tapeworm and Wenham circulate. Thackeray captures the quality of such "scandal" and makes it an attribute of the novel itself through the form he imposes on the events recorded in it. His narrative "redoublings," as John A. Lester first called them,[18] imitate exactly a gossip's manner of telling a story. The narrator is not content simply to double back in time to pick up the story of the character he has temporarily ignored; such disruptions in the chronology of a tale are a narrative necessity faced by any novelist interested in treating the lives of various groups of people. Thackeray, however, further complicates his chronology by presenting a new turn of events in a dramatic scene or as a fait accompli, and only then does he narrate the events which have led up to it. A gossip like Tapeworm or Tom Eaves uses the same strategy. He tries to surprise or interest his listener with the startling announcement of his news and then goes on to elaborate, with background information, details, and ramifications. The gossip would tell the story of Sedley's bankruptcy in precisely the achronological fashion Thackeray employs to set out the information in chapters 17 and 18. He would say, "Did you hear about the auction? . . . It was held at Sedley's house in Russell Square. . . . Well, you know they're now living off the Fulham Road. . . . Yes, for some time now Sedley's business has been going downhill." Like the narrator who listens to Tom Eaves's version of Lady Steyne's past, the reader learns of crucial events such as George Osborne's death and Becky's marriage as if they had been recounted by a gossip. The technique appears in countless major and minor instances, but Thackeray uses it most extensively to recount the event in the plot which involves the greatest moral ambiguity: Becky's evening with Lord Steyne. At the end of chapter 51, Rawdon, accompanied by Steyne's agent, Wenham, is arrested by Moss's men. In chapter 52 the narrator doubles back to present several events removed some distance in time from the night of the arrest. The reader waits in some suspense over Rawdon's fate while the narrator explains what he ironically calls Steyne's "kindness towards the Crawley family" (p. 501). Before Rawdon's capture, Steyne has helped enroll little Rawdon in a boarding school and has found Briggs, Becky's moral "sheep-dog" (p. 466), a position in the country. This redoubling cannot but rouse the reader's suspicions of Steyne's motives and of Becky's possible complicity. It both explains Rawdon's arrest—he is the last guardian of Becky's virtue to be removed from the house in Mayfair—and prepares for the even greater crisis which is about to occur. Here Thackeray creates an analogy between the reader and Rawdon. Like Becky's bewildered husband, we are asked to put the pieces of the puzzle together without any certain assurance that the resulting picture is an accurate image of events. Such implications are characteristic of Thackeray's fiction. In *The Newcomes* he would use other social forms, portrait paintings and dinner gatherings, as the basis of his narrative technique, so that he could insure that reading imitates the experiential quality of his characters' lives.

When Thackeray turns *Vanity Fair* into "a history of which every word is true," he adduces the reconciliation between life and art that is the goal of Victorian fiction. Almost as unexpected and marvelous as the moment when the statue of Hermione becomes a woman who moves and speaks, this transformation reveals the wit and assurance of Thackeray's art at its best. If the world of *Vanity Fair* allows little of the idealism of the *Carol* or the moral earnestness of the *Scenes*, its comic energy more than adequately supplies their place. The narrator's quick-change act is a piece of narrative magic that the reader is expected to enjoy, and it is akin to the joke at the end of *A Christmas Carol*. After representing through the ghosts his most extensive ambitions as a novelist and his most serious social concerns, the narrator prophesies that Scrooge will see no new spirits now that he has embraced the Total Abstinence Principle. Only an author who trusts the goodwill and the capacities of his audience would so freely compound facetiousness and earnestness. *Vanity Fair* displays something of the same good faith. Here Thackeray has come into his own. He bases his art on the analogical processes already evident in Dickens's work, but he does so in a way that could never be confused with Dickens's approach. In a fashion typical of his later fiction, Thackeray concentrates on the relation between his characters and his narrator; in turn, this bond becomes the source of the reader's connection to the story. In *Vanity Fair* Thackeray has clearly discovered the power inherent in this circle of linked analogies.

When Thackeray was a young man idling away his time on the Continent or in London, studying the part that his narrator would later play in chapter 62 of *Vanity Fair*, he spent a great deal of time reading fiction. On one occasion he confided in his diary, "The day spent in seediness repentance & novel reading" (*Letters*, 1 : 206). It is impossible to be sure whether, in 1832, the novels pertained to the seediness or to the repentance, but it is not hard to guess. Thackeray seems to have been reading Scott at the time, but that fact would be evidence in the case against repentance. The year before, in his introduction to *The Fortunes of Nigel*, Scott himself had admitted that he was "no great believer in the moral utility" of the novel (p. viii), and he had gone to great lengths in *St. Ronan's Well* to prove that a taste for fiction is only one easy step from the willing submission to seduction, the spawning of illegitimate and syphilitic children, and death by puerperal fever. Soon, however, Carlyle's practice in *Sartor Resartus* would demonstrate some of the ways in which fiction might redeem itself. Although Carlyle would never become a kindly critic of the novel—

"Dickens writes a *Dombey and Son*, Thackeray a *Vanity Fair*; not *reapers* they, either of them!"[19]—he formulated the principles by which the novelist might take his proper place in society and recover from his former disrepute. Ultimately, the Victorian novelist made more of the potential inherent in the narrative form of *Sartor Resartus* than Carlyle himself did. Nor were Dickens, Thackeray, and George Eliot the only novelists to exploit its possibilities. Reading the account of Teufelsdröckh's life in the summer of 1850, Melville came upon a narrative mode that he adopted in the mediating voice of *Moby-Dick*. Ishmael is in fact such an effective bridge between our own land-locked experience and life on board the *Pequod* that, by the end of the novel, the reader whom he had addressed as an "ignorant landsman" is conceived to be, in spirit at least, a Nantucketer and a whaleman. With something of the same sense of shared experience, the author of *The Newcomes*, who had earlier expressed his hostility to his audience, would offer to take his reader by the hand. Like the Editor of *Sartor*, Thackeray would come to see the publication of his works and, partic-ularly, serial publication as a kind of "confidential talk between writer and reader" (*Pendennis*, p. xxxv). The bonds of reading, the analogical relations wrought by the author's imagination in the act of creating the story and by the reader's in the act of perceiving it, had established a firm basis for such communion.

For the Victorian novelist the opposition between art and life is the problem that must be confronted in every narrative that presumes to be more than "mere Lying." The moral value of his fiction depends upon persuading the reader to entertain the possibility that art is expe-rience, "nearer" to life than he had ever imagined. Carlyle had stated a cardinal point when he wrote, "Only in so far as Imagination, were it but momentarily, is *believed*, can there be any use or meaning in it, any enjoyment of it" ("Biography," CME, 3 : 50). Victorian fiction responds consistently and energetically to this challenge; it is a rhetorical art born out of moral necessity. If the romantic conception of the imagina-tion outlines one answer to the problem of belief, the novelist's typ-ically generous definition of mimesis suggests another. As George Eliot proved by quoting Dante in *Theophrastus Such*, vision and fact are both "true" and "not untrue" (p. 198). Dickens, as usual, was the first of the Victorian novelists to come to such a conclusion. *Oliver*

Twist, product of the year in which Victoria came to the throne, contains one of the first and most impressive images of the interpenetration of fact and vision, reality and imagination, that would characterize the novel at mid-century. Late in the story, the rescued orphan dozes as Fagin and Monks stand outside the window of Mrs. Maylie's country home, and the narrator comments on this, the second of Oliver's dream-visions:

There is a kind of sleep that steals upon us sometimes, which, while it holds the body prisoner, does not free the mind from a sense of things about it, and enable it to ramble at its pleasure. . . . Words which are really spoken, or sounds which really exist at the moment, accommodate themselves with surprising readiness to our visions, until reality and imagination become so strangely blended that it is afterwards almost a matter of impossibility to separate the two. (pp. 227–28)

The fiction of Oliver's dream is determined by the reality beyond it. The words spoken at the window are transformed, by Oliver's sleeping awareness of them, into a visual image of Fagin in the London slum which Oliver has escaped. When Oliver wakes, he sees the subject of his vision standing before him. Like the narrator of *Vanity Fair* as well as Keats's Adam, he awoke and found it true.

The Victorian novelists capable of creating such transformations for their characters or narrators aspired to effect them for their readers as well. To do so, Dickens, Thackeray, and George Eliot developed the wide range of narrative techniques that identify their works as participants in a mid-century tradition. They experimented with the reader's temporal relation to the story so frequently that unconventional present-tense narration became a convention of their art. They adopted techniques from the divergent realms of history and poetry to illustrate the shifting boundaries between reality and romance. They extended romantic modes of narration to satisfy the demands of quite Victorian aesthetic assumptions. And, most consistently, they explored with great energy and persistence the possibility of using their narrators as voices mediating between the fictive life of the novel and the world of the reader. The actual achievement of this aim is not a matter open to empirical proof or critical demonstration; only the individual reader can say whether he has accepted the invitation to enter the bonds of reading. That the novelist always remained blithely confident that such a goal might be attained is, in fact, not a conclusion one would draw from even the most sanguine of their mid-century works. Yet the impact of their ideals on their narrative techniques, on their practice as storytellers, is a demonstrable fact. Indeed, in their desire to create an occasion for the analogical powers of narration, these three novelists engaged all the impressive technical ingenuity and vigor of their art.

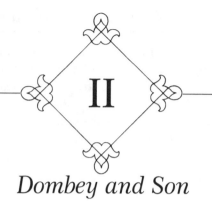

II

Dombey and Son
Temporality and Transcendence

In *Dombey and Son* (1846–48) Dickens re-creates Oliver's initial waking dream of Fagin, with several elaborate and revealing alterations. At the beginning of chapter 34, Good Mrs. Brown, the female Fagin who years ago had lured Florence to her den, sits motionless before a "sullen" fire. Unlike Fagin, she is alone. There is no dreaming child, no female Oliver, present to witness this particular nightmare. The fire itself, "like the eye of a fierce beast," both creates and perceives a demonic vision of the old woman: "A gigantic and distorted image of [her is] thrown half upon the wall behind her, half upon the roof above." This broken image suggests an interpenetration of reality and imagination that has become more perplexing than illuminating. The movement of Good Mrs. Brown's chattering jaws is "too frequent and too fast" to be captured in the shadow cast by the "slow flickering of the fire"; paradoxically, therefore, it seems "an illusion wrought by the light" on a "motionless" face. Moreover, the truth of this image is mnemonic, but it evokes a memory that no one actually experiences. If Florence were present, the narrator explains, the shadow on the wall would recall a terrifying event in her past. Only so "grotesque and exaggerated a presentment of the truth" would conform to Florence's "childish recollection" of the woman's witchlike figure (p. 465).

Although the very complexity of this passage manages to relate, at least hypothetically, the realms of reality and imagination, it reveals a potential discontinuity that threatens both Florence and her creator. The crucial point of this description is, of course, Florence's absence. By the time this chapter opens, she has long inhabited a world where fact and fancy, circumstance and desire, have no relation to each other; she lives "in a dream wherein the overflowing love of her young heart expended itself on airy forms, and in a real world where she had experienced little but the rolling back of that strong tide upon itself" (p. 624). Even though her essential innocence, like Oliver's, cannot be tarnished by this world, Gorgon-like reality may turn her into a stone incapable of experiencing even the feeblest of dreams. Conversely, like Miss Flite of *Bleak House*, Florence may come to live in a world of dreams that have only the most bitterly ironic of relations to actuality. Preferring to notice only the ideality of her characterization, most modern readers have overlooked Florence's difficulties, but they have found Dickens's quite similar situation genuinely disturbing. Such readers tell us that the seductions of an irrelevant fantasizing have obscured his perception of fact. He is accused of being more naive than even the Neapolitan storyteller of *Vanity Fair*. *Dombey and Son* is often judged to be the product of an imagination in touch with neither its own strengths nor its "proper" material, of a vision as divided as Wemmick's private and professional lives. Dickens's original outline of the plot is repeatedly used as evidence against him—he supposedly began a "business" novel, gave it up when he heard the music of the waves, and never found a unifying focus to take the place of his original theme. According to such readings, reality and imagination in this novel never attain the coherence exhibited in Oliver's dream-vision. For this reason Dickens fails to make *Dombey and Son* one of his later, "great" social novels.[1]

Yet Dickens clearly understands the dangers of this duality. If he proposes the frightening disjunction of dream and reality, shadow and substance, he does so only because he knows he can ultimately avert an unthinkable outcome. Before reaching a conclusion in which reconciliation is possible, Dickens acknowledges the realities of a social world that stubbornly stand in opposition to such endings. The dehumanization and literal deadliness of a world given over to the worship of Mammon are as central to this novel as they are to *Bleak House* or *Our Mutual Friend*. If *Dombey and Son* often seems to be an earlier version of *Little Dorrit*, if the issues of the two novels, some of the characters, and their relationships are strikingly similar, Dickens's approach and his solutions to their difficulties are not. *Dombey* is far from the fragile and muted consolations of *Little Dorrit*. Its music is composed in a different key. "Hope," as Captain Cuttle says, "Hope. It's that as animates you. Hope is a buoy" (pp. 667–68). Hope is certainly the animating force of *Dombey and Son*. It is the only one of Dickens's major novels that shares the spirit of the Christmas books. Its insistent fairy-tale elements continually assure us that a happy ending is around the long narrative corner of this twenty-number serial. Dick Whittington never drowns at sea; he will return to become the rightful Son and Heir. Like Captain Cuttle on the night of Walter's return, the narrator will tell us a story equal to our longings; the shadow on the wall will suddenly turn into the long-lost brother we had given up as dead. The perplexity and fear that characterize Mrs. Brown's distorted image will resolve into the simplicity of a "pure embrace" (p. 662). Desired outcome and actuality will be united at last.

The nature of such faith and Dickens's need to articulate it have confused and embarrassed modern readers. To some effects of this impulse toward affirmation we cannot and perhaps should not be reconciled; Lord Jeffrey might have been willing to cede critical judgment to weep over the happy death of Paul, but we are less attuned to such consummations. Some careful distinctions, however, would help. It is not so much this quite powerful and restrained deathbed scene that is likely to disturb us; it is rather the narrator's pontificating rhetoric, his self-conscious rhythmic invocations of whispering waves and faraway countries that create the modern reader's discomfort. If we try to uncover the relevance of this strained poetry to the prose of Dombey's commercial world, we might begin to comprehend the logic of even Dickens's most fantastic visions. Florence and the narrator of *Dombey and Son* face the same essential problem. They both confront a world in which imagination and its attendant virtue, hope, seem irrelevant; they both confront others skeptical of such values. In this sense the reader of *Dombey and Son* finds his analogue in Dombey himself. The rift between father and daughter represents the adversary relationship that might obtain between reader and narrator. By exploring the analogy between Florence and the narrator, we can understand the impulse behind the distinctive narrative technique of this novel. If it is Florence's mission to redeem her father, it is equally the narrator's task to liberate the reader from his conventional attitudes. In both cases, time is the medium for such acts of illumination; in both cases, reconciliation is their goal. The events of the story constitute the process which must unite character and character; their narration will presumably unite narrator and reader. If this is to happen, however, narrative technique must equate living and reading, equate the experiences of the Dombey family and the experience of reading about them.

Carlyle's *Sartor Resartus* offers the most revealing perspective from which this process and its resulting analogies can be approached. Dickens was always attuned to the lessons of Carlyle's satiric denunciations, but in *Dombey and Son* he seems closer to Carlyle's positive assertions than in any of his other novels.[2] The issues raised in the sage's early works allow us to comprehend the aspects of the novel that seem least congenial to our tastes—its characterization of Florence as well as its self-conscious symbolism, its fairy-tale qualities, and its refusal to remain bound to the social themes it inaugurates. There is nothing new about the questions that both Carlyle and Dickens explore; time, change, death, rebirth, and eternity, the river of life and the sea of transcendence can all be found in Christian contexts. Tennyson's *In Memoriam* is the most obvious Victorian analogue. Yet like George Eliot's fiction, both *Dombey* and *Sartor* draw on the symbolism of conventional religion as they free it from its doctrinal implications. It is striking, for instance, that Paul, not the narrator, makes the only specific reference to Christ in the novel. While Dickens and Carlyle might posit a reality beyond this life, they both focus on the same, more immediate question: what is the relation between a man caught in temporality and the transcendent realm for which he longs? As Carlyle explains, life in time involves pain and paradox:

For man lives in Time, has his whole earthly being, endeavour and destiny shaped for him by Time: only in the transitory Time-Symbol is the ever-motionless Eternity we stand on made manifest. And yet, in such winter-seasons of Denial, it is for the nobler-minded perhaps a comparative misery to have been born, and to be awake and work; and for the duller a felicity, if, like hibernating animals, safe-lodged in some Salamanca University, or Sybaris City, or other superstitious or voluptuous Castle of Indolence, they can slumber-through in stupid dreams, and only awaken when the loud-roaring hailstorms have all done their work, and to our prayers and martyrdoms the new Spring has been vouchsafed. (SR, p. 91)

The characterizations of *Dombey and Son* are patterned on such an attitude toward time. Dombey is the "man [who] lives in Time," and his children are defined by their awareness of "ever-motionless Eternity." The novel explores what is for Dombey's "nobler-minded" children a "winter-season of Denial." While he presides in his castle of monomaniacal egoism, they long for his recognition of their reality. Like Teufelsdröckh, "Son of Time," who speaks of his "glimpses of our upper Azure Home" which he will reach on a sea of eternity (SR, p. 104), the Dombey children respond to the "waves" that speak of an "invisible country far away" (p. 773). A less morbid version of Hardy's Little Father Time, Paul can only peer over some great Atlantic of Time or cling to Florence, the embodiment of unchanging love. The realm of temporality is one of suffering and denial; the rule of life, which man tries to deny, is change. In a later passage that seems to describe both Dombey and the climactic event of the novel, Teufelsdröckh notes, "By nature [man] hates change; seldom will he quit his old house till it has actually fallen about his ears" (SR, p. 189). Although they are merely shadows, time and change are the only means by which man, imprisoned in the present, can perceive eternity, the Everlasting *NOW*. "Yes here, in this poor, miserable, hampered, despicable Actual . . . here or nowhere is thy Ideal" (SR, p. 156).

The ideal is necessarily hampered by the fact of temporality, but, as Scrooge's story had shown, the quality of Victorian life makes its bondage all the more intolerable. In *Dombey and Son* the commercial world imprisons individuals in a circularity of routine that blinds them to both time and change. Life, which was once natural and vital, has become simply mechanistic. As Carlyle sarcastically explains, "Here, circling like the gin-horse, for whom partial or total blindness is no evil, the Bread-artist [doctor, lawyer] can travel contentedly round and round, still fancying that it is forward and forward." Man becomes "an additional horse's power in the grand corn-mill or hemp-mill of Economic Society" (SR, p. 97). Morfin makes the same point in *Dombey and Son* when he comments on the "jog-trot life" of habit: "We go on in our clock-work routine, from day to day, and can't make out, or follow, these changes. They—they're a metaphysical sort of thing. We—we haven't leisure for it. . . . In short, we are so d——d business-like" (p. 459). Although Dombey is a remarkably inattentive businessman, his indifference to "metaphysical" realities makes him the appropriate head of his firm. His only concern is to speed up time, to dominate an indomitable medium, so that Paul can become his partner. The irony needs no elucidation. Paul, the "*Boy born, to die,*"[3] should teach Dombey that time leads inevitably to death, but his father ignores both the frightening lesson of time—*edax rerum*—and its paradoxical consolation: change, the process that exists in time, can also lead out of temporality. As Dombey becomes increasingly blind and rigid, he epitomizes the time-bound man to an ever greater degree.

Florence, the character who seems untouched by change, attuned to eternity, is the figure through whom Dickens further explores the conditions of paradox that temporality imposes on human life. It is precisely Florence's connection to the Everlasting *NOW* that puts her humanity in doubt. She is a vacuum, in Kathleen Tillotson's memorable phrase, a "space where [a] character ought to be."[4] Dickens warns against the cruelty of using people as symbols—the elder, erring John Carker is forced to serve as a "cheap example" to the other clerks in the Firm (p. 615)—but Florence is clearly a symbol. She stands for love, as Teufelsdröckh defines it, a "discerning of the Infinite in the Finite, of the Idea made Real" (s r, p. 115). She consistently embodies the ideals that Carlyle outlines in his essay on Dr. Johnson: Reverence and Humility, as well as Love. In a chapter called "The Study of a Loving Heart," Dickens provides a narrative illustration of the maxim that Carlyle states in the essay on "Biography": "A loving Heart is the beginning of all Knowledge" (c m e, 3 : 57). Yet the world Florence inhabits ignores her relevance, and her life is genuinely one of contradiction. The vacuity of her characterization is a function, not of her identity, but of her situation. The failure of the descendental world to recognize and thereby substantiate her virtues insures that the idea of her character never achieves the status of the real. Florence learns that her father's hatred necessarily alienates her from other potential sources of affection; to admit that she feels a need for love would be a public indictment of his neglect to satisfy that need. For all her integrity, Florence leads a life of division. Just as her father causes a separation of fact and fancy in her life, she causes the alienation of those she loves. Paul ignores his father because of his love for his sister. Edith's attachment to Florence further divides both wife and daughter from Dombey. Walter is exiled from his uncle because Dombey resents his interest in and concern for Florence. The unchanging, time-bound father must reject both Florence, *Veritas filia temporis*, and any character who betrays a knowledge of her worth.

The contradictions of Florence's life are exactly those faced by the narrator as he tries to embody the transcendent values she represents in the temporal medium to which the novel binds him. He works in a genre necessarily defined by time—as the derivation of the word implies—and the reader who follows the story from page to page is necessarily, like Dombey, a being who "lives in Time." The novel is certainly not the most appropriate medium for capturing a glimpse of what Tennyson in "The Ancient Sage" calls "the single world"; its form is obviously more conducive to temporality and its "double seeming." Yet novelists repeatedly try to escape this generic limitation and evoke a sense of the transcendent. In a fashion reminiscent of Carlyle, D. H. Lawrence manages to capture it in the intoxicating vision in the last paragraph of *The Rainbow*, but such attempts usually lead to the uneven success evident in novels such as *Pierre* and *Daniel Deronda*. *Sartor Resartus* suggests one possible solution to this problem. Although Teufelsdröckh asks, "How paint to the sensual eye . . . in what words, known to these profane times, speak even afar-off of the unspeakable?" (s R, p. 148), Carlyle himself responds by resorting to the "words" of a narrative. He tells the story of Teufelsdröckh's life, but he chooses to paint what G. B. Tennyson calls "a *Märchen* figure . . . in a *Märchen* world."[5] Carlyle liberates narrative from the traditional realistic restraints that had come to define the novel in the eighteenth century. He sees no inconsistency in blending social fact with fairy tale; the old clothes men of Monmouth Street are, if we only knew it, perfectly appropriate symbolic figures. The motifs of a *Märchen* world dominate *Sartor Resartus* because they suggest a form of narrative that is both timeless and universal. But Dickens is more troubled than Carlyle is by the contradictions that such elements create. His early attempts to account for Sol Gills's shop in economic terms are misleading and unconvincing. When the novel opens, he seems reluctant to admit that the Wooden Midshipman stands for the inviolable sanctuary cherished in every child's dreams. Unlike *Sartor Resartus*, in which transcendent and temporal coexist from the first page on, *Dombey and Son* opens with a tentative formulation of temporality's dominion; only as the plot develops do transcendence and the *Märchen* world succeed in relegating the actual to its proper place. Only then is the reader allowed to escape the temporality in which reading a novel threatens to entrap him.

Through Phiz, Dickens even offers an iconography by which we can evaluate his changing conceptions of the novel. The monthly-number cover, a reflection of his initial sense of the action, is an image of temporality. The frontispiece to the first book edition, which was originally published in the final double number of the serial, offers an image of the temporal from the perspective of the transcendent. One detail of the monthly-number cover (see p. 75) suggests that Dickens's initial plan was more specifically topical than has been previously noticed and its final form much less so. Both *Dickens at Work* and the introduction to the Clarendon edition of the novel note without explanation that this scene seems to place Dombey in Parliament.[6] The startling rise of George Hudson, the Railway King, suggests what Dombey might be doing there. By 1845 Hudson had become a lionized and prominent member of Parliament, all on the strength of the fabulous fortune he made in railway investments. Since all proposals for new lines and companies had to be approved by Parliament, Dombey's place in the House of Commons might have involved him in the increasing mania for financial ventures. Dickens, I think, planned a plot in which Dombey would invest the funds of his traditional import/export business in railway speculations, rise into prominence and Parliament, and finally lose both his investments and his business as the result of a Merdle-like collapse. (For this point Hudson could not have served as an example; his good luck held throughout the bursting of the Railway Bubble, and the fraud by which he made his wealth was not discovered until 1849.) This scheme would explain why the M.P., Sir Barnet Skettles, is introduced into the novel for a prominent role he never is called upon to perform, why Dickens insists on mentioning

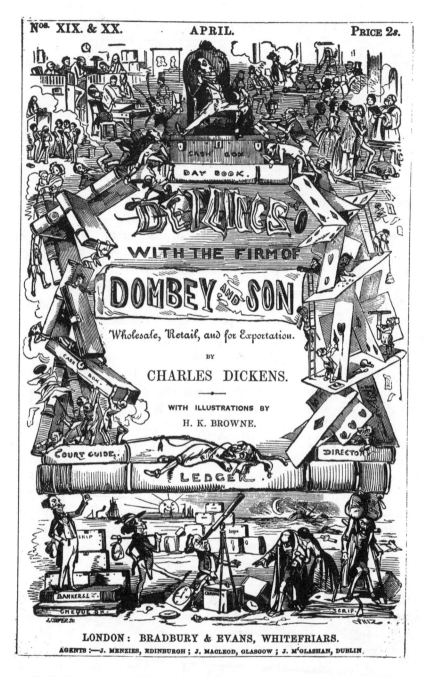

H. K. Browne, monthly-number cover, *Dombey and Son* (April 1848)

Miss Tox's uncle the Magistrate, a character who could have been involved in Dombey's ensuing legal embarrassments. Such a plan also explains the image of Dombey that we see in the bottom right-hand corner of the monthly-number cover. A broken man, bent under the weight of moneybags, perhaps a symbol of debt, Dombey stands on a sheaf of papers labeled "scrip," the contemporary term used for railway shares. This drawing recalls another topical allusion, the "stag" or investor who might have had something to do with the early treatment of Staggs's Gardens. This scheme finally explains why Dickens was uncomfortable with Phiz's cover illustration and found "a little too much in it" (Pilgrim *Letters*, 4:620). It certainly suggests a more specific plot than the one to which Dickens ultimately gave his wholehearted imaginative commitment.

The plot suggested by the number cover never, of course, came into existence. Dombey in no way resembles the Arthur Clennam he would have become if Dickens had adhered to his initial intentions, and Staggs's Gardens are less the product of outrageous speculation than the name suggests. Dickens carefully limits any topical sources of reference; the subjects that overwhelm the pages of *Punch* in 1845 and 1846—railway charters, scrip, stags, Capel Court, and the gauge controversy—have no place in the text of the novel.[7] The nature of Carker's disastrous investments, in which Dombey plays no part, is not specified. The railroad in *Dombey and Son* is neither a symbol of progress nor "The Railway Juggernaut of 1845," whose engine is marked "SPECULATION" in John Leech's famous cartoon (*Punch* 9 [1845]:47). Even less does it symbolize the perversion of values that Carlyle was soon to castigate in the seventh of the *Latter-Day Pamphlets* (1850) where King Hudson and scrip again play a major role. Rather the train resembles the more generalized and universal winged-and-bearded figure marked "TIME" in a less well known cartoon by Leech (see p. 76, *Punch* 9 [1845]:188). The figures of a specifically timeless and non-topical popular imagination have come to dominate the novel. In the frontispiece Phiz emphasized images of transcendence; the far-away country with its waves and angels frame the characters who are caught in temporality as they suggest a release from its grasp. Here, as in the text, Carker is destroyed by a train which recalls Carlyle's image of the mechanistic universe that Teufelsdröckh must reject: "One huge, dead,

H. K. Browne, frontispiece, *Dombey and Son* (1848)

Detail, monthly-number cover, *Dombey and Son*

immeasurable Steam-engine, rolling on, in its dead indifference, to grind me limb from limb" (s r, p. 133). The train in Phiz's drawing stands opposite an image that Carlyle calls the Time-Prince, the Devil. A demonic version of Leech's *Punch* figure, this winged and bearded devil, complete with hourglass, stands before a skeleton poised to strike Mrs. Skewton (see p. 78); the traditional connection that Carlyle invariably makes between time, the devil, and death is given pictorial representation here. The fairy-tale motifs that are faintly sketched in the bottom of the monthly-number cover are now replaced by a visual design in which they are the predominating features.

Yet even a narrative based exclusively on such timeless symbols—as *Dombey and Son* is not—will never succeed in concealing the fact that every story exists in time. Carlyle again defines the problem and proposes a solution. In "On History" he explains the inevitable temporal limitation of prose fiction: "All Narrative is, by its nature, of only one dimension; only travels forward towards one, or towards successive points." Narration, then, is like a train—the reader, its passenger. But a recognition of transcendence demands that the writer present

John Leech, "Anti-Railway Meeting of Fox-Hunters" (*Punch*, 1845)

more than a sequential progression in time: "The whole is a broad, deep Immensity, and each atom is 'chained' and complected with all" (CME, 2:89). Conventional narrative also assumes the completion of the action in time past; but Teufelsdröckh declares that "nothing is completed, but ever completing" (SR, p. 197). Conventional narrative forces the reader to distinguish between the fictional action and his own experience. Although both move inevitably forward in one direction, one exists in the past, and the other exists from moment to moment in the present. Carlyle's use of the historical present in *Sartor Resartus* solves this problem. By treating the fictional action as if it existed in a present coincident with the reader's experience of the novel, the writer can bridge the gap between real and fictive; moreover, he can diminish the temporal distinctions that subvert the potential moral analogies of reader, character, and narrator. The historical present in *Sartor* often evokes both the sense of a reality that never is relegated to the past and the transcendent values that are always present. Similarly, the Editor of *Sartor*, like the editors of Richardson's epistolary fiction, naturally offers his commentary on Teufelsdröckh's life in the present tense; the form of his comments inevitably suggests the immediacy of his conversational attitude toward the reader. Although Dickens adopted these two uses of the present tense frequently in the course of his long career, their treatment in *Dombey and Son* is uniquely extensive and effective. They provide the analogies that link the three agents of narration as they define the quality of both day-to-day experience and aesthetic apprehension.

The most lengthy and perhaps even infamous example of present-tense narrative commentary in *Dombey and Son* appears at the opening of chapter 47.[8] It is a key to both the difficulties that the narrator faces and his willingness to go to extremes to solve them. Here we have unabashed moralizing. The strenuous rhetoric of this sermon threatens to turn the novel into a version of the fairy tale *moralisé* that Dickens would not accept from Cruikshank. Hard pressed to find space in the fifteenth number to prepare the reader for Edith's betrayal of Dombey, Dickens nonetheless decided to introduce this "thunderbolt" into the plot by beginning with some "opening . . . matter" on a "sanatory" topic ("Plans," p. 850). It is certainly a climactic moment for a tirade on a subject close to the narrator's heart; at the end of the

Detail, frontispiece, *Dombey and Son*

chapter, Dombey, maddened by shame and frustration, actually strikes his long-suffering daughter. Yet here the narrator asks us to be "just" to Dombey and his "unnatural" feelings by examining "what Nature is, and how men work to change her, and whether, in the enforced distortions so produced, it is not natural to be unnatural" (pp. 618–19). From this question proceed five paragraphs of often frenzied discourse on physical and moral diseases. The narrator challenges the reader to go out into the city streets and witness the degradation in which the "millions" live. He measures Dombey's world against the yardstick offered in the New Testament—"Ye shall know them by their fruits" (Matthew 7:16)—and finds it a "foetid bed" in which there is no chance of "natural growth." Soon the reader finds himself indicted for the disease "we generate . . . to strike our children down and entail itself on unborn generations." Here the analogy which links the reader and Dombey becomes explicit; in their blindness they will both soon "strike" their children. The narrator waxes hysterically prophetic by the end of the passage. We are given alternative visions of the future which will inevitably result from this situation: the appalling prospect of universal blight—or the new heaven and new earth that would be won if we, like Scrooge, could only avert the "tremendous social retributions" that await our blindness and inaction (p. 620). By the end of the passage, the reader seems to have come a long way from the case of Dombey, Sr.

Yet there can be no doubt about the thematic relevance of this "moral address . . . (punctuated with thumps)" (p. 69). *Dombey and Son* is a novel obsessed, as its title implies, with the processes of generation and their resulting generations. Most of its characters are children or childlike adults. Even the mature characters, Carker excepted, are presented in the context of the childhoods that have made them what they are. Paul, Edith, Alice, Toots, Rob the Grinder, Susan Nipper, Blitherstone, Alexander Mac Stinger, even the faded Miss Tox, product of Mrs. Pipchin's "child-quelling-line of business" (p. 687)—all are or have been, as children, morally, physically, or spiritually deformed by the world in which they live. Dombey himself is no exception. His only past is that of a son in the Firm subjected to the same process that will kill his own son. Bound as the "prisoner to one idea," he naturally cannot see Nature in "her comprehensive truth" (p. 619).

Dombey may bear responsibility for the world around him, but his very blindness to that responsibility is a social condition which he did not create. No wonder Dickens claims that the sins of the fathers will be visited on generation after generation. With the ineffectual exceptions of the Toodles and Sol Gills, the parental figures in this world are irresponsible—either indifferent, like Dombey himself, or exploitative, like Mrs. Skewton—and institutions of education simply compound their mistakes. When almost all the characters believe, with Dr. Blimber, that "nature [is] of no consequence at all" (p. 142), the narrator must state his case. Nature has its laws; only when roses bloom in a city churchyard will a healthy generation spring from "such seed." Moreover, he feels he must clarify the reader's relation to this urgent message. By couching it in the present tense, the narrator escapes the time-bound characteristics of narration which conventionally distinguish between reader and character. He equates the reader's presumed irresponsibility with both the conditions that have created Dombey and his own pressing need to change them.

Such sermonizing is not, of course, unknown in Dickens's earlier novels, but the way in which the narrator coordinates his own speech with the attitudes of the characters reveals his specifically mid-century handling of this technique. Just as the narrator calls upon his readers to see the evidence of the judgment rendered against them, Edith twice challenges her mother: "Look at me," she cries out, "a judgment on you! well deserved!" (p. 381). After a long absence, Alice greets her mother, the Good Mrs. Brown, with the same denunciation. Objectifying her own past in a third-person narrative, Alice explains, "There was a child called Alice Marwood . . . born among poverty and neglect, and nursed in it. Nobody taught her, nobody stepped forward to help her, nobody cared for her." She describes her trial on the charge for which she was transported, and offers a concrete example of the hypothetical magistrate and judge invoked in chapter 47. "And Lord, how the gentlemen in the court talked about it! and how grave the judge was, on her duty, and on her having perverted the gifts of nature—as if he didn't know better than anybody there, that they had been made curses to her!" Finally, Alice imagines her own death. "But the gentlemen [in the courts] needn't be afraid of being thrown out of work. There's crowds of little wretches, boy and girl, growing up in any of the streets they live in, that'll keep them to it till they've made their fortunes" (pp. 468–69). Both Alice and the narrator point to the streets as the text of their lessons; both rail against examples of judicial complacency and self-righteousness. Alice, like the narrator, suggests that her story is the beginning of a process which will "overrun vast continents with crime" (p. 620). Both this speech and the opening of chapter 47 recall passages in earlier novels. In chapter 46 of *Nicholas Nickleby* (1838–39), for instance, Charles Cheeryble, the embodiment of Good Nature and Good Will, makes a similar speech. In the Christmas book for 1844, *The Chimes*, the Bells are more competent to offer the lesson than the oppressed and oppressive victim of society, Trotty Veck. Here, however, Dickens uses both the voice of his narrator and the dialogue of his characters to implicate the reader in the social criticism they offer. That his narrator substantiates the viewpoints of questionable moral authorities such as Edith Dombey and Alice Marwood suggests the range and freedom of sympathy in *Dombey and Son*. The repetition of this crucial message identifies these characters and the narrator while it indicts the reader on charges of having caused the misery of the world they inhabit.

The opening of chapter 47 also clarifies the status and quality of temporality in *Dombey and Son*. The worst years of the hungry forties, 1846–48, the times which seemed most urgently to demand action, were exactly the years in which *Dombey* was written and published. They were years of anxiety, and the widespread fear was justified. Dickens had a wealth of compelling topical problems from which to choose material for his "new English story." As the number cover suggests, the Railway Mania of 1845 had become the Railway Bubble of 1846. While Dickens worked on the novel, the problems multiplied: the Irish famine, the 1846 Repeal of the Corn Laws which followed agitation by the Anti-Corn Law League, a recrudescence of Chartism at home and, by early 1848, revolution on the Continent. Yet another fear provides the terms of the sermon in chapter 47. When Dickens refers to the "noxious particles that rise from vitiated air" (p. 619) in the London slums, he invokes a specter that every contemporary reader would have understood, of fever and the current zymotic or miasmic theory of its contagion. *Fever* was a term which covered a wide variety of undifferentiated diseases; it was both an endemic and

epidemic condition in Victorian England.[9] Yet Dickens's reference is
not at all generalized. When this chapter was written, cholera had
spread from Egypt to Malta and Russia, typhus was rampant in Ireland, epidemics had invaded the industrial towns, and influenza was
in London itself—all evidently the precursors of the cholera epidemic
that would surpass in mortality the one of 1831–32 and kill over
55,000 by 1849. Earlier in 1847, *Punch*, with a characteristic pun, had
called for a "sweeping reformation" to clean up the "reeking courts
and noisome alleys" which were breeding "fatal pestilence."[10] Chapter
47 of *Dombey and Son*, published in December, made the same timely
plea. The specter of an imminent plague is, however, only the first indication of this sermon's journalistic flavor. Dickens uses this passage
to strike out at another favorite *Punch* target. His generalized example
of the "magistrate or judge" who admonishes "the unnatural outcasts
of society" (p. 619) is another attack on Sir Peter Laurie, the alderman
who earlier served as the model for Alderman Cute in *The Chimes*.[11]
Like the *Punch* writers, Dickens adopts the editorial imperative mood;
he challenges the reader to follow Sir Peter's foolish example, and asserts his faith that a closer knowledge of the poor would eliminate the
stupidity evident in the alderman's statements. His methods resemble
those of the famous 1841 editorial in which Douglas Jerrold demands,
"Now ask the Paisley weaver what is Life?" Dickens simply asks that
we see the world "lying within the echoes of our carriage wheels and
daily tread upon the pavement stones" (p. 619). The ability to find sermons in stones is characteristically Victorian. Writers from Carlyle and
Mayhew to Ruskin and even Arnold suggest that their readers look
into the city streets to discover the genuine Condition of England.[12]
They had all heard the call that Dickens records in an *All the Year
Round* essay of 1860; he walks "the streets of a city where every stone
seemed to call to me, . . . 'Turn this way, man, and see what waits to be
done!'" (*Uncommercial Traveller*, p. 28).

Even the apocalyptic tones of the narrator's commentary have their
topical source and their analogues in *Punch*—paradoxically, Dickens's
movement away from the subjects typical of the late 1840s is itself a
distinctively topical feature of the novel. The "bright and blest" morning that Dickens envisions will reveal that we are all members of "one
family." "The Reconciliation," another of Jerrold's Q-editorials, the 1845

"Prophecy by Punch" (8 [1845] : 122), foretells the "glorious sight" we will see when the rich and the poor hold a "parliament of the heart." This movement from present woes to a healing future is characteristic of *Punch*'s many New Year's greetings. More significant is a later poem that may itself be indebted to *Dombey and Son*, as is Leech's famous 1847 Big Cut cartoon. In "Britannia's Thanksgiving Day Dream," *Punch* celebrates the 1849 cessation of the cholera with a vision like that of chapter 47. Death, seated on Mammon's throne, declares that its subjects will eventually discover, by the "light of Heaven," the "bond of brotherhood" (17 [1849] : 206). When the narrator of *Dombey and Son* invokes tomorrow's "bright and blest" dawn, he is resorting to journalistic rhetoric that his contemporary readers would easily recognize.

The source of such rhetoric, with its characteristic progression from now to forever, is, again, Thomas Carlyle. Either his 1831 essay "Characteristics" or "The Phoenix" of *Sartor Resartus* could have served as a model for Dickens's sermonizing. His distinctive combination of topics and his perspective became almost conventional by the 1850s and 1860s—they appear in Mayhew's work and Thackeray's review of *London Labour and the London Poor*, and they are even echoed in the reports of medical inspectors [13]—but in the 1830s these tones were uniquely Carlylean. In "Characteristics" he begins by discussing the physical diseases of present-day society, then turns to its "Spiritual condition." He finds spread before him "lava-torrents of fever-frenzy," a nation "sick to dissolution" with "a whole nosology of diseases" (CME, 3 : 21–22). Against the present—the world of time, mortality, and mutability—Carlyle posits the "truly Great and Transcendental [which] has its basis and substance in Eternity" (p. 38). At the close of the essay he envisions a new day dawning, a day of changeless Truth and Goodness. Here Carlyle offers a simplified version of the *Palingenesia; or, Newbirth of Society* that he describes in *Sartor Resartus*. There Teufelsdröckh asks us to see with his eyes a society that has "not so much as the Idea of a common Home," the world "under a process of devastation and waste." Yet we also see the effects of that process. The Phoenix Death-Birth, the "fire-creation," promises a new "Living Society" in which community will become the rule (SR, pp. 173, 185–89). Although Dickens refers to the Destroying

Angel in chapter 47, he proposes a vision of the future that is more Carlylean than Christian. Like Carlyle, he evokes a vision of the mysterious and invisible forces that will lead to ruin and then consoles his readers with the hope that such destruction could ultimately reestablish the family of man. Like Carlyle, he announces that the outcome of this inevitable process depends on man, not God. The sermon in chapter 47 ends with a vision of an apocalypse which has its analogue in the image of the World-Phoenix. Like Carlyle, the narrator of *Dombey and Son* responds to the plight of the present world by looking toward a future in which its conditions will be transformed and transcended.

Yet for all its thematic and topical relevance, this passage, like earlier invocations of waves and faraway countries, strikes a false note. The narrator's intentions and the justifications one can marshal for his rhetoric inevitably seem more convincing than the rhetoric itself. In this sense, the narrator again resembles Florence; and like the Dombey who remains unmoved by her appeals, the reader may find himself more, not less immured in his conventional temporality. By trying to evoke the transcendent, the narrator reveals the irrelevance of its ideality, not its substantiality. The quality of his narrative activity here corresponds to the futility of Florence's daydreaming. At the end of the chapter, she runs away from the father who strikes her; at its beginning, the narrator tries to escape into a futurity that has, as yet, no real existence. No wonder his tone becomes strained. Yet, as the plot of the novel develops, Florence begins to find a situation in which her virtues can be substantiated; similarly, the narrator discovers a less abrasive and more effective way of inviting the reader to comprehend the paradox of temporality and transcendence.

The technique the narrator chooses to achieve this end—unconventional present-tense narration—would be used so frequently in later Victorian fiction that it became almost commonplace. Its appearance in the work of the second-rate or inexperienced writer is a sure sign of his inability to trust the power of character and event to engage the reader's attention. Before writing *Dombey*, Dickens himself was not above employing it for the most melodramatic of effects; it serves, for instance, to intensify the "drama" of Kit's trial and release in *The Old Curiosity Shop*. George Eliot's dependence on the technique in the *Scenes of Clerical Life* is, at one point, only a step removed from that of the pornographic Victorian romance, *Varney the Vampire; or, The Feast of Blood*: "With a plunge he seizes her neck in his fang-like teeth—a gush of blood and a hideous sucking noise follows. *The girl has swooned and the vampire is at his hideous repast!*" [14] Such passages explain why Thackeray finds the historical present a convenient way to parody Newgate fiction in *Catherine*—ironically, it becomes one of the great weaknesses of his last novels. But the present tense has its legitimate effects, and it became a distinguishing feature of the Victorian novel. In *Dombey and Son* Dickens offers one of the earliest and, ultimately, one of the fullest explorations of its capacity to set reader, character, and narrator in analogous relation to each other.

There is ample evidence that Dickens's eye was on his readers when he first turned to this unusual mode of narration. Paul, the character most likely to engage the conventional reader's attention, was slated to die almost immediately, and Dickens was worried about losing readers. Little Nell, after all, had survived through seventy-one chapters of *The Old Curiosity Shop*, and the enthralled Lord Jeffrey fueled Dickens's anxiety by asking if Paul's early death had not already expended all the novel's potential for powerful effects. Dickens's head literally ached with these difficulties; in his number plans he admonishes himself, "Great point of the N° to throw the interest of Paul, *at once on Florence*" ("Plans," p. 840). Falling sales later substantiated his fears, and an 1860s American abridgment of the novel called *Little Paul* actually ends with the voice of the waves at the conclusion of the fifth number. But Dickens tried to avert such responses; his first uses of extended present-tense narration occur in the two numbers that follow Paul's death. He seems to have hoped to increase the reader's involvement in the story by inviting him to participate, like a theatergoer, in the events unfolding on the narrative stage. Significantly, Dickens reverts to the practice in his later novels when he has a similar problem. He abandons conventional past-tense omniscience in *A Tale of Two Cities* when he wants to transfer the interest from Carton's coming execution to the fleeing Darnay family, and the reader is told what "the agony of our impatience is" (p. 339). In *Dombey and Son*, however, he eschews any simply melodramatic effects; neither of the two most sensational scenes in the novel, Dombey's striking of

Florence and Edith's disabusement of Carker, takes this form. After its initial use in parts of chapters 18 and 20, it reappears in sections of four other chapters. More important is the fact that fully five chapters are narrated entirely in the historical present, and all five of these chapters occur at the end of a monthly number (31, 41, 51, 57, and 62). The technique must have implied, for Dickens, a clearly defined effect. It would leave the reader with the proper perspective for a month's contemplation between parts as it insured his interest in the coming resumption of the action. It would create, in short, the appropriate reverberating note at the end of an installment.

Yet even in his first, apparently experimental use of the technique in chapter 18, Dickens initiates what is the consistent function of such narration, to set the characters (and not incidentally the reader) in a specifically defined relation to time. Only toward the end of the novel does the historical present serve consistently to evoke, as it does in *Sartor Resartus*, the transcendence that Florence embodies. Earlier the present tense is Dombey's mode. Its form is the form of habit— circularity, the inability to change or progress from one point to another. In each instance, the narrator, highly self-conscious about his role, "orchestrates" the action and underlines its circularity by repeating tag-lines or by returning, at the end of the passage, to the subjects with which he began. The paradoxical effect of these chapters is emphasized by the subject matter they invariably treat: weddings, funerals, deaths, all those marked points in the journey of life that should lead out of time but only further imprison characters like Dombey, Edith, and Mrs. Skewton. The past-tense description of Paul's death and the present-tense depiction of his funeral make this distinction in a particularly cogent fashion. In dying Paul has been slowly released from the present, and time itself becomes whole to his altered perception: "what was then and what had been" are "blended like the colours in the rainbow" (p. 200). Paul himself realizes that he is being released from temporality. He says to his father, "Remember Walter. I was fond of Walter!" (p. 224). Paul already inhabits the past, and his death is depicted in the tense that mirrors the completion of his life. But Dombey, confronted by this mockery of his hopes and further hardened by it, inhabits a narrative present. There is no release for him. "He is not 'brought down'"; his face "bears the same expression as of old" (pp. 236–37). As soon as the narrator turns to consider Florence, whose grief is compared to the "width and depth of vast eternity" (p. 238), the past-tense narrative resumes. Until then the historical present depicts both the habitual activities of the servants and passers-by whose lives go on in their accustomed ways or Dombey's attempt to remain impervious to change. Similarly, Mrs. Skewton's death occurs in the "static, tragic" and "unredeemable" time that Steven Marcus finds characteristic of life in *Dombey and Son*.[15] Dickens frames the chapter with the eternal message of the waves, and in their "mar-vellous song" Florence hears Paul's "little story told again" (p. 554). Yet Mrs. Skewton dies in the present, never to be released into the past. In contrast, Alice Marwood's death is presided over by a redeeming angel, Harriet Carker, whose function resembles Florence's earlier atten-dance at Paul's bedside;[16] Alice's death, like Paul's, is a sanctified past-tense release from temporality.

The two "Wedding" chapters of *Dombey and Son*, 31 and 57, de-pend on the same contrast, and they constitute yet another instance of the distinguishing imaginative impulse of the novel—the movement from temporality to transcendence. Both are chapters of present-tense narration. In chapter 31 Dombey and Edith are married, and the self-consciously poetic qualities of the narration, its circular movement as well as its constant focus on images of mortality, emphasize one cru-cial fact: this marriage will lead, not to new life, but to the continuation of death-in-life. Even the coming of a new day, described at both the beginning and end of the chapter, is not a rebirth. Rather, day causes night and then dawn to retreat into the vault below the church and sit upon the coffins. The pew-opener and the beadle enter the church, "treading the circle of their daily lives, unbroken as a marriage ring" (p. 436). To highlight the folly of such habitual complacency, Dickens allows death, the breaking of the circle, to sound its note at the end of the wedding ceremony: a "thousand sober moralists" claim that "these people little think such happiness can't last" (p. 428), and the sexton "tolls a funeral" as the wedding party leaves the church (p. 431). Al-though the characters themselves cannot yet recognize its import, the lesson of the church bell is clear. Neither this marriage nor life itself will remain unbroken.

Dickens asks his readers to participate in this stasis, to share

Dombey's imprisonment in temporality by depicting it in the tense associated with their own current experience. In a telling detail Dickens describes the young ladies who witness this marriage, "every one of whom remembers the fashion and the colour of [Edith's] every article of dress from that moment, and reproduces it on her doll, who is for ever being married" (p. 428). These young ladies are an analogy for the reader's own peculiar temporal relation to the event he watches. For every reader who picks up *Dombey and Son*, Edith is again and forever being married; the present tense simply emphasizes each reader's renewed and always new imaginative engagement with the event. (That, of course, is the reason why critical accounts of the action of a novel are conventionally couched in the present tense; the event always has the potential to take place.) Yet the novel, like both the individual reader's experience of it and his own life, eventually ends. Writers like Dickens and Thackeray frequently regretted completing a novel because it meant the death of their characters, and Trollope's grief over the untimely demise of Mrs. Proudie is simply an exaggerated version of a normal tendency. For the reader the ending has resonances equally personal and immediate, in that the end of a particular reading experience is a prelude to the end of all experience. In chapter 31 Dickens draws attention to the paradox inherent in any heightened awareness of the present, its triumphs or its pleasures. The reader, like the fictive audience of young girls at the wedding, is invited to participate in the mode which epitomizes the paradox. The present seems endless because every moment that passes is, as we experience it, the present, yet there is no way to retard its inevitable progress toward death. Like the effect that his falling fortunes have on Dombey, this emphasis on the present should heighten the reader's desire for a release from a merciless temporality.

As usual in *Dombey and Son*, expectations are aroused to be met, desires created to be satisfied. The plot confirms the strength of Florence's unchanging love and loyalty, and the present tense finally comes to stand for transcendence. Chapter 57, "Another Wedding," begins in the dusty church where Edith and Dombey were married. Florence and Walter go there to pay their respects to the past and the memory of Paul's death. The narrator insists upon the death-in-life of the world these two characters inhabit. The young couple walks through the streets, the light and shade of which prophesy the marriage at the end of *Little Dorrit*. They come to "darker, narrower streets" and finally reach a dustier and more confined church that smells "like a cellar" (p. 768). The marriage itself is a kind of death: "No gracious ray of light is seen to fall on Florence. . . . The morning luminary is built out, and don't shine there" (p. 769). The witnesses of this ceremony fully comprehend its meaning as the prelude to an imminent separation, but they refuse to pretend that Walter and Florence's story is over. As Sol Gills so rightly decides, this is not the appropriate time to drink the last bottle of Madeira. This chapter has no circular return to the point at which it began. In a strange but apt fulfillment of the seemingly impossible prophecy of chapter 47, roses have bloomed in a churchyard sated with the graves of the dead. The chapter specifically opens out both spatially and temporally at its conclusion. Paul and Florence are at sea; the waves they hear speak of love, not death, "of love, eternal and illimitable, not bounded by the confines of this world, or by the end of time" (p. 773). The present tense serves here the function that it fulfills in a moment of transcendence in *In Memoriam*. Tennyson normally uses the present tense in his lyrics to denote the fact that he is recording his immediate, first impressions of his grief and his slow movement toward faith. It is the sign of his temporality. In lyric 95, however, he uses the past tense to depict an experience that happened in time and led to a release from time. When he reaches that point and participates in a mystical awareness of "that which is," a movement into the present of transcendence is necessary. In Tennyson's lyric and Dickens's novel, the present tense invites the reader to experience "that which is," both time and eternity. The technique creates a middle ground between the aesthetic object and the reader's experience; awareness is "not bounded by the confines of this world," the world of the work of art, "or by the end of time," the end of the reader's perception of the work.

Yet *Dombey and Son* does not end on the note of this marital consummation. The event that in *Little Dorrit* signals the only conceivable fruition of man's desires is, in this earlier novel of hope, a merely partial satisfaction. Florence and her father must be joined in a final embrace of mutual love and forgiveness, just as the narrator and the reader are united by the transcendence represented in the histor-

ical present. Again *Sartor Resartus* offers a perspective which explains why this is so. For Carlyle, the aim of human life is to establish
relations between ideal and real, time and eternity, self and community. In the chapter called "Organic Filaments," Teufelsdröckh explains that the human community encompasses not only all men who
live in a given time; "the immeasurable, universal World-tissue" also
spreads from generation to generation. One must establish one's identity within that "living indivisible whole" (s r, pp. 195–96). Similarly,
each individual must reconcile his past to his present and his present
to his future. He can do so only through memory, the record of the
past, and hope, the promise of the future. "Is the Past annihilated,
then, or only past; is the Future non-extant, or only future? Those
mystic faculties of thine, Memory and Hope, already answer: already
through those mystic avenues, thou the Earth-blinded summonest
both Past and Future, and communest with them, though as yet
darkly, and with mute beckonings. The curtains of Yesterday drop
down, the curtains of Tomorrow roll up; but Yesterday and Tomorrow
both *are*" (s r, p. 208). Before the "Retribution" of chapter 59, Florence and her father have only partially united themselves to the World-
tissue of generations; they have only begun the process by which they
will reconcile past and future. Without each other, Florence and Dombey are, in Teufelsdröckh's terms, less than wholly human.

Chapter 59 begins in the apparently "unredeemable" present tense.
Dombey's situation here recalls Scrooge's confrontation with the Ghost
of Christmas Past. The initial step in the "Retribution" that awaits him
is a birth into memory. The narrator has continually prophesied the
fate Dombey faces; throughout the novel, the cry of "let him remember" has established Dombey's inability to find in memory either consolation or moral awareness. As soon as Dombey begins to remember,
the narration shifts into the past tense. But he awakens to memories
that reveal only irrevocable loss and stasis: "She had never changed to
him—nor had he ever changed to her—and she was lost" (p. 796).
Florence's supposed virtue, her immutable love, has no saving power;
her love, as Dickens told Forster in his original outline, has become
Dombey's "bitterest reproach" (Pilgrim *Letters* 4:590). Yet even now
Dombey's ego, his self-sufficient isolation, will not allow him to recognize her relationship to him. In his thoughts of her, Florence is already

dead. Inhabiting a decaying house where time has ceased to have any meaning, he lives like Miss Havisham in the desolating memories of the past. Dombey becomes an animal pacing the cage of his house, a ghost, an "it"; suicide seems to offer the only release. Dombey has discovered his past, but he has no future; his daughter's case at this point is exactly the reverse of his. By marrying Walter, she has prospectively joined herself to the organic filaments of the coming generations, and their union is the hopeful promise of perpetuation. Yet the blow that Dombey delivers in "The Thunderbolt" has violently severed Florence's present from her past. "She saw she had no father upon earth, and ran out, orphaned, from his house" (p. 637). Even before the moment which "orphans" her, Florence has been forced to think of her father as "some dear one who had been" (p. 621), so that the thought of him might not be an intolerable recognition of her unfulfilled need for his love.

Family, for Dickens as for Carlyle, constitutes the reconciliation of past and future, memory and hope; without such connections the individual suffers what Carlyle calls in *Past and Present* the "frightfulest enchantment": "Isolation is the sum-total of wretchedness to man. To be cut off, to be left solitary: to have a world alien, not your world; all a hostile camp for you; not a home at all, of hearts and faces who are yours, whose you are!" (p. 274). In a manner that would strike most modern readers as an outright denial of Walter's importance in her life, Florence begs hysterically for her father's forgiveness, "Papa, don't cast me off, or I shall die!" (p. 801). Her desperation, however, is comprehensible. She needs him as a tie to the past fully as much as he needs her as a tie to the future. Before Florence returns, Dombey has seen visions of a "figure, childish itself, but carrying a child" (p. 797), clearly a memory of Florence carrying his own son Paul. When she returns, she comes carrying, metaphorically if not literally, that same child; her son Paul is the consolation Florence offers her father. The shadow of the past has become both the reality of the present and a prophecy for the future. Dombey does not respond to any of her entreaties until she speaks of her own son, "the little child who taught me to come back" (p. 802). Like Eppie in *Silas Marner*, the second Paul stands for hope and community; both children are described by the lines from Wordsworth's "Michael" which George Eliot chose as

her epigraph: "A child, more than all other gifts / That earth can offer
to declining man, / Brings hope with it, and forward-looking thoughts."
Florence, the supposedly immutable embodiment of love and fidelity,
admits that she too has "changed," that she knows the "fault" of her
betrayal of her father (p. 801). Dombey's acceptance of her appeal does
not release him into a transcendent present; rather, in an appropriately
Carlylean fashion, the movement of the chapter is descendental. Both
characters finally accept the temporality which defines human experience, and that acceptance is itself the promise of a future release from
time. By embracing each other, the two characters embrace their own
integrity and the fullness of their humanity.

The present tense employed in the "Final" chapter of *Dombey and
Son* suggests that the resolution of the characters' difficulties has put
an end to the narrator's problems as well. Before writing this novel
Dickens had often used the present tense in his conclusions. By dating
the action of his novels before the period of their publication, he could
go on to trace the course of his characters' lives after the close of the
action proper. The past-tense narrative yields to the present tense; the
characters exist in a future already realized, and their fates coexist
with the reader's experience of the novel. Dickens ends both *Pickwick
Papers* (1836–37) and *Oliver Twist* (1837–39) with a final paragraph
in the present tense, and in *Martin Chuzzlewit* (1843–44) he extends
this practice in several pages of direct address to the character Tom
Pinch. *Dombey and Son*, however, is the first example of a final chapter written exclusively in the present tense. One can easily see why
such an ending would be appropriate. As Florence and Dombey have
discovered in each other the transcendence that their very temporality
permits them, so the narrator has found a way to tell his story that embodies both change and the changeless. The reader, like Dombey, has
learned to put the two in their proper perspective. The details that the
narrator emphasizes continually point to this triumph. "The fulness
of the time and the design" (p. 830) has allowed both Sol Gills's investments and the narrator's experiments to come to fruition. The repeated references to the cobwebs on the buried wine express, not an
imprisonment in time, but a movement toward a release from it. Significantly, when Dickens was forced to shorten his final chapter so that
he could include a reference to Miss Tox and Diogenes, he cut the final

invocation of the voices in the waves. Such direct addresses to the reader were no longer necessary. Dombey's relation to his granddaughter and the present-tense depiction of that bond now constitute an adequate expression of a timeless reality that the reader can be trusted to recognize.

Although we might wish to accept, at least partially, the witty conclusion of Julian Moynahan's psychological analysis of the novel—"At the end of *Dombey and Son* Dickens is saying that things would be all right if men of Dombey's class and function made their daughters their mothers and lay down"[17]—it is also possible to admire the clarity and logic of the novel's more specifically social orientation. Dombey, like Pip, lives through an illness in which he loses his grasp on time, so that he can be reborn to the values he should have cherished in the past. If he is an aged, broken man at the end of the novel, it is only because time, so long ignored, will have its revenge, a lesson even Dorian Gray is forced to learn. Dickens's contemporaries would have understood this logic. The process at work in *Dombey and Son* is apparent in the action of *In Memoriam*. The speaker in the poem at first exists in a present defined only by lacerating memories of what he has lost. Yet in the marriage song at the end of the poem, Tennyson can speak, in the present tense, of the enduring reality that has appeared only briefly in the ninety-fifth lyric. Here faith has made possible not only the memory that sustains and sanctifies the present, but also the hope that promises reunion in the future. *The Mill on the Floss* ends with a similar reconciliation. For George Eliot, however, it is a regressive gesture, a union purchased at the cost of life itself. Like Florence, Maggie reaches out to embrace the human being who constitutes her relation to the past. For Florence the effect of that gesture is a beneficent beginning. At least in *Dombey and Son*, Dickens posits in life what both George Eliot and Carlyle find possible only in death, the "confluence of Time with Eternity" (SR, p. 178).

Love and procreation are the principal ways in which man achieves transcendence. Art, of course, is another. As Cousin Feenix and Jonson say of Shakespeare, the artist is a man who is not "for an age but for all time" (p. 828). There is some evidence that Dickens thought of his novels and, particularly, his experimental use of the present tense as means to this end. In 1851 he asked Charles Knight, one of his *House-*

hold Words contributors, to consider using the unconventional technique he had explored in *Dombey and Son*: "I understand each phase of the thing [your subject] to be *always a thing present before the mind's eye*—a shadow passing before it. Whatever is done, must be *doing*." At first Dickens suggests that he wants the "picturesque effect" that the present tense will create. Then, imagining a hypothetical case in which he would rewrite an eighteenth-century novel, he offers another more revealing explanation:

For example, if I did the Shadow of Robinson Crusoe, I should not say he *was* a boy at Hull when his father lectured him about going to sea, and so forth; but he *is* a boy at Hull. There he is, in that particular Shadow, eternally a boy at Hull; his life to me is a series of shadows, but there is no "was" in the case. If I choose to go to his manhood, I can. These shadows don't change as realities do. No phase of his existence passes away, if I choose to bring it to this unsubstantial and delightful life, the only death of which, to me, is *my* death, and thus he is immortal to unnumbered thousands. (*Letters*, 2:334)

In *Dombey and Son* Dickens had given such "unsubstantial and delightful" life to the "Shadows" and "Deeper Shadows" of his chapter titles. Here he suggests that the life of his creation is a triumph over his own mortality. The novel becomes an "organic filament" in the ongoing web of generations; it is "immortal to unnumbered thousands." Steven Marcus has presented the convincing argument that Dickens became more and more obsessively concerned with his past as he was writing *Dombey and Son*.[18] Yet, like Florence, Dickens seems to have envisioned at least a potential reconciliation of memory and hope: his past would be linked by the creative energies of the present to the generations of the future. Significantly, a few months after *Dombey* began its "brilliant" career, Dickens arranged for the Cheap Edition of his novels, an edition dedicated "to the English people, in whose approval, if the books be true in spirit, they will live, and out of whose memory, if they be false, they will very soon die" (*Life*, pp. 448–49). In a manner wholly characteristic of mid-century Victorian fiction, Dickens defines his reader and the bonds he establishes between his novels and his audience as the basis of his most far-reaching ambitions.

Yet as his career progressed, Dickens's hopes for personal or artistic transcendence diminished. In *Bleak House* (1852–53) the present-tense chapters reveal, not a realm of immutable spiritual realities, but the hopeless intransigence of a dehumanized society. Dickens uses the technique in a way that recalls the first chapter of *Past and Present*; there Carlyle describes events "not of this year, or of last year," but events that occur every year and reveal the "chronic gangrene" of society and its institutions (p. 3). The present tense is the appropriate form for the anecdotes of the Irish widow or the Stockport Assizes because such atrocities are always happening. Similarly, in *Bleak House*, the omniscient narrator presents a world which exists concurrently with that of the reader, a world in which the poor, like Jo, are "dying thus around us every day" (p. 649). In *Little Dorrit*, the possibility of transcendence has receded even farther; the "invisible region, far away" is now beyond man's grasp. It stands at an "untraversable distance" from the "mists and obscurities" of this world (p. 632). Man is simply a pale imitation of a "better order" that he "mimics" as feebly as fireflies mimic the stars (p. 14). All facets of life, not merely its temporality, have become prisons, and the present tense is no longer an appropriate way to distinguish one kind of reality from another. "The Study of a Loving Heart"—in *Dombey* the promise and preparation for reconciliation—has become, chillingly, a sketch for Miss Wade's cruelly perverse "History of a Self-Tormentor." In *Dombey and Son*, stories, such as Polly's account of the first Mrs. Dombey's death or Feenix's tactless anecdote of the bought bride, may be painful, but they are true. The shadow of the dream is not inevitably alienated from its substance. In *Little Dorrit* stories are too often lies. If Dickens is to find a consolation for this pervasively hopeless condition, he must refashion the accommodation between reality and imagination; but now any such accommodation must occur within a realm that is wholly human, wholly temporal; it must, therefore, bear the taint of the prison.

III

Little Dorrit
Necessary Fictions

On the last page of *Little Dorrit* (1855–57), Dickens describes the wedding day of Amy Dorrit and Arthur Clennam. Literally the last words accorded to a character are spoken by the most minor of them all, "the sexton, or the beadle, or the verger, or whatever he was" (p. 170) of St. George's Church. He explains the "special interest" that observers take in Little Dorrit's wedding: "'For, you see,' said Little Dorrit's old friend, 'this young lady is one of our curiosities, and has come now to the third volume of our Registers. Her birth is in what I call the first volume; she lay asleep on this very floor, with her pretty head on what I call the second volume; and she's now a-writing her little name as a bride, in what I call the third volume'" (p. 801). The implications of this comment justify the place of distinction it is given. In *Little Dorrit*, more directly than in any of his other novels, Dickens explores the moral status of fiction, and here he makes a final self-conscious reference to his own literary form. By parodying the conventional narrative pattern which opens with a birth in the first volume and ends with a marriage in the final volume, he juxtaposes the actions of individual characters against the ultimate realities of birth and death that had been so prominent in *Dombey and Son*. Yet the passage also provides a telling perspective on *Little Dorrit* itself. The official unwittingly compares the biography of Amy Dorrit to the fictional form it assumes, the actual novel that the reader is holding. His displacement of the conventional order of the three elemental human experiences—birth, death, and union—traces sequentially the three main events of Little Dorrit's life: her birth, her father's death, and her marriage to Clennam. There is an even more complicated reference involved here. The functionary's concern for his three volumes is a veiled allusion to the form of publication that rivaled Dickens's twenty-number serials. Within a few sentences, Dickens has created a comparison between the novel he has written about Amy Dorrit's life and the pattern that St. George's three registers impose on her life. Clearly, this witty allusion sets up a competition which Dickens knows he has already won; his twenty numbers are undoubtedly a more adequate record of his heroine's experience than anyone else's volumes could be.

Yet, like the consummation of generations reached at the end of *Dombey and Son*, the triumph implicit in this assertion of the serial's integrity is a conclusion achieved only after the obstacles in its way have been fully confronted and overcome. Throughout *Little Dorrit*, Dickens repeatedly draws attention to the moral ambiguities involved in any attempt to present life in a fictional form. The nameless church appendage, whose functions and motives are both indeterminate, embodies one of these ambiguities. If he is kind to Little Dorrit, he is also insensitive; he finds her a place to sleep when she has been locked out of the Marshalsea earlier in the novel, yet he also regards her as an object, merely "one of [his] curiosities." Here Dickens seems to suggest one of the fears that worries Hawthorne in a novel like *The Blithedale Romance*, the fear that the novelist is a voyeur who violates the lives of those around him. More relevant to *Little Dorrit*, however, are Carlyle's doubts about the legitimacy of the novel. The social criticism of this work owes a great deal to Carlyle's thought, and his conception of the questionable moral status of fiction, particularly his definition of the popular novel as "mere Lying," is central to its form. Surprisingly enough, by mid-century Carlyle's early attacks on the novel, the passages in an essay like "Biography" and the famous castigation of *Pelham* in *Sartor Resartus*, had lost none of their sting, although the respectability of the form had increased markedly and Carlyle's own popularity and influence had waned. Long after Trollope had become a successful novelist who could take comfort in the fact that a great man like Thackeray was his colleague, he recorded the pain he felt when he had first read Carlyle's remarks. Even though he had come to realize that the attack was "silly and arrogant," it still troubled him. In a speech he delivered in 1867 as a tribute to Dickens, Trollope was still referring to Carlyle's conception of the "perilous and close . . . cousin-ship" of fiction and lying. In the 1850s Dickens himself had good reason to acknowledge the moral ambiguity of the term *fiction*. When he countered the *Edinburgh Review* censures on *Little Dorrit*, as he had earlier refuted Sir Peter Laurie's comments on Jacob's Island, he ironically described the Circumlocution Office as an "idle fiction."[1] Yet unlike Trollope, who protests against Carlyle's viewpoint by speaking of the novelist as teacher and prophet, Dickens in *Little Dorrit* tends to acquiesce in the terms of Carlyle's arguments. Paradoxically, he makes of the novel's dubious status its greatest strength. He develops a correlation between the fictions, the lies, that his characters tell and the novel that he is writing, and at its center stands the unlikely figure of Little Dorrit. For all her traditionally estimable female qualities—humility, perseverance, loyalty, and selflessness—her equally characteristic female traits of evasiveness and subterfuge fully qualify her for a central role in a novel replete with deceptions. Little Dorrit is the appropriate eponymous heroine for two reasons; the novel is her story, and her creator adopts her way of telling that story, even though much of the action is seen through Arthur Clennam's eyes. By proposing a correlation between his central character and the role of his narrator, Dickens, oddly enough, defines fiction as one of the arts of How Not to Do It. As he approaches that definition in the course of telling the story, Dickens outlines what the reader should and should not expect from a novel. The bond between narrator and character becomes, as it is in *Dombey and Son*, the source of the reader's relation to the fictive world and, indeed, the basis of the relation between art and life.

By the time Dickens wrote *Little Dorrit*, the equation of the narrator's role as storyteller and his heroine's actions within the story had become a characteristic feature of his major fiction. Although the narrative difficulty that this analogy addresses changes with the changing context and character of both narrator and heroine, the apparently passive figure of Florence Dombey, Esther Summerson, Sissy Jupe, or Little Dorrit is, in the alchemy of Dickens's creative processes, the crux of the particular imaginative problem of the novel which gives each heroine her existence. The correlation between the contradictions of Florence's life in time and the narrator's ideals in *Dombey and Son* leads to some of Dickens's most extensive experiments in narrative form. In *Bleak House* the analogy is both self-evident and oddly reminiscent of the subtler case of *Dombey*—the raging voice of the omniscient narrator must be augmented by both the ideality and the sometimes perverse acuity of Esther Summerson. Illegitimate, defensive, insecure, always ready to do good so that she can compensate for the disadvantage of her birth, Esther reveals the fears about the novelist's doubtful social status which Dickens would not more openly acknowledge. She also embodies fears about the novelist's usefulness. Perhaps, after all, he can offer only the tidying-up of a few households, not the rebirth of society envisioned in *Dombey and Son*. In *Hard Times*, the analogy again becomes the imaginative strength it had been in *Dombey*. Sissy Jupe stands for an entire realm of imaginative activity from circus acts to fairy tales and *The Arabian Nights*. Like the narrator she mediates between the fanciful and the real; by bringing circus values into the Gradgrind household, she reveals the moral dimension of entertainment and humanizes a family dedicated to steam engines and statistics. The narrator writes his story in a fashion imitative of Sissy's presence in an otherwise imaginatively barren world. If Gradgrind refuses to let fairy tales into his home, Dickens proposes to establish the language of the fairy tale in every home that contains a copy of *Hard Times*. Gradgrind's children may not know what an ogre is or what Peter Piper picked, but the narrator makes sure that the reader does. The factories that epitomize the grim environment of Coketown are themselves fairy palaces giving off "monstrous serpents of smoke," equipped with machinery in the form of "melancholy mad elephants" (p. 69). By bringing imagination into the realm of everyday experience, Sissy and the narrator avert the threat of dehumanization that contemporary life poses and encourage the old virtues and sentimental values embodied in the traditional nursery tale.

In *Little Dorrit*, however, Dickens must ring another change on this analogy. Unlike Sissy, Amy Dorrit does not bring the underestimated virtues of art into a materialistic world. Born in a prison, the product of poverty and debt, Amy partakes of the qualities of the world she would cure. The values that Dickens sets in opposition to this world are not those of the circus or the library; rather, he invokes the values of a lost pastoral realm that Little Dorrit has experienced only on her brief Sunday outings with her old friend the turnkey. The defenses and modes of accommodation that she develops to sustain herself in the atmosphere of the prison no longer suggest an opposition between art and life that at least insures the integrity of the imagination. The collapse of that traditional contrast had disclosed the frightening possibility that art is as sordid as life. At times Dickens comes close to such a vision. The characters in this novel—and Little Dorrit is no exception—continually create "fictions" to hide the "reality" of their feelings or their social positions. Like Thackeray's treatment of gossip in *Vanity Fair*, Dickens's continual reference to the traditional narrative forms that define his characters' lives is one way of bridging the gap between the real and the fictive. But that process has little comfort to offer. Involved "legends" surround the name of Bleeding Heart Yard or explain Frederick Dorrit's odd behavior in the theater where he plays the clarinet, and "stories" account for Edmund Sparkler's dim-wittedness. None of them, of course, can be verified. According to Tite Barnacle, Dorrit is the subject of "a good story, as a story"; he is granted his freedom when "the fairy [comes] out of the Bank and [gives] him his fortune" (p. 547). But we know that Dorrit's life is no fairy tale. The tendency to encapsulate experience or identities in narrative formulas is apparent in the deceptive names that characters give others or assume for themselves. The villain uses names as a disguise. He is, variously, Rigaud, Lagnier, and Blandois. Flora calls Clennam "Doyce and Clennam" in a preposterously halfhearted attempt to disguise her early attachment to "Arthur." The fictions that Dickens presents in this way are, clearly and simply, lies. Throughout *Little Dorrit* he insists upon this interpretation of the word. The narrator's disgust with Dorrit's pretensions to the status of a gentleman is transparent; he speaks of "the miserably ragged old fiction of the family gentility" (p. 207). As Dickens knew too well, debt is not genteel, and the narrator is angered by any attempt to pretend that it is. The "little fiction" that Mrs. Plornish creates by having her shop wall "painted to represent the exterior of a thatched cottage" is a "most wonderful deception" (p. 556). Wonderful, but still a deception.

The characters of *Little Dorrit* continually create self-conscious, sustained narratives from their own experience. Dickens's use of the first person in the memorandum book which he began to keep six months before he started writing *Little Dorrit* suggests that he was increasingly anxious to let his characters present themselves in their own voices—literally, to identify narrator and character as he does later in *Great Expectations*. In *Little Dorrit* characters speak of themselves by constructing narrative frameworks for their lives. Flora falls back on various literary sources, including the myths of Cain and Pygmalion, *The Prelude*, and *The Winter's Tale*[2] to re-create the past in the present. Like her drinking habits, the peculiar conventions of her speech reveal her tenuous hold on actuality. Young John Chivery, that "pining shepherd" in his "tuneless groves" of laundry (pp. 290, 252), composes epitaphs for his own gravestone that follow the course of his love for Little Dorrit. At the end of the novel, his imagined tomb triumphantly proclaims that he "FOR THE SAKE OF THE LOVED ONE . . . BECAME MAGNANIMOUS" (p. 714). Clennam can express his feelings only by creating an objectified version of himself, "Nobody." After he "decides" not to fall in love with Pet Meagles, his references to "Nobody's State of Mind" are patent though futile attempts at self-deception. Meagles fosters this subterfuge with his own fiction of the continued growth of Pet's dead twin; the idea is so powerfully conceived that Clennam imagines himself as the twin's widower. When Dickens is finally ready to reveal the events surrounding Arthur's birth, he notes in his number plans, "Tell the whole story, *working it out as much as possible through Mrs. Clennam herself.*"[3] The characters involved in this revelation are fully aware of its status as a story. Blandois confronts Mrs. Clennam and offers to tell a "ravishing little family history" (p. 750). He assumes the role of the entertainer: "I perceive I interest you. I perceive I awaken your sympathy" (p. 751). But like Paul Dombey rejecting Mrs. Pipchin's cautionary anecdote, Mrs. Clennam will not accept the "glass" in which Blandois offers to present her: "I will tell it with my own lips, and will express myself throughout it. . . . I will be known as I know myself" (pp. 753–54). Her version of events, weighted down by vindictive Calvinistic language, is simply a modern Old Testament story. Both the reader and the listeners in Mrs. Clennam's room are asked to believe that God's righteous fury works itself out through his human instruments. Miss Wade's story is an even more conspicuous example of such storytelling. Her autobiographical account is an interpolated narrative with its own grandiose, self-advertising title—"The History of a Self-Tormentor"—its own plot, characters, and moral. Dickens describes this history in his memorandum for the chapter: "From her own point of view. Dissect it" ("Plans," p. 822). The narrative is to be Miss Wade's own peculiar paranoid reconstruction of events. She uses both Clennam, her audience, and the narrative itself as a "looking-glass" to reflect the version of reality she wants to see. That Mrs. Clennam and Miss Wade both explain their activities by referring to a mirror is not accidental. Their fictions are appropriately defined by the traditional symbol of both art and narcissism. Their stories are signally faithful measures of their moral blindness; their mirrors reveal the shadows cast by their tormented psychologies, not clear visions of their actions.

To propose that Little Dorrit stands at the head of this group of deceptive, perverse, or simply disingenuous characters may seem, at first, surprising. Little Dorrit is a good woman. She is a dutiful daughter, a loving sister, and presumably she will be a dutiful and loving wife. No one can fail to notice Amy's goodness; Trilling even calls her "the Beatrice of the Comedy, the Paraclete in female form." F. R. Leavis exults in Little Dorrit's goodness: "Her genius is to be always beyond question genuine—real. She is indefectibly real, and the test of reality for the others. . . . The characteristic manifests itself in her power to be, for her father and brother and sister, the never-failing providence, the vital core of sincerity, the conscience, the courage of moral percipience, the saving realism, that preserves for them the necessary bare minimum of the real beneath the fantastic play of snobberies, pretences and self-deceptions that constitutes genteel life in the Marshalsea."[4] This description of Little Dorrit's role is eloquent, indeed moving, and it does conform to one's sense of her status in the moral hierarchy of the novel. There is only one problem: it is patently inaccurate. Leavis's comment refers to Amy specifically when she and her family inhabit the Marshalsea. Is she the "saving realism," or does her experience there resemble the contradictions of Florence Dombey's imprisonment in her father's castle? Is even Little Dorrit enmeshed in the pretences and self-deceptions that imprison her family?

Of course, Dorrit himself creates the fiction that he is a gentleman, a public figure with a public duty among the Collegians, but Little Dorrit—not her father or brother or sister—is the character who "preserves" the "genteel fiction that they [are] all idle beggars together" (p. 72). She is the one who tells her father stories to conceal the shaming fact that Fanny dances for a living. She never questions the "family fiction" that she knows nothing of the world beyond the prison (p. 227). She is the one who maintains the "pious fraud" that her brother Tip is a visitor, not an inmate, in the debtor's prison. Tip himself demonstrates some healthy skepticism about the need for all this prevaricating. He candidly tells Clennam that he is a prisoner, "only my sister has a theory that our governor must never know it. I don't see why, myself" (pp. 75, 83). Little Dorrit is not particularly pleased with her role—she does not like "becom[ing] secret with" Mrs. Clennam (p. 83)—but she insists that her role is necessary. She explains to Clennam that, in order to see Fanny in the theater, she must "pretend" that she is going to a party: "I hope there is no harm in it. I could never have been of any use, if I had not pretended a little" (p. 162). At the end of the chapter, the narrator presents his own bitter evaluation of the "party" that Amy has supposedly attended: "This was Little Dorrit's party. The shame, desertion, wretchedness, and exposure, of the great capital; the wet, the cold, the slow hours, and the swift clouds, of the dismal night. This was the party from which Little Dorrit went home" (p. 171). The disjunction between the "white lies" Little Dorrit tells and the reality she experiences could hardly be more complete.

As long as Little Dorrit can sustain the fiction of her father's love and concern, she and the rest of the family can survive. She is utterly defeated by any event which reveals the true nature of his feelings. Florence keeps alive a fiction of her father's love by imagining him already dead, and she loses even that consolation when he strikes her. Dorrit attacks his daughter's devotion in a less violent but no less effective manner. In two scenes in the Marshalsea, he confronts her with the reality of his position. When Little Dorrit fails to humor John Chivery, Dorrit rebukes her and describes himself as a "poor prisoner, fed on alms and broken victuals; a squalid, disgraced wretch" (p. 221). The line literally brings Amy to her knees. Later, he is "cut to the soul" because she has been seen in public with the pauper Old Nandy, and he sobs while Fanny tells her exactly what she is, "you Common-minded little Amy! You complete prison-child!" (p. 361). Again, she kneels before her father and begs his forgiveness. The fictions that Little Dorrit sustains are among the most morally debilitating in the novel. Like Tip, the reader may wonder whether she actually helps her father by fostering his self-deceptions. Like Fanny, the reader may question the value of a "flat sister" (p. 571)—Little Dorrit might do both Fanny and her father some good if she would boldly speak the truth.

A similar situation in one of Dickens's earlier stories reveals how thoroughly he understands the issues involved in his complex characterization of Little Dorrit. In *The Cricket on the Hearth* (1845), the roles are reversed: Caleb Plummer treats his daughter Bertha, the Blind Girl, as Little Dorrit treats her father. He invents stories and tells lies so that he can conceal the abject poverty in which they live. Like Little Dorrit's, Caleb's impulses are only the best. He loves his daughter, and he wants to shield her from the truth she literally cannot see. But he learns to regret his self-denying deception. He has convinced her that his Scrooge-like employer is a generous patron, and the Blind Girl, of course, falls in love with this figment of her father's imagination. When the employer becomes engaged to another woman and Caleb realizes what he has done, he confesses: "I have wandered from the truth, intending to be kind to you; and have been cruel" (p. 221). The highly charged dialogue that follows applies directly to Little Dorrit's treatment of her father:

"My dear blind daughter, hear me and forgive me! The world you live in, heart of mine, doesn't exist as I have represented it. The eyes you have trusted in, have been false to you."

She turned her wonder-stricken face towards him. . . .

"Your road in life was rough, my poor one," said Caleb, "and I meant to smooth it for you. I have altered objects, changed the characters of people, invented many things that never have been, to make you happier. I have had concealments from you, put deceptions on you, God forgive me! and surrounded you with fancies." . . .

"Oh, why," cried the Blind Girl, tortured, as it seemed, almost beyond endurance, "why did you ever do this? Why did you ever fill my heart so full, and then come in like Death, and tear away the objects of my love? O Heaven, how blind I am!" (p. 222)

In *The Cricket*, we see visions of "Household Spirits to whom falsehood is annihilation" (p. 212). In *Little Dorrit* falsehood has become a way of life, the only possible way to protect oneself and others from annihilating visions of the truth. When the Dorrits leave the Marshalsea, Amy does assert her human reality, her inability to deal in fictions. Yet while she still inhabits the prison, she is what Fanny calls her, a "prevaricating little piece of goods" (p. 361). She is an unrepentant Caleb Plummer.

If, in the second half of the novel, Little Dorrit's presence invalidates the fictions on which her family depends, she maintains, in persistent and baffling ways, some extraordinary fictions about herself. This point explains her repeated insistence that her name is Little Dorrit, not Amy. As Flora comments earlier in the novel, it is "of all the strangest names I ever heard the strangest, like a place down in the country with a turnpike, or a favorite pony or puppy or a bird or something from a seed-shop to be put in a garden or a flower-pot and come up speckled" (p. 265). One does expect a little dorrit to come up speckled; it is hardly a human name. Like Florence's conviction that she is Walter's "sister," Amy's use of this name conceals the human potentiality of her relationship with Arthur Clennam. Throughout the two chapters which recount her early history, Dickens refers to her either as Amy or as the Child of the Marshalsea, but he prepares for her later deception of Clennam by reserving the name Little Dorrit until Clennam sees her enter the Marshalsea at the end of chapter 7. Clennam has a tendency to think of her as "his adopted daughter" (p. 184), and Little Dorrit uses her diminutive name to sustain that fiction. She writes him about her friendship with Pet: "She speaks to me by my name—I mean, not my Christian name, but the name you gave me. When she began to call me Amy, I told her my short story, and that you had always called me Little Dorrit. I told her that the name was much dearer to me than any other, and so she calls me Little Dorrit too" (p. 536). Appropriately enough, the repressed child of the prison tells only a "short story," but it contains a full measure of untruth. Though Clennam has accepted the practice of calling her Little Dorrit, he is not responsible for giving her that name—Affery first mentions it when he asks who she is. Amy herself prefers the name of a "poor child" because it conceals the fact that she is old enough to love Clennam. This deception persists through the last chapter of the novel. Arthur refers to her as Amy, and she responds by correcting him: "Little Dorrit. Never any other name" (p. 796). Even their mutual protestations of love do not dissolve the fiction of her daughterliness. As the church functionary says on the last page, Little Dorrit signs her "little name" into the marriage register.

Just as Miss Wade tells her "History of a Self-Tormentor," Little Dorrit tells her own story earlier in the novel when she entertains Maggy with a fairy tale.[5] This interpolated narrative is the counterpart of Clennam's conception of himself as Nobody. A "poor little tiny woman" (p. 284) spins in her cottage while she mourns the loss of "Some one who had gone by long before" (p. 285). Eventually the little woman dies and the shadow of "Some one" descends into her grave. The little woman is obviously Little Dorrit; Clennam is "Some one." In a curious way both their tales reduce him to an indefinite pronoun. Just as Clennam turns himself into a ghost wed to Pet's dead sister, Little Dorrit's storytelling makes a grotesque comment on her sense of identity: she becomes a corpse united to a shadow. Captain Cuttle's fairy tale has been the source of consolation and reconciliation, but here the fairy tale reinforces the fiction that Little Dorrit is somehow insubstantial, unreal. It is consistent with Fanny's calling her "amiable and dear little Twoshoes!" (p. 678) and with Flora's addressing her as an "industrious little fairy" (p. 276). When Clennam later proclaims that he is beyond the age of marriage and Little Dorrit conceals her feelings, Maggy refers to the story of the little woman. Little Dorrit has said, "I have no secret," but Maggy senses the truth: "It was the little woman as had the secret." She begs Little Dorrit to tell the story, but Amy refuses, dismissing it as "only a Fairy Tale" (pp. 374–75). The irony is apparent. If she did tell the story, her story, she and Clennam might have a chance to comprehend the reality of their feelings for each other; they might even embrace as Walter and Florence have.

The ambiguity of Little Dorrit's role in the creation of fictions within the novel is definitely and finally established in the last scene she shares with Clennam. Dickens's memorandum—"Scene (*reserve carefully till now*) between Little Dorrit and Arthur" ("Plans," p. 828)—suggests the particular importance of this scene within the narrative pattern of the novel. On the morning they are to be married, Amy joins Arthur in his room at the Marshalsea. She has told him that she is poor again, and Doyce has returned from the Barbaric Power with the money needed to free him. Amy has sent Meagles to the Continent to retrieve the original copy of the codicil which proves that Mrs. Clennam had cheated her of a legacy of one thousand guineas. Tattycoram has saved the papers, and Little Dorrit can maintain the fiction that Arthur's suspicions about his mother were unfounded: "The secret was safe now! She could keep her own part of it from him; he should never know of her loss" (p. 788). In this last scene, Little Dorrit asks Clennam to burn a piece of paper, the codicil he is never to know about:

"My dear love," said Arthur. "Why does Maggy light the fire? We shall be gone directly."

"I asked her to do it. I have taken such an odd fancy. I want you to burn something for me."

"What?"

"Only this folded paper. If you will put it in the fire with your own hand, just as it is, my fancy will be gratified."

"Superstitious, darling Little Dorrit? Is it a charm?"

"It is anything you like best, my own," she answered, laughing with glistening eyes and standing on tiptoe to kiss him, "if you will only humour me when the fire burns up." . . .

"Does the charm want any words to be said?" asked Arthur, as he held the paper over the flame. "You can say (if you don't mind) 'I love you!'" answered Little Dorrit. So he said it, and the paper burned away. (pp. 798–801)

The surface sweetness of this dialogue belies its essential meaning. Here Little Dorrit continues to maintain surfaces and sustain fictions. Clennam asks of the codicil, "Is it a charm?" She responds with a patent deception, "It is anything you like best"—certainly an interesting case of the transforming powers of the imagination. Their life together is begun with the inception of a new fiction, a new instance of secrecy. Only by withholding the "reality" of their legal and financial relationship, whereby Clennam, through his "mother," stands in debt to Little Dorrit, can their emotional relationship survive. Unlike Florence, who must unite both past and future in her married life, Little Dorrit assumes that by burning the paper she can destroy the past. From the very opening of the novel, Clennam has suspected that his mother is guilty of some wrong. Here he is deprived not only of the opportunity to make reparations, but also of the very knowledge that reparations are at all appropriate. Little Dorrit assumes that in destroying the evidence of the "curse" of the past she can transform that curse into a "charm" to bless the opening of their life together. Well-intentioned as she is, she enacts a lie, a crucial deception. Here Little Dorrit creates her ultimate fiction, her last "odd fancy."

But Little Dorrit and Arthur are blessed; they are, as the narrator tells us, "inseparable and blessed." And we know that Little Dorrit, that "prevaricating little piece of goods," is good. On the one hand, unless we question the wisdom or the moral implications of her fictions, we cannot hope to perceive the meaning of the novel. On the other hand, such questioning is almost rendered pointless by her irrefutable status as the embodiment of the novel's highest moral values. It is true of the novel as a whole, as it is true of what Clennam calls "his own poor story," that Little Dorrit is "its vanishing-point. Everything in its perspective led to her innocent figure. . . . It was the centre of the interest of his life; it was the termination of everything that was good and pleasant in it; beyond there was nothing but mere waste, and darkened sky" (p. 714). Little Dorrit's role can be both ambiguous and unquestionably moral because of the context, the novel, in which she appears. Her lies are peculiarly like the "lies" that the novelist tells: she deals with Clennam in much the same way in which the narrator deals with the reader. Like Little Dorrit, the narrator fails to confront certain facts; he ignores certain problems and suggests that others cannot be solved. But such acts of deception do not undercut the moral status of the novel. Rather, like Thackeray's more playful attempt to turn *Vanity Fair* into a history, Dickens's definition of fiction as a lie actually substantiates the novel's claims for moral relevance. Lies are acceptable simply because they are necessary. Telling the "truth" inevitably involves such deceptions, such failures to tell the whole story.

The narrator's handling of the plot reveals one facet of the kinship between Little Dorrit and her creator. From the earliest reviewers such as Fitzjames Stephen to the most recent critics of the novel, readers have complained of the complexity of its plot.[6] Dickens himself displayed a good deal of concern about its ramifications. As he repeatedly affirmed, and as Forster emphasized in his account of *Little Dorrit* in the *Life*, Dickens hoped to do something new with the plot and its effects on his readers. His memorandum for the first number explains his intentions: "People to meet and part as travellers do, and the future connexion between them in the story, not to be shewn to the reader but to be worked out as in life. *Try this uncertainty and this not-putting of them together, as a new means of interest.* Indicate and carry through this intention" ("Plans," p. 806). "As in life"—again, the form in which the reader perceives the story is itself a mimetic process. Dickens repeated this intention to Forster in a somewhat more conventional manner; he said he would "connect [the characters] afterwards, and . . . make the waiting for that connection a part of the interest" (*Life*, p. 624). The common assumption, made first by Forster and echoed by later critics, is that Dickens failed to follow this plan. In one sense, that is true. By presenting one group of travelers in quarantine in chapter 2 of the first book and another group in the monastery of the Great Saint Bernard in the first chapter of Book the Second, Dickens has already made "connections" between them. Yet in another sense this plan became his ultimate narrative strategy. In the second chapter, Miss Wade delivers an oracular comment that seems to promise that the patterns of the novel will work themselves out in a neat imitation of fate: "In our course through life we shall meet the people who are coming to meet *us*, from many strange places and by many strange roads . . . and what it is set to us to do to them, and what it is set to them to do to us, will all be done" (p. 24). In his remarks at the end of the chapter, the narrator adopts Miss Wade's metaphor of life as a journey: "And thus . . . journeying by land and journeying by sea, coming and going so strangely, to meet and to act and react on one another, move all we restless travellers through the pilgrimage of life" (p. 26). The narrator here promises that the characters will meet and act and react on one another. According to this definition, the "connections" Dickens speaks of in the number plans are the primary, vital connections of human responsiveness. The reader ultimately learns that both the narrator and Miss Wade have issued empty promises. Sixteen numbers later we discover that Miss Wade's manipulations, not the workings of blind chance, have brought her into proximity with the Meagleses. At the end of the novel, the reader realizes too well that the narrator's intentions have been equally deceptive. The entire action of the novel might be described as an attempt to get answers, allay suspicions, and establish connections. The most typical activity within the novel is a search for information or for certainty that leads to nothing. Dickens develops supposedly solvable mysteries and he suggests potential relationships, but in the end, he refuses to fulfill the expectations he arouses. He does not provide the conclusive statements characteristic of a conventional narrative pattern. Yet as the possibility of creating "connections" between his characters diminishes, Dickens continues to propose the analogies which will link them to both his narrator and his reader.

The mysteries of *Little Dorrit* are so prominent that they seem obsessive. The need to elicit the reader's interest would hardly justify their role in the novel. Because of its baffling complexity, the plot cannot serve, in the words of one critic, as a way of "reassuring the reader, of promising that some, at least, of the novel's problems can be solved like a puzzle—simply by persistence and ingenuity."[7] Clennam is the focus of the suspicions and secrets which pervade the novel. If Little Dorrit is the narrator's analogue, Clennam is the reader's. He is always asking questions. He is always assuming that the concerns of other characters relate to his own. His persistence borders on the neurotic: "I want some light thrown on the secrets of this house" (p. 669); "I want that suspicion to be cleared away" (p. 725). His first confrontation with his mother emphasizes his role: "I want to ask you, mother, whether it ever occurred to you to suspect—" (p. 46). Although his father's deathbed behavior serves as a partial pretext for his uneasiness, Clennam suffers from an exacerbated sensitivity to suspicion; even his father's portrait, "earnestly speechless on the wall," seems "to urge him awfully to the task" (p. 54). There is no logical reason why he should connect his mother's silence with Little Dorrit's presence; but "involuntary starts of fancy" take "possession of him" (pp. 85–86), and the connection becomes so vivid that he can hear his mother's voice justifying the actions he attributes to her. Here he resembles the reader of conventional romance; like Catherine Morland of *Northanger Abbey*, he imagines motivations that are phantasmagorical while he remains blind to the more frightening actuality around him.

Clennam, of course, asks all the questions that the reader longs to see answered. First for Dorrit and then for Doyce, he attempts to fathom the secrets of the Circumlocution Office. His first visit there is an allegorical journey through the levels of bureaucracy: Christian has been replaced by the persistent inquirer. He repeats his request, "I want to know," twice to Barnacle Junior, once to Barnacle Senior, then to Wobbler, to the four storytelling clerks, and finally to his fellow pilgrims, Meagles and Doyce. But he gets nowhere; by trying to search out a mystery, he only manages to become, in Clarence Barnacle's eyes, the "mysterious Clennam" (p. 203). When he is not actually pursuing other characters' mysteries, he is busy suspecting that those mysteries might relate to him. *Little Dorrit* is peopled with characters, from Merdle and Miss Wade to Tattycoram and Maggy, who constantly entertain paranoid suspicions. Even the extremely minor character who makes up Clennam's bed in the Snuggery suspects that the governor of the prison is defrauding him of three and ninepence a week. Clennam stands at the head of this group of characters. His insistence on following clues and revealing secrets is neither entirely normal nor very productive. What happens to his efforts epitomizes what happens to many of the secrets in the novel. His attempts are rendered useless. Instead of removing secrets, he becomes involved in creating them. When he reveals to his mother that Blandois is a murderer, she retorts, "It is you who make this a secret. . . . You, Arthur, who bring here doubts and suspicions and entreaties for explanations, and it is you, Arthur, who bring secrets here." As Arthur realizes only too well, Mrs. Clennam succeeds in the "turning of his intelligence, and of his whole attempt and design against himself" (p. 664). The reader of *Little Dorrit* often feels similarly baffled. Later in the novel, Clennam's ineffectuality is even more apparent; his imprisonment for debt renders him literally motionless as the time for the final confrontation between Blandois and his mother approaches—he cannot "stir hand or foot" (p. 728).

The notation in Dickens's number plans for *Little Dorrit* suggests that his conscious narrative method was to retard the events or withhold the connections that might ease both Clennam and the reader's perplexity. The effect he wanted to create was a sense of "strengthening mystery" ("Plans," p. 821). By beginning with such a large number of characters and so many complicated events, the narrator could reserve a major portion of the action for long sections of the novel. The notes for chapter 30, Book the First read: "Pursue Rigaud, and the beginning of his influence over Mr. Flintwinch and Mrs. Clennam

Suspend it all. Hanging Sword" ("Plans," p. 815). By withholding developments in certain segments of the plot, Dickens could make the
narrative approximate a hanging sword, a sword that might or might
not fall. Similarly, he delays telling Miss Wade's story throughout most
of the novel. In the memorandum for number 3, Dickens asks himself,
"Miss Wade in the prison?" and answers, "Not yet." While planning
number 4, he suggests that he could tell her history—"Miss Wade.
Her surroundings and antecedents?"—and the answer is an emphatic
"*No.*" This pattern is repeated in the memoranda for numbers 5, 6, and
7. Finally, in the plans for number 8, the answer is "*Yes,*" and Miss
Wade again appears. But it is not until number 16 that Miss Wade tells
her story; twelve numbers have intervened since Dickens first saw the
possibility of revealing her "antecedents." He withholds the crucial
revelation of her motivation until the action of the novel is almost completed. That Clennam serves as the audience for this explanation
again suggests his analogous relation to the reader of *Little Dorrit*
itself.

   The fate of this story once it is told demonstrates the way in which
Dickens refuses to make significant moral connections between his
characters. Clennam has gone to Calais to ask Miss Wade if she knows
where Blandois might be, but she refuses to give him any information.
Instead she offers him her "History of a Self-Tormentor." One expectation is frustrated by the unexpected fulfillment of another, which has
been so long delayed that it may have ceased to exist. Clennam leaves
Calais with this history in hand, and, in the following chapter, the narrative itself appears. It is a powerful, almost explosive document, but
after its actual appearance, it is never mentioned again. The reader
presumes that Clennam has read it. His ideals of conduct, we are told,
are "duty on earth, restitution on earth" (p. 311). It would be interesting to discover what he thinks of a woman whose entire existence is
motivated by passion and vindictiveness, but the reader never does
find out what Clennam thinks. In the following chapter, he is back in
London, and he has resumed his search for Blandois. Miss Wade has
acted, but the reader never sees Clennam react. It is as if the history
had disappeared into thin air. Of course, one might suggest that Dickens is to blame for his failure to present Clennam's response; he has
complicated the plot to such an extent that he simply has more mate-

rial than he can handle. But such an explanation clearly is not satisfactory. A line or two might have supplied Clennam's opinion of Miss Wade. The analogy between Clennam and the reader indeed evolves in the reading experience "as in life." Clennam acts out the reader's desire for information, but even when information is made available, the reader and Clennam remain confused about its import.

The narrator's treatment of this history is completely consistent with other instances in which he refuses, throughout the second half of the novel, to show one character reacting to another. In the plans of number 17, Dickens asks himself if he should "close with a Letter from Little Dorrit?" His answer is emphatic, "*No—Not to weaken her next appearance*" ("Plans," p. 823). The reader therefore never knows how Little Dorrit reacts to the most radical change in her life, the deaths of both her father and her uncle. She does not appear again until the end of the next number. There her role is not that of the grieving child but that of the comforting nurse; her loss is never mentioned. The fate of Clennam's mother is a similar case. We are told that she lives for three years after the collapse of her house, yet in the scenes that take place between Clennam and Little Dorrit, she is never mentioned. How does Little Dorrit explain what has happened? The house collapses, but the reader is never given the chance to see the dust settle. This technique extends to various minor elements in the story. We know what the Nation thinks of Merdle's death, but how does Fanny respond to the use her father-in-law has made of her penknife? Or, in the case of the Gowans, we know that Blandois suspects Little Dorrit of delivering a love letter from Clennam to Pet. Does he share this information with Gowan? If so, how does Gowan react? And, of course, we never see Clennam respond to the truth about his birth. Little Dorrit promises to tell him—"in time to come, he should know all that was of import to himself" (p. 788)—but for all the reader knows, that time might never come. Unlike Caleb Plummer's daughter, Clennam may never be given the opportunity to understand the reality of his relationship to others; he is denied the past that, in the context of *Dombey and Son* or *The Mill on the Floss*, is vital to the individual's integrity. Forster thought that a major fault in *Little Dorrit* was "the want of ease and coherence among the figures of the story" (*Life*, p. 625). The narrator's handling of the events in the second half of the novel suggests that this supposed incoherence is not an oversight, but a consistent plan of narrative presentation. He does not forget to inform the reader of certain events; he purposely excludes them so that he can demonstrate the lack of "connections" between his characters.

The care with which Dickens planned the ending of *Little Dorrit* is obvious. Before determining what to include in the final double number, he reconsidered all the previous action; he reread parts of the novel and made notes in two separate sets of "*Mems: for working the Story round*" ("Plans," p. 825). Like Little Dorrit's final scene with Clennam, the resolution reached by the end of the novel suggests the limitations involved in what fiction can ultimately reveal to the reader. Because there is so much "story" in *Little Dorrit*, it is possible to forget just how much of it Dickens chooses not to tell. Merdle's business dealings are never explained. Arthur's question—"How connected with the Dorrits?" ("Plans," p. 825)—is answered, but not for him. Most of the Dorrit story remains a mystery. Tite Barnacle cannot remember the nature of Dorrit's original business. It could have been "spirits, or buttons, or wine, or blacking, or oatmeal, or woollen, or pork, or hooks and eyes, or iron, or treacle, or shoes, or something or other that was wanted for troops, or seamen, or somebody" (p. 547). This question is never resolved. The reader never even finds out how Dorrit gets into debt, or, for that matter, how he gets out; where that fortune has been resting for all those years remains a mystery concealed in Pancks's "hand." Nor do we ever understand the nature of Doyce's invention. Though he explains it to Clennam with the utmost clarity, that courtesy is never extended to the reader. Nor do we learn the nature of his business with the Barbaric Power. As Meagles points out, Doyce must "hide" his works and labors "under lock and key" (p. 796) when he returns to England. And, as J. Hillis Miller has noted, Clennam's attempt to find justice in the Circumlocution Office reaches no conclusion; it "remains at the end of *Little Dorrit* like a loose thread of the plot dangling unresolved."[8] Just before the collapse of the Clennam house, Flintwinch promises that he will explain his theft of the codicil in twenty-four hours. This elucidation, however, is withheld: "His taking himself off within that period with all he could get, was the final satisfactory sum and substance of his promised explanation" (p. 773). By the end of the novel, the narrator, who has

pledged earlier that he will be explicit, leaves such points open to speculation. This effect is playfully underlined in the last appearance of Mr.
F's Aunt. Throughout the novel, she has been the source of "mysterious communication" (p. 149). In the last chapter, she sits in the
kidney-pie shop, "addressing the following Sibyllic apostrophe, . . .
'Bring him for'ard, and I'll chuck him out o' winder!'" (p. 794). The
narrator refuses even to guess the meaning of this invective: "It has
been supposed that this admirably consistent female intended by
'him,' Arthur Clennam. This, however, is mere speculation; who the
person was, who, for the satisfaction of Mr. F's Aunt's mind, ought to
have been brought forward, and never was brought forward, will never
be positively known" (p. 795). "Mere speculation," in even this most
minor of matters, is all that remains.

In all his major works between *Dombey and Son* and *Little Dorrit*,
Dickens had adhered to the practice of ending his novels with a present-tense chapter like the one with which he had concluded Florence's
story. While Dombey and Sol Gills and Captain Cuttle "drink" the
Madeira, Mr. Dick "plays" with David Copperfield's children, and Esther Summerson tells the reader how happy she "is" after seven years
of marriage. The main purpose of these endings is simply to convey
information. As Humphry House noted, "Dickens was enough of a
pure story-teller to want to answer the child's insistent question, 'What
happened next?'"[9] The reader therefore learns "what happens" to
most of the major and to many of the minor characters. In *Hard Times*
Dickens varies this practice, but only slightly. He conveys this information by allowing his characters to see into the "futurity" he has
planned for them. But information has become remarkably scarce in
Little Dorrit. Although the events of the novel sufficiently antedate its
appearance to allow Dickens to follow the procedure he had established, he chooses to do otherwise. He concludes his narration when
the action proper is completed; the novel ends with the marriage of
Little Dorrit and Clennam, not with the history of how many children
they had or how many of the other characters they could include in
their happy family. What would have been present-tense narration in
an earlier novel is a continuation of the conventional past tense. The
reader learns as little about the future as Clennam has learned about
the codicil. The reader knows that Fanny will neglect her children and

that Amy will nurse the dying Tip. The narrator notes, in parentheses, that Pancks will become chief clerk, then partner, of Doyce and Clennam. But all this information is subordinated to the main action of the wedding. Dickens seems less interested in narrating the fates of Amy and Clennam than he is in including the dog Diogenes in the final tableau of *Dombey and Son*. An entire chapter of sustained promise in *Dombey and Son* shrinks to two paragraphs of vaguely projected events in the later novel. The figures of Woodcourt, Esther, and Ada in *Bleak House* are comparable to Clennam, Amy, and Pet. We know a great deal about "what happens" to the former and practically nothing about what will happen to the latter. Carlyle's great web of generations is given no substantiation here. This sense of relative incompletion extends to details of presentation. The last paragraph begins with an incomplete sentence; the narrator has relinquished even the desire to sustain the normal patterns of grammar. Although these paragraphs are a masterpiece of balanced tone, they constitute something less than a neat conclusion. Indeed, the resonance of this ending depends on the narrator's ability to balance the inconclusiveness of the information he offers against his use of the conventionally "tidy" marriage ending.

Although Dickens cannot end with the tag-line, "and they lived happily ever after," *Little Dorrit* does not ultimately conclude on a note of defeat. It is true that Dickens's conception of what the novel can achieve is now distinctly limited. It cannot create connections between characters when the world they inhabit precludes such bonds. Unlike *Dombey and Son*, this novel cannot turn the shadow of a wish into the reality of an embrace. The conclusion of the work is the narrator's exercise in How Not to Do It.[10] He refuses to tidy up the plot. He is not Mrs. General; he does not believe in varnishing the narrative's surface, and he will not "cram all articles of difficulty into cupboards, lock them up, and say they had no existence" (p. 438). Yet if the conditions of the world of *Little Dorrit* threaten to break down the analogies that have identified reader, character, and narrator in Dickens's earlier fiction, that event is averted. The reader is asked to share the experience of some of the incomprehensibility that plagues the characters. When Plornish tries to understand his poverty, he becomes like a "blind man" with a "tangled skein" of yarn; he futilely tries "to find some beginning or end to it" (p. 137). Clennam complains that the world is a labyrinth. The complexity of the novel's plot and the narrator's treatment of its events mirror this labyrinthine quality. Like the gossip's redoublings in *Vanity Fair*, this plot defines both the limitations and the mimetic strengths of the novel. Dickens balances knowledge and ignorance, revelation and deception, awareness and blindness, in a manner that resembles the tensions characteristic of Thackeray's best work. In *Little Dorrit* as in *Vanity Fair*, both character and reader must live with what Dickens calls the "contradictions, vacillations, inconsistencies, the little peevish perplexities of this ignorant life, mists which the morning without a night only can clear away" (p. 618). At mid-century both novelists embody in their work an understanding of fiction that is comprehensive enough to suggest its relevance to both art and life, to include its moral ambiguities without allowing them to undercut its moral utility. Approaching this question from a different direction than he had chosen in *Vanity Fair*, Thackeray arrives at much the same conclusion in *The Newcomes*, although there, as in *Little Dorrit*, the analogies are sustained against considerable odds.

If in *Little Dorrit* Dickens has come a long way from the hard-won but fully satisfying enactment of romance that he created in the ending of *Dombey and Son*, he still offers persuasive consolations. Limited as Arthur Clennam's knowledge may be, he does wed Little Dorrit in the end, and this consummation, like the reconciliation of Florence and her father, comes to represent, by analogy, the union of narrator and reader. The marital image is wholly appropriate, and it is not confined to Dickens's fiction. In "Janet's Repentance" George Eliot equates her narrator's role with that of the Rev. Mr. Tryan and the reader's role with Janet's; at the end of the tale, the two characters exchange a pure kiss of spiritual marriage. As the narrator notes, the fellowship in suffering creates ties closer than those of mother and child, brother and sister; the only closer tie, one assumes, is that of husband and wife. Similar relations in Thackeray's fiction reveal his characteristic uneasiness. Becky Sharp, we are often told, is a performer, an artist; her handling of her human material, coldblooded, ruthless, or even generous, as on occasion it can be, reveals Thackeray's attraction to a conception of an art divorced from the constraints of social responsibility. But such art, the novel proves, leads to no lasting unions. In

Henry Esmond, romance is equated with the sexual attractions of Beatrix. To give her up is to cease having a story to tell; a record of life with Rachel Esmond cannot pretend to engage the reader's interest. In the mid-century novel marriage or the failure to marry often reveals not only the quality of the society being depicted, but the quality of the reader's presumed imaginative relation to the narrative itself. In Dickens's later works the analogical bonds become more tenuous, but still conceivable, as the studied enigma at the end of *Great Expectations* suggests. In *Little Dorrit*, unions, both fictive and aesthetic, are still possible. The comment made by the church functionary at the end of *Little Dorrit* is a case in point; the narrator offers it in the confidence that his reader will share both his amusement and his self-confidence. Moreover, the joke is immediately followed by the extraordinarily restrained and balanced tone of the closing lines: "They went quietly down into the roaring streets, inseparable and blessed; and as they passed along in sunshine and in shade, the noisy and the eager, and the arrogant and the froward and the vain, fretted, and chafed, and made their usual uproar" (p. 802). If Dickens refuses to offer final assurances or a sense of ultimate clarity, he brings *Little Dorrit* in its last page to a conclusion worthy of the complexity and profundity of his heroine's characterization. Like Little Dorrit herself, Dickens could say, "I could never have been of any use, if I had not pretended a little."

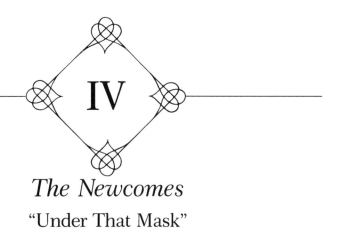

IV

The Newcomes
"Under That Mask"

The plot of *The Newcomes* (1853–55), like that of *Little Dorrit*, turns on matters of speculation. The fate of the Bundelcund Banking Company, a financial bubble as fragile as Merdle's empire, dictates the radical changes in fortune on which the characters rise and fall. Arthur Clennam and Colonel Newcome, anachronisms of gentility and honor in an era of charlatans, accept responsibility for a turn of events that neither could foresee, while Ethel Newcome and Amy Dorrit manipulate their own fortunes in generous but covert attempts to aid the men they love. The manifold narrative speculations of *Little Dorrit*—whether Mr. F's Aunt means to defenestrate Clennam, for instance—are replaced at the end of *The Newcomes* by a series of questions posed to determine whether Clive and Ethel will marry after all. Such unsettled issues point to the conclusion that both novels draw: in love as in finance, instability is the only certainty. As Plornish notes in his typically befuddled way, man stands on a wheel of fortune. One moment his head is held high, the next moment he finds himself turned upside down. Again and again in *The Newcomes*, Thackeray treats the aesthetic equivalent of these economic and marital uncertainties; literary fashions and literary tastes are as much subject to change as any other facet of human experience. When Colonel Newcome first returns from India, he cannot comprehend or accept the critical judgments that he hears from his son's bright young friends—it is simply impossible that

Sir Walter is now considered a second-rate poet, that the younger generation reveres the author of the ridiculous "Peter Bell," or that Carlyle
is the "great man" of the day. That Thackeray should present popular
taste as an indication of mutability is only appropriate. His own uneasy
and tentative relation to his audience led to ironies and paradoxes that
he himself might well have appreciated. Although he often belittled
his audience and mocked its limitations, the narrative form of his fiction, more than that of either Dickens or even George Eliot, was determined by his preoccupation with his readers and his presumptions
about their responses to his work.

Carlyle defined the central problem of Thackeray's career when he
said of himself, "I never know or can even guess what or who my audience is, or whether I have any audience: thus too naturally I adjust
myself on the Devil-may-care principle."[1] Both men were, as George
Eliot would later describe herself, "much in need of the warmly expressed sympathy which only popularity can win" (*Letters*, 3 : 6). But
for the first ten years of both their careers, popularity was elusive. As
late as 1845, one of Thackeray's spokesmen, George Savage Fitz-
Boodle, complained of the public's "unmerited obloquy and inattention
. . . that meanest of all martyrdoms, indifference, with which a callous
age has visited" him. Fitz-Boodle, like both his creator and Carlyle,
might well label himself "a *grande âme inconnue*, a *génie incompris*"
(6 : 521–22). At comparable periods in their careers, when Carlyle was
writing the studiously ignored *Sartor Resartus*, Dickens had already
demonstrated his ability to capture the public's imagination with such
characters as Pickwick and Little Nell, and George Eliot was being offered £10,000 for the copyright of *Romola*. Even after the popularity of
The French Revolution (1837) and the favorable reception of *Vanity
Fair* ten years later, distrust and the expectation of disappointment
were engrained in both Carlyle and Thackeray; there was no way of
insuring that past failures might not prophesy the fate of future works.
In the preface to *Pendennis* (1850), the novelist noted that he had
"found many thousands more readers than [he had] ever looked for."
The way he reacted to such popularity, however, suggests that he
thought it fortuitous and perhaps transitory: "I can no more ignore
good fortune than any other chance which has befallen me" (12 :
xxxv). As Plornish would point out, this piece of good luck might aban-

don him; the wheel of fortune, an apt image for his readers' favor, might turn again. By 1850, the wheel had indeed turned for Carlyle. Even Trollope, a devout admirer, Dr. Pessimist Anticant notwithstanding, had decided that *The Latter-Day Pamphlets* were not worth the eight shillings they had cost him. In *The Newcomes*, Thackeray's reference to the "great" Carlyle is patently ironic; its lesson could not be ignored. What had happened to the man whom Thackeray now nicknamed Gurlyle could happen to him as well. Yet, at the height of his powers and his popularity, Thackeray was able to postpone that fate. In novels like *Vanity Fair, Henry Esmond,* and *The Newcomes,* he balanced his own distrust of his readers against his need for their approval. By doing so, he gained the popularity he had earlier seemed to disdain.

Before that time, however, Thackeray had adopted the devil-may-care principles and approaches that characterized Carlyle's early work. Both men published their first substantial works in *Fraser's Magazine* in the 1830s; both had found productive and congenial the journalistic convention that *Fraser's* had adopted from *Blackwood's,* the repeated appearance of fictitious narrators with well-developed personalities and distinctive perspectives. Diogenes Teufelsdröckh, the Editor of *Sartor Resartus,* and Sauerteig allowed Carlyle to distance himself from attitudes that his readers might be only too ready to reject. Impersonating Oliver Yorke, the editor of *Fraser's,* Carlyle explains the fugitive quality of his own authorial identity: "With us even he still communicates in some sort of mask, or muffler; and, we have reason to think, under a feigned name" (s R, p. 9). Devil's-dung and Sourdough are reminiscent of Sir Walter Scott's best-known persona, the schoolteacher Jedediah Cleishbotham, or Thwackass, but Carlyle's use of such "mufflers" and Thackeray's adaptation of the same technique are marks of what Teufelsdröckh calls the ironic man. The Editor of *Sartor Resartus* offers a perceptive analysis of this "too defensive" mode. The assumed identity of the persona with its supposed indifference and sarcasm is the "buckram case" in which the speaker tries to shield his vulnerability. Although the ironic man wants to "unite" himself with those he addresses, "division, not union, is written on most part of his procedure" (pp. 104–5). Thackeray's early narrative personas have precisely this self-defeating effect. Drawing on eighteenth-century conceptions of fiction in *Catherine* (1839–40), as Dickens had done in *Oliver Twist*, Thackeray distinguishes virtue from vice as he tries to establish the similarities shared by the murderess Cat Hayes and the "vicious" readers who thirst for narratives of bloody crime. The genuinely emetic function of the tale, however, caused and perhaps still causes his readers to reject the quite healthy attitude that stands behind his ironic approach. Thackeray's mask here is Ikey Solomons, the well-known model for Fagin, and his identity calls into play the anti-Semitic tendencies of the audience. After Thackeray speaks as Oliver Yorke to explain that Ikey is safely locked away in Newgate, the narrator's familiar attitude toward the reader, his references to "us," become even more unsettling. Thackeray's attempts to identify the reader with this narrator, to create the analogies that would become so effective in his later work, actually encourage the reader to reject both Ikey and his characters. In some ways, the parody of Newgate fiction here is too complete; as Thackeray lamented in 1850, *Catherine* was declared "horridly immoral" (10:590). Division is the fate of the ironic man. No wonder Carlyle was one of the few readers of *Catherine* who understood and appreciated the goal of Thackeray's indirections.

By mid-century, Thackeray had created seemingly countless masks and established the fictitious persona as a distinguishing mark of his fiction, but the device had become a mode of mediation rather than alienation. Whenever Thackeray created a voice with a story to tell, he seemed impelled to endow it with a personality and a history, as chapter 62 of *Vanity Fair* attests. *Pendennis*, his sole mid-century attempt to do without such a persona is, to my mind at least, one of his weaker performances. Even so thoroughly disguised an autobiography cannot succeed unless a narrative mask sets Thackeray at a distance from his subject; both the autobiographical clarity and consummate art of *Henry Esmond* suggest what is missing in the earlier novel. Part of the motivation behind such masks was, like Scott's, a gentlemanly disinclination to identify himself as the author of "trifles." Yet Scott's personas—Cleishbotham, Peter Pattieson, and Chrystal Croftangry—stand as blinds between the Great Unknown and his public. Thackeray's, though, are a means of communication. In *The Newcomes*, Arthur Pendennis, himself the author of *Leaves from the Life-book of*

Walter Lorraine, becomes the storyteller; as a man of letters whose personality the audience has already come to know, he is an obvious narrative vehicle. Years before Thackeray had transformed the voices of his early reviews, Yellowplush and Titmarsh, into narrators; now Pendennis would serve the same function. Thackeray described his "uncontrolable modesty" as the basis of Pendennis's function: "Mr. Pendennis is the author of the book, and he has taken a great weight off my mind, for under that mask and acting, as it were, I can afford to say and think many things that I couldn't venture on in my own person, now that it is a person, and I know the public are staring at it" (*Letters*, 4:436). Scott had explained in his 1831 introduction to *The Fortunes of Nigel* that his use of Captain Clutterbuck had allowed him to depart from "the rules of civility and good taste" (p. xiii). For Thackeray the persona was also a source of freedom; but by 1853 it afforded him the freedom to define himself and his readers in a relation which could offer them both ease and dignity.

At first Thackeray seems to have been unsure about the extent of his narrator's role. In chapter 1 Pendennis asks permission "to accompany [the characters] for a short while . . . until, familiarized with the public, they can make their own way" (14:7). Perhaps he originally planned to dispose of Pendennis after the plot and its characters had been introduced. The subtitle of the first volume (1854) of the first edition suggests such a strategy: *The Newcomes: Memoirs of a Most Respectable Family . . . Edited by A. Pendennis Esqre*. Like Laurence Templeton of *Ivanhoe* or Cleishbotham in *The Tales of My Landlord*, Pendennis would edit a family's papers. Yet the revised title of the second volume (1855) implies that Pendennis's presence as narrator has become indispensable; here *The Newcomes* is described as *A History of a Most Respectable Family by A. Pendennis Esqre*. It must have seemed clear to Thackeray that, if there were psychological and professional reasons for adopting "that mask" and for "acting," there were aesthetic reasons for continuing the practice. Like the evolution of the narrator's role in *Vanity Fair*, this handling of Pendennis's role suggests the extemporaneous quality of Thackeray's narrative technique; he allowed it to develop according to the evolving demands of the narrative. In *The Newcomes* he seems to have begun with Scott's example in mind. Pendennis would be an editor not personally involved in the story he tells. Whether provided by a retired soldier like Captain Clutterbuck, an antiquary like Dryasdust, or a retired lawyer like Croftangry, the narrative frames of Scott's novels are consistently and purposefully unrelated to the stories they introduce. In the case of a novel like *The Heart of Mid-Lothian*, the frame may seem tonally irrelevant or even misplaced. Thackeray could easily have maintained Scott's distinction between the substance of his tale and the occasion of its telling. That practice, of course, would have rendered difficult the creation of any analogies that might link reader, narrator, and character. Yet, as he had done earlier, Carlyle provided a more productive model. Like the Editor of *Sartor Resartus*, Pen becomes the intermediary, the agent who creates a bond between the reader and the characters. Moreover, Pen exemplifies the impulse that both Carlyle and Thackeray share. As Carlyle said of Richter, the "author . . . generally becomes a person in the drama himself, before all is over" (CME, 1:12).

The Newcomes is, as Pendennis announces, a "book . . . all about the world and a respectable family dwelling in it" (p. 502). The "world" is the "great world," the moneyed society of West End London in the 1830s and early 1840s. As Ethel Newcome notes, it consists of wealth, rank, fine houses, and titles. Juliet McMaster has succinctly characterized the values of this society; Thackeray's subject, she says, is the "complex union of, or confusion between, financial and moral values, good and goods, which constitutes 'respectability.'"[2] The great world exists on the principle of a dog-eat-dog struggle for social survival. The mock-moral of *The Newcomes*, exemplified by the family of the title, expresses this principle: "To push on in the crowd, every male or female struggler must use his shoulders. . . . Is there a good place at table? Take it. . . . If your neighbour's foot obstructs you, stamp on it; and do you suppose he won't take it away?" (pp. 95–96). Everything in this world has its price. Literature, religion, art are all offered for sale, hawked in the streets, and sometimes sold at a discount. The plot centers on one aspect of this rapacious world; the marriage market in *The Newcomes* replaces the marriage booth of *Vanity Fair*. Parents sell their marriageable children, as Ethel Newcome implies when she attends a family dinner wearing a green ticket with her price written on it, and men buy the wives who will promote their status.

The story focuses on Clive and Ethel, cousins in two branches of the family, but it records the *mariages de convenance* contracted by three generations of Newcomes. Clive's grandfather marries twice, first for love, to a poor factory-girl; the second time for gain, to the rich daughter of his former employer. Of the love-match is born Thomas, later Colonel Newcome, Clive's father; the results of policy are the twins, Brian and Hobson. The second generation repeats the pattern begun by the father's unhappy second choice. Thomas is thwarted in his attempt to marry Léonore, daughter of a noble French émigré. She is married off to the old Comte de Florac, and Newcome goes in self-exile to India. There he marries a poor widow who makes him quite miserable. Colonel Newcome's half-brothers, partners in a rich and powerful banking firm, fare no better. Brian marries the scatterbrained countess, Lady Ann Kew, and becomes Sir Brian. Hobson marries a vulgar woman obsessed with laughable intellectual and social pretensions. None of these households is happy; each demonstrates one of Thackeray's favorite themes, the inevitable isolation of individuals and generations. Their children, alienated from their parents, continue the pattern. Sir Brian's son, Barnes, after a liaison with a Mrs. Delacy which yields two illegitimate children, marries the heiress Lady Clara Pulleyn. Barnes abuses his simple, pathetic wife until she is literally beaten into running off with Lord Highgate, the former Jack Belsize, to whom she had been attached until her family intervened. Barnes's sister Ethel would like to marry Clive, but he has chosen to become an artist and therefore is socially beyond the pale. She is engaged first to Lord Kew and later to Lord Farintosh. Both "catches" are pitilessly pursued until captured by her grandmother, the old Countess of Kew, much to the humiliation of Ethel, who cannot but admit that she is "bandied about from bidder to bidder, and offered for sale to a gentleman who will not buy" her (p. 504). The failure of Barnes's marriage makes Ethel understand that the marriage market consumes its wares, and she breaks off her engagement to Lord Farintosh. Her cousin Clive makes the mistake she avoids. He is bright, talented, good-natured, charming—something of a prig, but, as Pendennis says, "everybody's favourite" (p. 523)—and he is effectively ruined by his marriage to Rosey Mackenzie, the niece of his father's closest friend. The marriage is dominated and finally destroyed by Rosey's mother, the Campaigner,

a military widow who has the effect of malaria on every man she
meets. Clive's role in this marriage is less than praiseworthy; he
cannot manage to care enough about his wife to prevent her mother's
worrying her to death. Each generation repeats the mistakes of the
previous generation. Throughout, these mistakes are the result of an
inability to realize that affective ties cannot be sustained on motives of
gain or family pride.

The man who tells the story of the Newcomes has an ambivalent
relationship to the world he describes. It is the world that Pendennis
inhabits, the world he understands, yet his own past allows him to see
it with some detachment, to judge it and often to feel superior to its
values. Of all the characters previously created by Thackeray, Pendennis is the one most suited to the role of narrator in *The Newcomes*. Like
Clive and Ethel, he has struggled to make a place for himself in the
"great world." Much of his social education, as it is presented in *The
History of Pendennis*, is presided over by his uncle, an "inveterate
worldling" (12:529). At this earlier stage in his life, Pen becomes a
dandy, fond of fine clothes, good dinners, and gambling. He develops a
"general scepticism and sneering acquiescence in the world as it is"
(12:800); as he tells Warrington, "I take things as I find them, and the
world, and the Acts of Parliament of the world, as they are." Like Ethel,
this younger Pendennis has been tempted by the marriage market;
Warrington denounces Pen's plans to marry for money in terms that
could be applied to her behavior: "You're going to sell yourself, and
Heaven help you! You are going to make a bargain which will degrade
you and make you miserable for life" (12:802). Yet Pendennis ultimately rejects the major's values and the marriage plans that his uncle
so ardently supports. Aided by his mother, his future wife, and his
friend, Pen learns the limitations of money and status. Yet if Pendennis
can judge the world in which Clive and Ethel become involved, his
role as the narrator of their story increases, in a rather paradoxical way,
our sense of the almost irresistible attractions of that world.[3] His rein-
carnation as the spectator of an initiation that so resembles his own is
a comment on his role as a character in the earlier story. It almost
seems as if Pendennis, or at least Thackeray, realizes that the happy
conclusion of Pen's story has been too pat, that he has too easily escaped the world's perennial temptations. Pen's profession, like his past,

increases the irony of his place in this social sphere. He is a novelist as well as a gentleman—a precarious balance, as Thackeray well knew. His own distrust of wealth and titles is therefore matched by the distrust with which the members of the Newcome banking family view him. Barnes does not even try to conceal his contempt for his cousin Clive, the painter, and his cousin's friend Pendennis: "Damn all literary fellows—all artists—the whole lot of them!" (p. 245). Yet the great world flatters itself with the company of the talent it despises, and Pendennis has enough social standing to be invited to dinner—if a seat should become empty at the last moment. Pendennis knows that his role in the great world is a minor one, and he indulges in self-mockery when he describes himself as "the explanatory personage . . . of quite a third-rate order," the gentleman-friend of Sir Harry Courtly or perhaps his valet (p. 319). He is the spectator, rarely the participant, in the little dramas enacted in fashionable drawing rooms.

Yet Pendennis has his own little domestic world, in which he is the central figure. In the second half of *The Newcomes* he marries Laura, and their sentimental love-match stands in rather obvious contrast to the typical *mariage de convenance*. Moreover, this event doubles the perspectives from which the action is seen. Along with two other men of letters, Fred Bayham and Warrington, Pendennis voices the attitudes of the world, if not of the great world. Laura stands for virtue and strict piety, so much so that she cannot even tolerate one of the world's victims, Lady Clara. Laura gives her husband access to new sources of information; as Pendennis is Clive's confidant, she is Ethel's. This chorus on the action allows Thackeray to avoid a great deal of the moral simplicity that vitiates *Pendennis*. Much as Pen cherishes the virtues and innocence of his wife, as cloying as his praise often becomes, his own ironic perspective reveals the narrowness of her principles. She is less the angelic figure than she appears to be in the title page of Pen's story. Laura's presence also leads to Pen's increasingly active involvement with the people whose story he narrates. The couple visits Clive and the colonel in Brussels, or the Floracs near Newcome. Pen inherits some money, which, deposited in the Newcome bank, entitles him to more frequent dinner invitations, and his wife and her social connections give him the respectability he has lacked. Pendennis even becomes something of a motive force in the plot when he discovers that the colonel has become one of the Poor Brethren, or pensioners of Grey Friars. Yet his role remains that of a spectator and a narrator. He advances the plot only because he sees the colonel at the annual school dinner and relates this turn of events to Léonore, Ethel, and the Prince de Montcontour.

A passage from Thackeray's speech "Charity and Humour" suggests that he was aware of the need for such a mediating presence in his fiction; describing the difference between the humor of Swift or Fielding and that of Steele, he commented indirectly on the transition that had taken place in his own career between the early 1840s and the 1850s:

And here, coming off the stage, and throwing aside the motley habit, or satiric disguise, in which he had before entertained you, mingling with the world, and wearing the same coat as his neighbour, the humourist's service became straightway immensely more available; his means of doing good infinitely multiplied; his success, and the esteem in which he was held, proportionately increased. It requires an effort, of which all minds are not capable, to understand *Don Quixote*. . . . Many more persons are sickened by *Jonathan Wild* than can comprehend the satire of it. . . . [The] distortions [of the satiric mask] appal many simple spectators; its settled sneer or laugh is unintelligible to thousands, who have not the wit to interpret the meaning of the visored satirist preaching from within. (10:621–22)

Thackeray here speaks from his own hard experience. Like *Catherine*, *The Luck of Barry Lyndon* (1844), another early work, had sickened without enlightening its readers. Although the social world it describes and Thackeray's attitudes toward that world vary in no essential way from the social criticism of *The Newcomes*, the voice of the earlier narrator had created considerable difficulties. There Thackeray identifies the speaker, Barry Lyndon himself, with the values he intends to invalidate. As the picaresque manipulator of a corrupt social system, Barry obscures the viewpoint of his creator, the "visored satirist" preaching from inside a mask. Thackeray had been forced to add editorial notes by another persona, George Savage Fitz-Boodle, to make his condemnation of Barry clear.[4] In *The Newcomes*, however, Thackeray discards "the motley habit, or satiric disguise," even though the mask itself is still retained, and his narrator is found "mingling with the world, and wearing the same coat as his neighbour." The author has become "more available" to his reader. Unlike Ikey Solomons or Barry

Lyndon, the narrator can use his commentary to suggest the analogical bonds that unite reader, character, and narrator without risking the reader's rejection of his propositions. Pendennis can maintain a sympathetic attitude toward the individuals in the great world as he deplores its customs and practices. By meeting his audience halfway, Thackeray has increased rather than restricted his artistic freedom; by decreasing the complexity of his ironic stand, he has created union out of the divisions that had perplexed Teufelsdröckh and Ikey Solomons. Moreover, he can safely complicate other issues that will extend the moral relevance of his work.

One such central issue in *The Newcomes*, as in *Dombey and Son* or *Adam Bede*, is the relation of the fiction to the "real world" it depicts. A novel like *Barry Lyndon* harks back to the simpler assumptions of Scott's historical fiction, but *The Newcomes* involves the reader in a process of discovering both the difference between fact and fiction and their frequent interpenetrations. Pendennis is both a historian— Clive's "biographer"—and a novelist. At the opening of *The Newcomes*, he describes Clive as the friend "of whose history I am the chronicler" (p. 43). He is continually trying to convince the reader of the factual authenticity of his narrative. He frequently cites the source of his information about a certain incident. Thus, his estimation of Mrs. Hobson Newcome is corroborated by her relative Giles; Tom Eaves, re-emerging from *Vanity Fair*, reports a conversation between Hobson and Barnes Newcome. Pendennis frequently gives his reader documentary evidence to validate his narrative. Letters constitute a significant part of the novel; as Clive's confidant, he receives accounts of his life in Rome and later in Baden. He even uses the records of the debates in the House of Lords to tell the story of Lady Clara's divorce from Barnes. Scott had offered the same kind of factual evidence to buttress the foundations of his fictions, but such material had been included in footnotes distinguished from the "imaginary" narrative; in *The Newcomes* this information provides the basis for and is included in the text. Yet Pendennis is a novelist by profession, and he once refers to the book the reader holds as the "present novel" (p. 462). The fact that he has written *Walter Lorraine* is mentioned several times. Mrs. Mackenzie even states that, though "a very *wicked* book; . . . it contains some sad, sad truths" (p. 287)—a judgment that a generous

Mrs. Grundy might make on *The Newcomes*. His identity as a novelist affects his roles as both character and narrator in this particular novel; the constant stream of literary allusions that embellish his commentary repeatedly remind us of his chosen craft. As Florac says, "He speaks like a book—the Romancier!" (p. 766).

Pendennis insists on the ambiguity of his dual roles in a way that eventually merges them into one. He chooses a peculiar method of inducing the reader's credulity in his role as the biographer of a real life when he comments that Clive "is, in a word, just such a youth as has a right to be the hero of a novel" (p. 75). This ambiguity reaches its height when he claims the right to invent what he does not know for a fact:

No doubt, the writer of the book, into whose hands Clive Newcome's logs have been put, and who is charged with the duty of making two octavo volumes out of his friend's story, dresses up the narrative in his own way; utters his own remarks in place of Newcome's; makes fanciful descriptions of individuals and incidents with which he never could have been personally acquainted; and commits blunders which the critics will discover. A great number of the descriptions in *Cook's Voyages*, for instance, were notoriously invented by Dr. Hawkesworth, who "did" the book: so in the present volumes, where dialogues are written down, which the reporter could by no possibility have heard, and where motives are detected which the persons actuated by them certainly never confided to the writer, the public must once for all be warned that the author's individual fancy very likely supplies much of the narrative; and that he forms it as best he may, out of stray papers, conversations reported to him, and his knowledge, right or wrong, of the characters of the persons engaged. And, as is the case with the most orthodox histories, the writer's own guesses or conjectures are printed in exactly the same type as the most ascertained patent facts. I fancy, for my part, that the speeches attributed to Clive, the colonel, and the rest, are as authentic as the orations in Sallust or Livy, and only implore the truth-loving public to believe that incidents here told, and which passed very probably without witnesses, were either confided to me subsequently as complier of this biography, or are of such a nature that they must have happened from what we know happened after. (pp. 296–97)

Pendennis justifies his imaginative endeavors not simply by suggesting that historians themselves tell lies, but by raising his fictive inventions to the status of history. What Pen does not know he invents, and what he invents is as true as anything he could know for a fact. The historical novelist like Scott might print his "ascertained patent facts" in a type unlike that used for the text, but Pen decides to follow the practice established by more conventional historians. Indeed, facets of *The Newcomes* suggest an even more venerable fictional model. If Colonel Newcome's simplicity and good nature qualify him for the title of Don Quixote, the voice who tells his story often resembles that of Cervantes's work. In both *Don Quixote* and *The Newcomes*, the boundaries of fiction and fact become so complicated, even at times comically confused, that the characters begin to assume a status of actuality that transcends such matters. If Cid Hamete Benengeli is the Arabic historian from whose work the narrator culls Don Quixote's tale, and all Arabs are notorious liars, is there any certain way of distinguishing between the real and the fictive? Pendennis's definition of his role has something of the same effect. Like the narrator of *Vanity Fair*, he is one of the characters; he lives in the "real" world Clive and Ethel inhabit. Aspects of that world and the activity that takes place within it are fictional, created by Pendennis; yet they are created only so that they can sustain and authenticate the status of the novel as history. When Pendennis speaks of the "part of [the colonel's] story to which we are now come perforce, and which the acute reader of novels has, no doubt, long foreseen" (p. 900), the reader is not at all surprised to discover that this authentic history is following the patterns imposed by fiction.

In *The Newcomes*, as in *Don Quixote*, the ability to recognize the difference between romance and reality is crucial. When Barnes Newcome can appear "romantic" to those around him, costly mistakes like Clara's marriage to him will inevitably occur. In the framework created by the "overture" and the epilogue of the novel, Thackeray challenges his reader to extend and then to test the traditional conceptions of romance and fable.[5] Here he speaks as the author; Pendennis does not introduce himself until the second half of the first chapter, and in the epilogue he has "disappeared as irrevocably as Eurydice" (p. 1008). In both sections of the framework, Thackeray recalls fables from Aesop and La Fontaine: the fox flatters the crow, the frog envies the ox, the wolf and ass dress themselves in sheep- and lionskins, and the owl claims superiority over them all. The ostensible point of these allusions is the universality of the story about to be told: "What stories are new? All types of all characters march through all fables: tremblers and boasters; victims and bullies; dupes and knaves; long-eared Neddies, giving themselves leonine airs. . . . With the very first page of the human story do not love and lies too begin?" (p. 5). Thackeray intimates that the moral of the story is not as unequivocal in his fable as it is in Aesop's or La Fontaine's. In fact, he turns the conventions upside down: "Rogues will sometimes triumph, and honest folks, let us hope, come by their own" (p. 6). The stress is on "let us hope"—he promises no poetic justice in his fictive world. At the end of the novel, Thackeray makes a surprising retreat from this position. As "Pendennis and Laura, and Ethel and Clive fade away into fable-land" (p. 1007), he asks questions about their futures that suggest that they inhabit a realm beyond his control. From the evidence Pendennis has offered, he draws the conclusion that Clive will marry Ethel. But the reader is perfectly free to come to his own conclusion. "But for you, dear friend, it is as you like. You may settle your fable-land in your own fashion." To offer such reassurance, however, Thackeray must return to the conventions he rejected in the "overture":

Anything you like happens in fable-land. Wicked folks die à propos . . . annoying folks are got out of the way; the poor are rewarded—the upstarts are set down in fable-land,—the frog bursts with wicked rage, the fox is caught in his trap, the lamb is rescued from the wolf, and so forth, just in the nick of time. And the poet of fable-land rewards and punishes absolutely. He splendidly deals out bags of sovereigns, which won't buy anything; belabours wicked backs with awful blows, which do not hurt, . . . makes the hero and heroine happy at last, and happy ever after. (p. 1009)

Like the reader of *Villette* or *Great Expectations*, the reader of *The Newcomes* must decide how the novel is to end. In doing so, he inevitably demonstrates the nature of his relation to the characters; if they are mere figures in fable-land, then the happy conclusion is possible.

If the author offers the reader this test, Pendennis has already provided the assumptions that will resolve the dilemma. Throughout the novel Pen adheres to the view of romance that appears in the "overture." He redefines the conventions of romance so that they correspond to the particular social world of *The Newcomes*. Clive is like one of "those guileless virgins of romance and ballad." "No giant waylaid him as yet; no robbing ogre fed on him; and . . . no winning enchantress or artful siren coaxed him to her cave, or lured him into her waters—haunts into which we know so many young simpletons are drawn, where their silly bones are picked and their tender flesh devoured" (p. 357). This passage is a radical retelling of several fairy tales; it counters every traditional and optimistic impulse that Dickens had put to such good use in *Dombey and Son*. Thackeray suggests that the heroes of romance are frequently eaten by ogres or have their bones picked and flesh devoured by sirens. But we know that in the realm of romance such things simply do not happen; the hero always emerges intact. The viciousness of the Newcome world extends to transform even the traditional stories it inherits. Furthermore, the import of the tale Pen tells defeats our usual impulses to indulge our longings for the consolations of romance. The action of the novel is destructive, not creative. Both Rosey and the colonel die after they have been reduced to near idiocy by the cruelty and domination of Mrs. Mac. Clive is transformed from a bright young man into a haggard, disappointed, and unsuccessful painter—the inheritance of six thousand pounds can hardly undo the damage he has suffered. The scandal and shame of adultery finally remove any possibility that Lady Clara might have had for happiness with Jack Belsize. The lamb is rescued from the wolf, but only to become the prey of social forces. And the wolf, with the help of Parliament, makes money by her escape. As early as *Barry Lyndon*, Fitz-Boodle stated that novelists who care about portraying "life as it really appears to them to be" must jettison the idea of "poetical justice." "Honesty is *not* the best policy" (6:310), and that point is eminently illustrated by the life of Colonel Newcome. Claiming that the hero and heroine could be "happy at last, and happy ever after" can only seem facile at this point; and the reader, granted the freedom to construct his own ending, will probably invent one that is more in keeping with the action that precedes it. Oddly enough, when Thackeray steps forward without his mask at the end of *The Newcomes*, his tone is more ironic than it has been since an earlier work like *Barry Lyndon*. But the effect of Thackeray's irony may attest to the faith he has in his reader's discernment as well as his desire to satisfy his reader's longings. At the conclusion of *Rebecca and Rowena*, for instance, he tells the reader that even the long-desired marriage of his characters will not make them particularly happy. Here the reader can be trusted to come to that conclusion on his own.

One facet of Thackeray's concluding statement suggests that his

characters have attained the status of actuality that defines their creator and his readers. In a letter Thackeray lamented the fact that he had
finished writing the novel: "I was quite sorry to part with a number of
kind people with whom I had been living and talking these 20 months
past, and to draw a line so ——————— on a sheet of paper, beyond
which their honest figures couldn't pass" (*Letters*, 3 : 459–60). In the
epilogue, he develops the idea of the line which signals "The End" and
creates a boundary between the fictional world of the characters and
the actual world that author and reader inhabit, but here he questions
its effectiveness: "Is yonder line (———————) which I drew with my
own pen, a barrier between me and Hades as it were, across which I
can see those figures retreating and only dimly glimmering?" (p. 1007).
The rest of the epilogue suggests that no such barrier exists, that once
Pendennis and Laura and Clive and Ethel have been created, they
cannot "fade away into fable-land." They go on existing in the minds of
both the author and the reader; perhaps they live "near us somewhere." Just as the "critic" in the "overture" provides the moral for the
tale, the reader in the epilogue prolongs the existence of the characters. He knows that some ten years have elapsed between Colonel
Newcome's death and the writing of the history of the family. Like the
narrator of *Dombey and Son* or *Little Dorrit*, Pendennis could reveal
their futures if he wanted to, but the reader is offered the opportunity
to extend their lives in any way he finds appropriate. This approach
suggests that the characters have assumed for the reader an authenticity that will not allow them to be confined or completed within the
realm of fiction. They refuse to become cardboard figures bound
within the covers of a novel. Thackeray's "lingering hold" (p. 1009) on
the reader's hand exemplifies the characters' lingering hold on the
reader's imagination and, indeed, on his sense of what life is "really"
like.

  Thackeray's narrative technique is designed to create and sustain
this sense of immediacy and authenticity. Part of his dismissal of the
conventions of fiction involves his studied disregard for plot, events
linked by cause and effect. In his principal explanation of the retro-
spective viewpoint created by the narrative, Pendennis dismisses the
idea of plot: "In such a history events follow each other without necessarily having a connexion with one another" (p. 296). Thackeray's

characteristic use of narrative redoublings is one way in which he thwarts the reader's normal plot-expectations. As Pendennis says, "I disdain . . . the tricks and surprises of the novelist's art" (p. 901). The narrative deemphasizes an event by focusing on the altered relations between characters that it has created. One of the climactic events of the novel, the collapse of the Bundelcund Banking Company, is narrated after the reader sees its primary result, the auctioning off of the colonel's house and goods. The following chapter explains how the auction came to be held. This redoubling is an exact copy of the way in which Thackeray relates the fall of Sedley's fortunes in *Vanity Fair*, yet in *The Newcomes* such techniques tend to slow the movement of the plot. Especially in the first half of the novel, the reader agrees with Thackeray when he says that the story "pretend[s] to march" (*Letters*, 3:355).

If Thackeray eschews the conventional concept of plot, he puts in its place a device more appropriate to Newcome society—narrative portraiture. The novel is the chronicle of a family with pretensions to an established genealogy and a place in the fashionable world. One way in which such a family advertises its sense of self-importance is by hanging portraits of its ancestors and present members. In *The Newcomes*, Thackeray repeatedly uses portraits and mirrors—looking glasses which reflect portraits of the characters—as expressions of the great world. Significantly, Laura is introduced first to Clive's portrait and only then to the man himself. In the famous excursus on the locked closets in Castle Bluebeard, Pendennis measures the splendor of this "English palace" by describing its family gallery: "the magnificence of this picture; the beauty of that statue; . . . the admirable likeness of the late marquis by Sir Thomas; of his father, the fifth earl, by Sir Joshua" (p. 150). After a particularly brutal confrontation between Barnes and Clara, Pendennis paints an ironic picture of Barnes "in his ancestral hall—surrounded by the portraits of his august forefathers—in his happy home" (p. 768). Mirrors create the same effect. The Princess of Montcontour, previously simple Miss Higg of Manchester, is terrified by the mirror-within-mirror décor of her bedroom at the Hôtel de Florac: "In her bed is an immense looking-glass. . . . Opposite that looking-glass, between the tall windows, at some forty feet distance, is another huge mirror, so that when the poor princess is in bed, in her prim old curl-papers, she sees a vista of elderly princesses twinkling away into the dark perspective." The princess' response to these mirrors is an apt metaphor for the position of the individual in the great world. She and her maid cover the mirrors, but she "never can get it out of her head that her image is still there, behind the jonquil hangings, turning as she turns, waking as she wakes" (p. 603). The façade of the great world never loses its power; its inhabitants are frozen by the desire for money and status into attitudes deemed appropriate by the family portrait painter. That Clive, who begins his career by painting heroic subjects, ultimately earns his living by painting portraits is significant. He succumbs to the usages of the great world as surely as his father does when he trusts the Bundelcund Banking Company.

Pendennis often narrates events as if they were static scenes or group portraits caught for a moment in the mirrors of a fashionable drawing room. Like Thackeray's use of gossip as a narrative representation of the social life in the fictional world of *Vanity Fair*, the way in which Pendennis tells the story in *The Newcomes* is mimetic. The narrative is literally a portrait of the Newcome world, and the reader's imagination becomes engaged in its creation as well as its apprehension: "The reader will be pleased to let his fancy paint for itself the look of courtesy . . . upon the colonel's kind face" (p. 200). At one point Pen decides that Clive's "face is so woebegone that we do not care to bring it forward in the family picture" (p. 696); the family picture is *The Newcomes* itself. The story consists, not of events completed in time past, but of scenes presently occurring in which the reader is invited to participate. Pendennis emphasizes this effect when he uses the second person to describe the interior of Colonel Newcome's grand house in Tyburnia: "Your face (handsome or otherwise) was reflected by countless looking-glasses, so multiplied and arranged as, as it were, to carry you into the next street" (pp. 824–25). The identity of "you" is purposefully generalized. It could be the reader, the character, the narrator, or an anonymous dinner guest. Allowing the reader to see himself as part of the company gathered in the great world, allowing him to feel the immediacy and power of its grasp on its members is the goal of Thackeray's narrative approach.

One of the principal means of attaining that goal is his use of a device Dickens had employed in *Dombey and Son* for quite other effects: narration in the present tense. In the eighth number, Pendennis calls attention to this technique and justifies it as a narrative necessity. "Our tale, such as it has hitherto been arranged, has passed in leisurely scenes wherein the present tense is perforce adopted; the writer acting as chorus to the drama, and occasionally explaining by hints or more open statements, what has occurred during the intervals of the acts" (p. 319). Thackeray may have been moved to make this explanation because "the publishers write and hint that the public has found that the story does not move." But he did not alter his practice—"I intend to disregard their petitions" (*Letters*, 3 : 346–47)—and the rest of the novel proceeds in "leisurely scenes wherein the present tense is perforce adopted." Unlike Dickens, who very consciously sets off chapters or parts of chapters from the more conventional past-tense narration in *Dombey and Son*, Thackeray unobtrusively slips in and out of the present tense. His use of this technique is fairly consistent. The characters who act as commentators within the novel—Pendennis, Laura, Warrington, and the major—often discuss the action in present-tense dialogues. Descriptions of places such as Honeyman's lodgings in Mayfair are conveyed in the tense appropriate to travel literature and guidebooks. Most often and most significantly, however, the present tense is used to narrate actions that typify the great world. The colonel returns from his long stay in India and is eager for a warm welcome from his family. The cold and condescending reception he finds at his half-brothers' office is a typical instance of how little blood relationships matter in the bankers' world. The conversation in which Clive and Ethel engage in the gardens of the Hôtel de Florac is also representative. Ethel asserts her allegiance to what she herself describes as a "life of vanity" (p. 627): love cannot withstand the appeal of fine houses, titles, and rank. Thackeray further emphasizes the typicality of the scene by moving from present-tense narration to the dramatic form of a dialogue. Ethel and Clive perform, as have others before them, "Two or Three Acts of a Little Comedy" (chapter 47).

The event most typical of the Newcome world is the society dinner, and Pendennis almost invariably narrates such occasions as if they were occurring in the present. They include, among others, various

dinners given by Colonel Newcome, by Mrs. Hobson Newcome, by
Lady Ann, and by Sherrick and Honeyman, along with the series of
dinners given by Barnes to celebrate the engagement of Ethel to Lord
Farintosh. The plot climaxes in a series of dinners—the Grey Friars'
event, the Christmas Eve dinner at which Pendennis reveals the colonel's plight, and the "day-after" dinner when Clive tries to eject his
mother-in-law. At one point, Pendennis makes a coy apology for the
time the reader spends at the dinner table: "I smile as I think how
much dining has been already commemorated in these veracious
pages; but the story is an everyday record; and does not dining form a
certain part of the pleasure and business of every day?" (pp. 651–52).
Pendennis knows well enough that the amount of dining described in
The Newcomes would be disproportionate even in an "everyday record." For the reader, the novel becomes one ongoing party; he moves
from table to table, from one gossip to the next. This point becomes
explicit when Pendennis tells the reader about Lord Kew's marriage to
Lady Henrietta Pulleyn: "All these interesting details, about people of
the very highest rank, we are supposed to whisper in the reader's ear
as we are sitting at a Belgravian dinner-table. My dear Barmecide
friend: isn't it pleasant to be in such fine company?" (p. 646). Reading
the novel is a way of joining the "fine company" dining within its
pages. As George Saintsbury explained, Thackeray's handling of the
Newcome family makes the "reader [feel] as if, on the humbler or less
humble side, he too were of the company, and all persons and their
affairs were naturally known to him."[6] The present tense is a way of
making the reader feel as if he were "of the company" the novel depicts. Like the gossip of *Vanity Fair*, it analogizes narration and the
uses of the world. As Major Pendennis says, "Gad . . . if we were not to
talk freely of those we dine with, how mum London would be!" (p. 54).

Thackeray's use of this unconventional form of narration in *The
Newcomes* is similar to Dickens's practice in *Our Mutual Friend* (1864–
65). From the first gathering of guests reflected in the mirror behind
the Veneering dinner table in chapter 2 to the final Veneering dinner in
Chapter the Last, Dickens conveys the pronouncements of the Voice of
Society in the present tense. The ultimate effect of this device in his
earlier novel *Dombey and Son* is exactly the opposite. Perhaps before

writing *Our Mutual Friend*, Dickens had learned something about its potential either from *The Newcomes* or from George Eliot's use of the device in the *Scenes of Clerical Life*. In *Dombey and Son*, sections narrated in the present tense eventually evoke the ultimate realities which undercut the supposed power and significance of temporal society. To Thackeray, such a perspective is not the proper subject of fiction. As Pendennis remarks of the piety of Lord Kew's mother, "Our history has had little to do with characters resembling this lady. It is of the world, and things pertaining to it. Things beyond it, as the writer imagines, scarcely belong to the novelist's province" (p. 485). In *Dombey and Son*, the present tense comes to evoke "things beyond" the world; in *The Newcomes*, it emphasizes the omnipotent and ever-present nature of "the world, and things pertaining to it." Just as all stories are old, have commenced with the beginning of time and continue in the present; just as all characters are typical; so too the usages of the world are universal and unavoidable. The reader cannot escape them; as Pendennis notes with the bitterest of ironies, he inevitably finds himself involved with "such fine company." It would be pleasant if, as Thackeray wistfully hopes in the epilogue, he and the reader could meet in "happy, harmless fable-land" (p. 1009), but his narrative technique dismisses, once and for all, that possibility. The novel, the self-avowed fiction, contains passages of present-tense narration so that he can equate the reader's experience of the novel with his experience of "real life." This narrative approach suggests that reader and author are more likely to meet at one of society's continuous dinner gatherings than in a nonexistent fable-land.

In a review that Thackeray particularly appreciated, Whitwell Elwin defined the process by which the reader of *The Newcomes* becomes convinced of its actuality: Thackeray brings "his mimic characters into competition with the living world, till forgetting they were shadows, we have followed their fortunes, and discussed their destinies and conduct as though they had been breathing flesh and blood."[7] This comment neatly summarizes the interdependent activities of creation and perception that constitute the aim of Victorian narration. The author acts, and his reader reacts in a way that raises art to the status of life. Almost twenty years earlier, when Carlyle offered his famous condemnation of Scott's romances, he suggested what would later become the basis for the difference between this mid-century demand for the reader's participation and earlier conceptions of narration. Not only does Scott not offer his reader anything of substance, Carlyle complained, he also asks nothing of his reader:

In this new-found poetic world there was no call for effort on the reader's part; what excellence [the romances] had, exhibited itself at a glance. It was for the reader, not the El Dorado only, but a beatific land of Cockaigne and Paradise of Donothings! The reader, what the vast majority of readers so long to do, was allowed to lie down at his ease, and be ministered to. What the Turkish bath-keeper is said to aim at with his frictions, and shampooings, and fomentings, more or less effectually, that the patient in total idleness may have the delights of activity,—was here to a considerable extent realised. The languid imagination fell back into its rest; an artist [whispered,] Be at ease, and let thy tepid element be comfortable to thee. (CME, 4:57)

In his best work Thackeray is anything but the Turkish bathkeeper, and his reader is never allowed to lie idle on his sofa. The conclusion of *The Newcomes*, in particular, suggests that at mid-century Thackeray was willing both to ask for his reader's active participation in the creation of the story and trust his audience's literary and moral sophistication. As Elwin implied, it is the reader who makes of the characters "flesh and blood" figures in a "living world."

Pendennis is the agent through whom this conclusion may be reached. By mediating between the reader and the characters, Pen establishes a creative relation between the author and his audience. For both Carlyle and Thackeray, the masks initially created to distance the author from his readers ultimately brought him into proximity with them. Early in *Sartor Resartus*, the Editor comments on Teufels-dröckh's Clothes-Philosophy and proposes a principle which describes Thackeray's fiction: "It seems as if the demonstration lay much in the Author's individuality; as if it were not Argument that had taught him, but Experience" (pp. 40–41). As *Vanity Fair* and *The Newcomes* prove, Thackeray raises his fictions to the level of experience by establishing and extending, through the presence of his narrators, the belief in the "Author's individuality." Yet even this approach could not solve the difficulties that Thackeray would face in his next novel, *The Virginians*. When he returned to the mode of historical fiction, the example of Scott, which had proved so productive in *Henry Esmond*, would reveal precisely those limitations that Carlyle had outlined in his comments on the Great Unknown and in his disdain for fiction in general. The author's individuality would become, not the source of experience, but the occasion for argument.

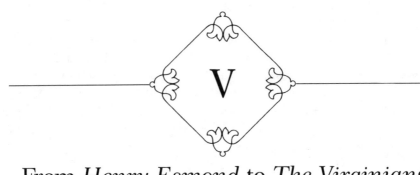

From *Henry Esmond* to *The Virginians*
The Loss of Faith

In 1861 Thackeray received this rather disconcerting piece of anonymous fan mail:

It is with great regret I write the following letter, regret that cause should have arisen for the writing of it. . . . [Its] subject is the great degeneration in your writings since you published your last great work, the Newcomes. The Virginians was a great falling off, but even that was immensely superior to the portion which has appeared of the Adventures of Philip. Surely, as an admirer of your genius, I have a right to appeal to you (even at an immense pecuniary sacrifice) to consult your future fame, and to keep it intact by writing no more novels, if you cannot improve on Lovel the Widower. (*Letters*, 4:242–43, n. 45)

The staggering presumption of this reader can be defended only by the justice of his case. *The Newcomes* is indeed Thackeray's "last great work"; *The Virginians* (1857–59), an equally "great falling off," marks the decline of both his powers as a novelist and his popularity. The respect and quite personal concern which motivated this plea constitute one of the signal ironies of Thackeray's career. Before and during the years when he was writing *The Virginians*, he constantly complained that his readers were tired of him and his work, but he made those complaints when his contemporary reputation had reached its height. The voice of Arthur Pendennis had succeeded in its work of mediation;

with *The Newcomes* Thackeray had reconciled himself to his audience. What we might consider to be sentimentality in his treatment of Colonel Newcome had finally invalidated the charge, as John Forster put it, that Thackeray could not raise himself "above the region of the sneering."[1] But Pendennis had spoken for his creator when he said, "If I were to write a book that should go through twenty editions, why, I should be the very first to sneer at my reputation" (12:932). Contrary to Thackeray's estimation of the case, his readers tired of his work after, not before they read *The Virginians*, and his own doubts about his reputation had created theirs. Thackeray had, in fact, followed Carlyle's lead—he alienated his readers before they were ready to reject him. Not halfway through the writing of the novel, he lamented, "The public does not care about the story nor about the Virginians nor I about either" (*Letters*, 4:110), but the last clause should have come first.

Thackeray began the novel that was to follow *The Newcomes* with reluctance and hesitation. He started a sequel to that novel of the great world, burned it, thought of "two or three schemes," was dissatisfied with them, and finally fastened on his old idea for an "American continuation" of *Henry Esmond*.[2] Even then he found himself sick and tired of what he had described as the wasting "idleness" of writing fiction. The composition of the novel went no more smoothly than its inception. Of the first third of the story he complained, "Nothing actually has happened" (*Letters*, 4:80). In 1858 he even asked a fellow novelist, John Pendleton Kennedy, to write a chapter for the upcoming installment. Clearly, his heart was not in his work. Thackeray pleaded every conceivable excuse for the weakness that he himself recognized. He complained of ill health, age, exhaustion, the pressures of financial worries, the problems of a "bachelor" father of two girls. He exhibited a desire to do anything but write another novel. He sought out distractions from his work, such as his bid for a seat in Parliament and the literary imbroglio with Edmund Yates, the so-called Garrick Club Affair, and then pointed to these distractions to explain his inability to write a good book. Yet often his excuses are themselves misleading. The brilliance of style and characterization, the psychological acuity of much of *The Virginians* bear witness against Thackeray's claim that there was "no go left in this dreary old expiring carcass" (*Letters*, 4 : 108–9). We have to look farther than Thackeray's comments on *The Virginians* if we are to understand the source of his difficulties.

The decision to write a sequel to *Henry Esmond* was, in some ways, unfortunate. Comparing the continuation to its parent novel, one is faced with the unavoidable conclusion that there has been a great falling off indeed; Thackeray's contemporary readers made the obvious comparison and came to the inevitable conclusion. Yet if *The Virginians* suffers when set against this measure, the comparison does give us a way to evaluate the novel and its shortcomings. In writing *Henry Esmond*, Thackeray had naturally turned to the example of Scott, as George Eliot did when she wrote *Romola*. The plot of *Henry Esmond* is clearly indebted to novels like *Woodstock*, *Rob Roy*, and *St. Ronan's Well*. Developing hints of narrative technique in Scott's work, Thackeray made of them what Scott himself had never intended— rigorous and subtle challenges on the reader's sense of moral life. As Scott had striven for transparence and ease of style, he had also proposed simple moral values that would not interfere with what were to him other, more significant facets of historical romance. In *Henry Esmond* Thackeray had shifted the focus of Scott's art and raised his assumptions to a level of moral complexity and ingenuity that places *Henry Esmond* in the first rank of mid-century fiction. In *The Virginians* he reverted to Scott's moral attitudes toward his art without achieving the force of Scott's dramatic confrontations and historical scope. Moreover, his awareness that he was failing to make moral demands on his work creates the impression that such attitudes are hypocritical and evasive. More importantly, however, *Henry Esmond* reveals the creative tensions characteristic of Thackeray's best work: affirmation balanced by doubt, ideals set in the perspective of actuality. In *The Virginians*, this equipoise is never attained, and its absence is nowhere more evident than in Thackeray's relation to his audience. Here again he returns to Scott's simpler, less demanding attitudes. Thackeray is clearly losing faith in the moral value of his art and in the intimate, responsive relationship between narrator and reader which is its source.[3] The form of his earlier novels engages the reader in a process which develops a liberating perspective on both life and art. Unlike

Henry Esmond, The Virginians is a denial of the possibility of such a narrative form. Thackeray specifically mocks the moral role of his novel, sabotaging at every turn his own imaginative endeavor.

In *The Virginians*, the plot, never the strong point of Thackeray's fiction, seems constructed to frustrate and exasperate both the author and his reader. The novel opens with an antithetical structure reminiscent of *Vanity Fair*. The twin grandsons of Henry Esmond, George and Harry Warrington, recapitulate as they reverse some of the qualities of Becky Sharp and Amelia Sedley. George is dark-haired, brooding, rebellious, as well as clever, witty, and learned. Harry is the fair-haired boy, loyal, generous, yet not very bright; he is the soldier in contrast to his twin, the scholar. Here the comparison with *Vanity Fair* breaks down: George, unlike Becky, is a "good" character, and his rebellion against his mother's domination is viewed with unalloyed sympathy. Chapters 5 through 13 (no. 2 through part of no. 4) deal with the adolescence of the twins on the Virginia estate of Castlewood. After a number of battles with his mother and his tutor, George leaves to join Braddock's campaign against the French and is reported lost in action. The next nine numbers (4 to 12) describe Harry's adventures in the motherland and the attempts of his English relations to lead him to ruin. Lo and behold, halfway through the novel, George, ransomed from his French captors, arrives in London—just in the nick of time— to rescue Harry from imprisonment for debt. A substantial part of the second half of the novel involves George's confrontation with eighteenth-century English society. The reader who has seen Thackeray's illustration on the monthly-number cover—one brother dressed in the king's colors shaking hands with a twin outfitted in revolutionary garb—may begin to wonder if this confrontation will ever occur. It finally does in number 23, after both men have married in opposition to their mother's wishes and after George has inherited the estate of the Norfolk Warringtons. As soon as the two meet in combat, George decides to retire from the field; his rather lukewarm devotion to the king's cause evaporates when he realizes that he might be forced to kill his brother. The central image Thackeray chooses for the novel, therefore, has nothing whatever to do with its main thematic concerns or, for that matter, with much of the plot. The novel ends, abruptly and gracelessly, with a cursory account of the American Revolution and a brief summary of George and Harry's later lives; one brother becomes an English squire, the other a Virginia planter.

The principal frustration of this plot is less its patent weakness than its potential for strength. Part of the brilliance of *Henry Esmond* results from its juxtapositioning of sexual and political questions. Henry's voluntary abdication of the role of Viscount Castlewood is aligned with and illuminated by the Pretender's selfish but self-defeating failure to take advantage of his one chance to become king. When James reveals his moral weakness, his lack of discipline, and his disregard for his subjects by pursuing Beatrix to Castlewood, Henry burns the papers that prove his own legitimacy and would confer on him the marquisate of Esmond if James were to be crowned king. The act is Henry's clear though tacit recognition that his love for Beatrix would make him as weak a leader of his family as James would be of his country. The Pretender clearly embodies and acts out the folly of Henry's love of Beatrix. *The Virginians* has the potential for the same kind of coherence. Here Thackeray explores, at some length and in detail, various aspects of rebellion against authority, whether it involves generations of a family or nations. The stories of George and Harry's refusal to submit to a domineering and wilful mother are nicely juxtaposed to the historical situation in the third quarter of the eighteenth century, and Thackeray achieves some of his most brilliant stylistic effects when he interchanges the metaphors of domestic and political life. As George, Prince Whippersnapper, defies both his mother and Colonel Lambert by marrying Theo, as Harry chooses to marry Fanny Mountain when his mother forbids it, so the American colonies revolt against the mother country. George, however, is a loyalist, and his political position contradicts the strong stand he takes for independence in personal matters. Yet Thackeray deftly handles this potential contradiction by allowing the older George, who narrates this part of his story, to realize that his loyalty to the mother country has been misguided. Even though his own situation has been complicated by his role as a parent, George admits that the revolt of the child against parental authority is normal and natural. The inevitability of this revolt is emphasized by the younger George's actions; he defies not only his mother, a woman who would exhaust a saint's patience, but also Colonel Lambert, the model of the just, reasonable, and loving parent.

Although Thackeray often complained that he was doomed to repeat past performances in *The Virginians*, and his readers would later agree with him, there is no simple repetition evident in his treatment of this theme. The problem of parental authority had been a major focus in his fiction from his early journalistic work on, but it had never been as cogently aligned with a political and historical background that enhances its significance and stature. In this respect, the conclusions to be drawn from *The Virginians* are even more radical than those of its predecessor.[4] In *Henry Esmond* Thackeray treats figures of authority who are deposed by their own incompetence to rule: family heads such as Lord Castlewood and Henry himself, political leaders such as the Chevalier de St. George, and emotional despots such as Beatrix and Rachel. In *The Virginians*, Thackeray considers sources of authority which are overthrown, not because they are too weak to rule effectively, but because the very nature of authority invites strenuous rebellion. He proposes as daring a critique of Victorian assumptions as Barry Lyndon or Ikey Solomons ever envisioned. The ideal of the autocratic family head is undercut by Thackeray's recognition that the politics of power are as futile and ineffective in domestic matters as they are in international relations. Far from becoming the old fogy he took himself to be, or the sycophant of aristocracy that Charlotte Brontë felt he had become, Thackeray was still quite capable of using his art to explore, in an honest and forthright fashion, a difficult and compelling subject.

There is, however, a significant difference between Thackeray's conception of this theme and his execution of it. It often seems more skeletal, more intermittently engaged, than my description suggests. The central problem is simple: Thackeray could not decide how to tell his story. In a sprawling, twenty-four number serial—longer than even Dickens's "big" novels—he evidently felt he could not sustain the ventriloquism of *Henry Esmond*, the only three-volume novel of his career. In that earlier novel Thackeray had chosen to use a variation of the technique of *Rob Roy*, one of Scott's uncharacteristic first-person narratives and the novel that treats the same historical period as *Es-*

mond. In *Rob Roy*, Frank Osbaldistone tells his friend Will Tresham the story of his youthful involvement in Jacobite plots, and he even contemplates using the third person as Caesar had done and as Henry Esmond would do. By another odd but telling coincidence, Thackeray adopts in *The Virginians* the mixed narrative modes of *Redgauntlet*, again the Scott novel which treats the comparable historical period; letters, journals, and first-person and omniscient narration are engaged and dismissed as the occasion suggests. While this freedom creates no problem in Scott's novel—indeed, *Redgauntlet* is one of his finest works—the reader of *The Virginians* finds himself confronting an unsatisfactory cross between the methods of *Pendennis* and those of *The Newcomes*. Thackeray's earlier openness of approach leads, in this late novel, to hesitation and confusion, though the narrative form that finally emerges resembles *Henry Esmond* more than one would expect from reading its first few numbers.

The narrative strategies of both *Henry Esmond* and *The Virginians* ultimately rest on a technique that has been given greatly different emphases in the two works. Esmond writes an autobiographical account in the third person, but about halfway through the writing of the story, as Sutherland's manuscript study of the novel has shown,[5] Thackeray began to add an editorial apparatus which includes comments by Esmond's wife, daughter, and grandsons, and is prefaced by Rachel Warrington's pious introductory account of her father. In the "American continuation" of *Esmond*, Thackeray turned the editorial apparatus into the chief means of narration. The narrator is a nameless friend of the Norfolk descendants of George Warrington—he could easily be Pendennis—and he undertakes to write the "memoirs" of the twin brothers (15:2). Like Scott's narrators in *Ivanhoe*, *Quentin Durward*, and *Woodstock*, he has access to the family papers. But, like Pendennis of *The Newcomes*, he claims the right to reconstruct a complete narrative from the "hints" and "indications" that such historical material offers: "I have drawn the figures as I fancied they were; set down conversations as I think I might have heard them; and so, to the best of my ability, endeavoured to revivify the bygone times and people" (pp. 2–3). This imaginative re-creation is supported by such materials as George's journal, the letters sent by the twins to each other and to their mother, and even a letter from Horace Walpole. Yet in number 19, three-quarters of the way through the novel, this impersonal editor disappears, and George, like his grandfather, writes about the central emotional crisis of his youth thirty years after the fact. Again like Esmond, he often writes in the third person. His account is recorded for the benefit of his descendants, and his opinions are confirmed or refuted by a series of footnotes by his wife and children. Thus *Henry Esmond* and the last part of *The Virginians* are both historical narratives in which the speaker, from the perspective of his late middle age, describes his own past. In both novels, the speakers attempt to "revivify" the past as well as record the workings of memory; Esmond, the omniscient editor, and George all use the historical present tense to convey their sense of the presence of the past. As *The Virginians* proceeds, its narrative method more nearly approaches that of *Esmond*, yet it never manages to create the analogies that identify reader, narrator, and character in the earlier novel.

In *Henry Esmond* Thackeray creates and sustains not only the illusion that an eighteenth-century gentleman is telling the story of his life, but also the illusion that there is a firm and satisfying bond between this narrator and his listeners. The basis of this relationship is as primitive and simple as it can be: kinship. Here Thackeray develops a narrative bond that Scott had created, not in his fiction, but in his historical and journalistic works. In general, Scott's novels reveal a remarkable lack of concern about the narrator's relation to his reader. Indeed, in Chrystal Croftangry's "Account of Himself" in *The Chronicles of the Canongate*, Scott playfully asserts his disdain for the common reader's opinion and even his comprehension. Croftangry decides to apply "Molière's recipe" and reads his work to Janet MacEvoy, his housekeeper. When his work fails the test—Janet responds like a "deaf person," trying valiantly to pretend that she has understood his story— he decides to forget her response, congratulating himself on writing in a figurative style that is "caviar to the multitude" (chap. 5, pp. 376–77). Such superiority toward the popular audience corresponds to Scott's opinion of the novel as the lowest form of "light literature." But Scott takes very seriously indeed one potential relation between a writer and his reader—the bond between a man and his progeny, his children and his grandchildren.

Whenever that relation between generations is the premise of a

reading experience in Scott's works, he reveals its efficacy and significance in a way that forecasts the analogical methods typical of
mid-century Victorian fiction. Chrystal Croftangry is a case in point.
Although he can easily dismiss Janet's response to his own works, he
cannot dismiss his own feelings about the family chronicle which his
grandfather has left him. He clearly sees that his forebear was narrow-
minded and self-righteous, but he cannot ignore the comments that
his grandfather makes on those who waste their inheritance, as Chrystal himself has done. At first tempted to burn the whole record as the
work of a "silly old man," Chrystal finally decides to try to regain his
estate, and when that effort fails, to preserve the heritage of his country by becoming an antiquary (chap. 2, p. 343). Reading here involves
its participant in the kind of morally effective process that would later
be evident in "Janet's Repentance" or *A Christmas Carol.* Scott's dedication to tradition and to the more specific heritage embodied in his
family was, of course, legendary; like Chrystal, he had been greatly
impressed by his reading of the poetic chronicle written by Walter
Scot of Satchells, and, as his son-in-law noted, he had seen his own
plight in those of his lame ancestors, John the Lamiter and William
Boltfoot. Scott's travel literature often takes as its premise this relationship between a man and his children. He speaks directly to his children in the 1814 diary of his trip on a lighthouse yacht and in his
account of the visit to Waterloo, published as *Paul's Letters to his Kin-
folk.* Scott's best-known use of this narrative stance is found, certainly,
in his *Tales of a Grandfather,* which began as a series of talks on Scottish history addressed to Hugh Littlejohn, his grandson John Hugh
Lockhart. Although he did not use this technique in any of his completed novels, Scott did begin one novel as a series of "private letters"
written in the time of James I. The result of this experiment, which he
ultimately abandoned, sounds surprisingly like *Henry Esmond.* In
printing the draft of this uncompleted work, Ballantyne was instructed
to imitate the form which an antiquarian society would use in the publication of such a manuscript—wide margins, archaic orthography,
and explanatory footnotes.[6]

Thackeray, of course, persevered in the experiment that Scott put
aside; the first edition of *Henry Esmond* imitates the physical features
of an eighteenth-century memoir, wide margins, the long "s," the for-

mal dedication, and the preface by the manuscript's "editor." More importantly, Thackeray adopted the narrative relation between grandfather and grandson that distinguishes Scott's historical writings. In doing so, however, he made it serve his own ends. In *Rebecca and Rowena* (1850), Thackeray had complained that Scott's mode of romance was a falsification of reality: "In the battles which are described by the kindly chronicler of one of whose works this present masterpiece is professedly a continuation, everything passes off agreeably; the people are slain, but without any unpleasant sensation to the reader; nay, some of the most savage and bloodstained characters of history, such is the indomitable good humour of the great novelist, become amiable, jovial companions, for whom one has a hearty sympathy" (10:531). Henry Esmond levels a version of this charge against Addison and his tendency to glorify even the most amoral of warriors. His own memoirs are to be written in opposition to such practices. Esmond proposes to "turn the perspective-glass" on the literary modes fashionable in his times by eschewing the heroic (13:244). Instead of the ideal figure of the "brave man in misfortune" that Addison offers in his *Cato*—or that Scott offers in *Old Mortality*—Esmond will depict "Cato fuddling himself at a tavern with a wench on each knee" (p. 15); the low level of his diction here indicates his desire to be faithful to commonplace experience.

Henry Esmond is a historical romance written to invalidate the very idea of romance, especially the myths of romantic love and heroic stature. To achieve this end, honesty must be the rule. Although Esmond would like to speak well of himself and those involved in his story, his sense of responsibility to his readers is an even stronger motivation: "But the present writer has had descendants of his own, . . . and as he would have his grandsons believe or represent him to be not an inch taller than Nature has made him: so, with regard to his past acquaintances, he would speak without anger, but with truth" (p. 76). This clearly defined relation between the speaker and his assumed audience, between a grandfather and his descendants, is a brilliant way of creating a moral perspective on the action. The memoirs are composed to prove that the venerated old man of Castlewood, the father whom Rachel Warrington praises so lavishly, is just a man like any other. Demythologizing the supposed perfection of one's parents or ancestors is a significant moral lesson that each child must learn before he can accept his own frailties, and Esmond's grandsons are therefore the most appropriate beneficiaries of this account of his life. The Warrington twins stand proxy for the reader in *Henry Esmond*; by putting his reader in the place of characters to whom the narrator has a clear and valid relation, Thackeray demands that the reader become involved in the process of narration. We are asked to make our own comments, our mental footnotes on the action. In the process that results, Thackeray reveals the clarity of Esmond's vision and its limitations, and the reader himself is made to evaluate and experience both the difficulty and the urgency of the narrative task Esmond has undertaken.

Esmond's sense of responsibility to his readers explains at least one aspect of his honesty. He is remarkably candid on matters of sexuality. In telling his story, he treats his grandsons as men who understand the force of sexual attraction, not as children who need to be protected from such knowledge. Lord Castlewood's Drury Lane mistress, the buxom Nancy Sievewright, and Beatrix herself all attest to one facet of a woman's power. When Frank undertakes a course of pleasure-hunting in Brussels, Esmond comments, "I am not going to play the moralist, and cry 'Fie!' For ages past, I know how old men preach, and what young men practise" (p. 321). One of the very old saws which constitute the wisdom of this novel is *cherchez la femme*, and Esmond does not refrain from pointing out what a woman's presence usually means. Rachel's outbursts about the blacksmith's daughter are uncomfortable and disconcerting, not because Esmond fails to present openly her sexual jealousy, but because he depicts so clearly the feelings that Rachel herself refuses to recognize. (Ironically, Thackeray's contemporary readers took umbrage less at the forthright treatment of Beatrix's physical attractions than at the studiously asexual union of Henry and Rachel.)[7] In dealing with such matters, Esmond creates the most forceful analogies between himself and his readers. He treats his attachment to Beatrix in a way that reveals that he has been "a silly fond fool" and not the "very wise old gentleman" that his grandsons might take him to be (p. 349). His past actions, moreover, are the basis of his bond with his grandchildren. Although his warning cannot keep his readers from making the same mistakes that he has made—"What can the sons of Adam and Eve expect, but to continue in that course of love and trouble their father and mother set out on?" (p. 375)—their common weaknesses and mutual needs are the premise of the sympathetic reading that Esmond expects his memoirs to receive.

Yet every man has his limitations, narrownesses, and failures of vision, and precisely because of its narrative technique, *Henry Esmond* makes this point as well. The novel continually treats blind loyalties, mistaken opinions, pride and prejudice; and another of its prominent old saws is that one ought to beware the beam in one's own eye. The editorial apparatus, significantly enough, first comes into play when Esmond speaks of his "private pique" against Marlborough, hoping that "any child" reading his "ancestor's memoirs" will be more objective in his judgment of "the great duke" (p. 243). Esmond is indeed rabid on the subject of Marlborough; at several points he even suggests that the hero was willing to sell both his body and his honor. But the footnotes added by his readers correct this situation and demonstrate that his grandsons have indeed learned to judge their grandfather's partiality, his penchant to adore General Webb or the young Frank Castlewood as wholly and as passionately as he despises Marlborough. In book 2, chapter 15, his grandsons explain that Esmond's stories about Marlborough have their source in the unreliable Father Holt, and they elaborate on the slight that won the duke Esmond's contempt. Even the footnotes added by Rachel and her second daughter stress the persistence of bias. The notes Rachel provides suggest that she is just as blind to her own motivations as Esmond portrays her to be. While Esmond's daughter never outgrows her slavish adoration of the courtly Colonel Esmond, the "perfect gentleman"—and it is consonant with the generally misogynist tendency of these memoirs that she remain well wadded with her stupidity—her preface and her notes do prove that his presentation of Rachel's character corresponds to her own experience; Rachel is clearly as jealous of her second daughter as she has been of her first.

While there is a good deal of this novel that seems to be motivated by Esmond's vindictive sense of wounded pride—the portrait of Beatrix may be as skewed as that of Marlborough—Esmond himself is the one who warns his readers to beware of his tendency to nurse slights and maintain unreasonable loyalties. Juliet McMaster has suggested that it is possible to read *Henry Esmond* as a "sustained piece of dramatic irony."[8] Esmond himself, his sense of his audience, and the record of its responses all make such a reading possible. Esmond admits that he is "perhaps secretly vain of [his] sacrifice" (pp. 184–85), that he is lowered to the level of conniving women and Jesuits when he becomes involved in the plot to regain the throne for the Stuarts, that much of his activity, in short, has a selfish motivation. Although he is not as straightforward in his self-criticism as he is in his attacks on Marlborough, he persists in maintaining that no man is a hero and that the women who come to worship him are as foolish as he himself has been. Moreover, he trusts that his readers—"his children who come after him" (p. 270)—will have enough intelligence and sufficiently firm moral values to read his work with both sympathy and objectivity.

Yet the clarity of this relationship and the confidence with which it is handled are thoroughly eroded by the time Thackeray undertakes the continuation of *Henry Esmond*. *The Virginians* is itself a denial of the moral claims Esmond makes for his memoirs. George is a diligent reader of his grandfather's manuscript, but Harry, "no bookman," has never read it "very carefully" (p. 555). The moral effects of this work, like those of all mid-century fiction, depend as much on the capacities and willingness of the reader as on the intent of the writer, but here Thackeray assumes that his readers cannot rise to the occasion. They are never as attentive or responsive as Scott's Hugh Littlejohn. Esmond's grandsons fail to learn the specific political lesson he hopes to inculcate. By using himself as an example, he reveals the folly of the Jacobite position, yet his grandsons are "staunch Jacobites"; Harry even risks saluting the heads on Traitors' Gate in Temple Bar when he visits London. Neither will they accept Esmond's moral judgments. They have no respect for the late Lord Castlewood, the patron Esmond so admires. Even George, so like his grandfather in temperament, misuses the memoirs. He cites the account of the duel between Castlewood and Lord Mohun as his authority when he plans to challenge Washington. He cannot see that the two situations are totally different: in *Henry Esmond*, Lord Mohun is quite sincere in his desire to seduce Rachel and dishonor her husband, but Washington is merely suspected—and, as it turns out, falsely suspected—of wanting to marry Rachel Warrington. George need hardly feel that his honor is endangered.

But the distrust of the moral value of fiction does more than simply reflect back on *Henry Esmond* and invalidate the confidence that the narrator displays in the earlier novel; it also thwarts any new attempt to create an acceptable relation between reader and narrator. The nameless editor of the Warrington papers in *The Virginians* is a man speaking to his contemporaries about the past, not a historical personage describing his own past to his descendants. The novel opens with the usual evocation of a friendly, casual implied discourse between reader and narrator that any reader of *The Newcomes* would expect. Yet Thackeray cannot sustain this pose, and soon the commentary implies bitterness or distrust on the narrator's part and stupidity or wilful incomprehension on the reader's. Both the reader and the narrator of *Vanity Fair* are outfitted as clowns, but here the reader alone wears long ears—ears more characteristic of an ass than of a clown. The reader is Mrs. Grundy, who is ready to "cry out fie and for shame" when George courts Theo, even though the hypocritical woman has allowed Mr. Grundy to court her (p. 725). Gone are the analogies that Thackeray creates in *Vanity Fair*, *Pendennis*, and *Henry Esmond*— the assumptions that narrator, reader, and characters share certain universal experiences. The narrator ironically speaks of his reader as if "she" were as pure and modest as anyone could wish: "You know (not, my dear creature, that I mean you have any experience; but you have heard people say—you have heard your mother say) that an old flirt, when she has done playing the fool with one passion, will play the fool with another; that flirting is like drinking; and the brandy being drunk up, you—no, not you—Glycera—the brandy being drunk up, Glycera, who has taken to drinking, will fall upon the gin" (pp. 737–38). Such an ironic approach betrays a crude hostility toward the reader. The narrator's denial that the reader has any experience in the sordid matters of alcohol and flirtation is clearly and purposefully undercut by the confusion of pronoun reference in the last clause: "you—no, not you— Glycera." Certainly "you," the reader, like Glycera, is suspected of having imbibed both the brandy and the gin. In Thackeray's earlier fiction, such complex turns of commentary would simply prove that the narrator can expect a certain understanding and sympathy from the reader.

This passage suggests, however, that forcing the hypocritical reader to admit to his own likeness to the character is an almost impossible task, one that can be achieved only by tricks of grammar. Although his subject hardly justifies such moral outrage, Thackeray has returned to the methods of *Catherine*. The reader is the speaker's adversary, never his companion.

Thackeray had begun *The Newcomes* with the admission that he was about to tell an "old story," but he had gone on to tell it anyway. In *The Virginians* such admissions prove to be more disturbing and more self-defeating. In chapter 18, "An Old Story," Thackeray presents the comic spectacle of Harry's love for his older cousin Maria. The narrator offers a long explanation of the continually repeated fable of "mischievous siren sluts" (p. 184) seducing a young Telemachus from the boat of a Ulysses too old to hear their song: "In the last sentence you see Lector Benevolus and Scriptor Doctissimus figure as tough old Ulysses and his tough old boatswain, who do not care a quid of tobacco for any siren at Sirens' Point; but Harry Warrington is green Telemachus. . . . The song is not stale to Harry Warrington, nor the voice cracked or out of tune that sings it. But—but—oh, dear me, Brother Boatswain! Don't you remember how pleasant the opera was when we first heard it?" (p. 185). At this early point in the novel, Thackeray establishes one of those delightful relationships one would expect to find in his fiction: the narrator, Scriptor Doctissimus, shares the experience and perspective of his Brother Boatswain, Lector Benevolus. If they no longer actually participate in the agonies of adolescent love, they can at least remember them and sympathize with the character's perplexity. Yet this relationship itself makes the telling of Harry's story an exercise in futility. The narrator expects that "any man or woman with a pennyworth of brains, or the like precious amount of personal experience, or who has read a novel before" (p. 185) must be bored with the story of Harry's love; his experience defeats instead of promotes his interest in the fictional character. Ironically, the very fact that he reads novels insures that he will not be interested in the conventional story that this particular novel has to tell. The narrator himself, unable to feel any such interest, has been off on a digression, and he assumes that the reader has been daydreaming. Because the reader is a tired old sailor like himself, the narrator knows he must be bored and disgusted: "And how did [Harry] come to want [the bunch of roses Maria gave him] and to prize it so passionately when he got the bit of rubbish? Is not one story as stale as the other? Are not they all alike? What is the use, I say, of telling them over and over?" (p. 186). The analogies that link reader and narrator preclude the possibility of their being linked to the character; we have come a long way from the mediating effect of Pendennis's interest in Clive Newcome's story. The assumption of common experience, once so necessary to the moral effect of Thackeray's art, has now become an invalidation of all fiction: "The incidents of life, and love-making especially, I believe to resemble each other so much, that I am surprised, gentlemen and ladies, you read novels any more. Psha!" (p. 186). In *Vanity Fair* Thackeray declines to explain the courtship of Becky Sharp and Rawdon Crawley because this refusal creates one of the most striking dramatic effects in the novel. Here he declines to offer similar information simply because it would be a vain retelling of a commonplace experience. Thackeray has extended his own lesson until it undercuts the mode by which that lesson has been conveyed. Earlier he had maintained that the art of telling stories should develop the reader's sense of his common humanity with the character. Now the very idea of common humanity renders the attempt to tell a story superfluous.

Some of these problems are alleviated, if not completely solved, when Thackeray decides to revert to the method of *Henry Esmond* and allow George Warrington to narrate the last quarter of the novel. Again the writer and reader are related by blood: George is explaining to "my dear young folks" (p. 814) the difficulties he and their mother encountered before their marriage. Thackeray replaces the previous rather trying relationships—of adversaries, of old fogies uninterested in the story, of contemporaries vainly trying to "revivify" the past—with the connection between George and his son and two daughters. In parts of chapters 76 and 77, this relationship is actually dramatized. George and his children discuss his story, and the narration itself becomes an event: "Here we have them all in a circle. Mamma is at her side of the fire, papa at his; Mademoiselle Eléonore [the French governess], at whom the captain looks rather sweetly (eyes off, captain!); the two girls, listening like—like *nymphas discentes* to Apollo, let us say; and John and Tummas (with obtuse ears), who are bringing in the tea-trays and urns" (p. 811). The natural affection and intimacy shared by Sir George and the readers of his manuscript often create an atmosphere conducive to the casual bantering exchanges between speaker and listener and the more general goodwill that have been missing in the earlier part of the novel. Because George can assume that his children have read his plays, that they understand the details of his daily life, Thackeray can justify not telling parts of the story that might tire the reader; there is no need to claim that storytelling itself is boring. Like his grandfather, George believes that his narrative does serve a useful purpose. He has a clear sense of his moral responsibility to his readers, and he rises on occasion to the kind of candor and honesty characteristic of his grandfather. "As a man and a father," he claims, he "ought to be very cautious in narrating" the story of his early and seemingly unwise marriage to Theo. He knows too well that the "pack of rash children round about [him] might be running off to Scotland to-morrow." But he refuses to "call out *mea culpa*, and put on a demure air" (p. 852). He maintains that, despite parental opposition, the marriage was justified, and he refuses to deceive his listeners simply because he is their father and he too may wish to veto their marital plans. Here George is living up to the narrative example set by his grandfather's memoirs. But even this device does not help Thackeray confront the central difficulty of *The Virginians*—the depiction of sexual behavior.

Thackeray's responses to Scott's fiction are again a touchstone here. In 1850, when he wrote his continuation of *Ivanhoe*, Thackeray had called for "middle-aged novels" to take the place of Scott's "extremely juvenile legends" (10:500). His adaptation of the plot of *Woodstock* in *Henry Esmond* is an even better example than *Rebecca and Rowena* of his desire to find in Scott's romances the subject-matter of adult fiction. In *Woodstock* the Pretender, later to become Charles II, is being hidden from Cromwell by Albert Lee; he transgresses against the principles of hospitality and honor by trying to seduce his ally's perfectly pure and innocent sister, Alice Lee. But the "kindly chronicler" will not countenance such villainy. Alice's cousin and suitor, Markham Everard, challenges Charles Stuart to a duel; and the royal roué, chastened by proofs of Alice's genuine virtue and Everard's honor, apologizes and promotes their union. Thackeray complicates the moral issues of this plot by combining the roles of Albert Lee and Everard in the less noble and more ambiguously motivated figure of Henry Esmond. He refuses to sanitize the portrait of his Pretender's moral qualities, though James too is shamed into recognizing his opponent's greater valor. Most significant, however, is Thackeray's depiction of Beatrix. Unlike Alice Lee, she not only understands the Pretender's advances, she meets them more than halfway. Yet, when Thackeray came to write *The Virginians*, he seems to have decided that such "middle-aged" versions of Scott were no longer possible. Indeed, his work is a good example of the Victorian prudery that Kathleen Tillotson has discovered less in the 1840s than in the 1860s.[9] Thackeray's letters repeatedly attest to his increased awareness of the children who constituted a segment of his audience. His own daughters, of course, served as a constant reminder of this fact. With Anne frequently serving as his amanuensis, he could hardly ignore the fact that his comments on his characters' sexuality might strike rather too close to home. For the sake of such readers, Thackeray himself would become a "kindly chronicler."

Although Thackeray thought the third quarter of the eighteenth century no less depraved than its first—contrary to the facts of social history, he claimed that George III inherited a "Court society as dissolute as our country ever knew" (13:757)—in *The Virginians* he refuses to portray this situation. Harry and George Warrington are perfect and perfectly vapid adaptations of the Scott hero. Everyone suspects them of having indulged in some fabulously naughty sexual adventures, much as Scott's Major Neville is suspected of being an actor in *The Antiquary*. There is talk of escapades with an Indian maiden or an actress, but the dear boys remain guiltless. This treatment of two young men let loose upon the loosest of London societies recalls the sometimes unsatisfactory depiction of Darsie Latimer in *Redgauntlet*. Darsie is considered a great rake by the puritanical father of his friend Alan Fairford, a genuine threat to Alan's moral and professional stability. But when forced to spend time with some rough characters, Darsie's purity shines through. One look at a "lewd jest book" and he throws it overboard, much to the disgust of the sailor who would have been happy to share its pleasures. Darsie's uncle loses all patience with him when he delays an early morning journey so that he can say his prayers. But even this rather cloying portrait of a decent young man does not damage Scott's novel as the corresponding portraits in *The Virginians* undermine Thackeray's work. Scott's treatment of Darsie's reputation as a bad influence is, after all, a joke leveled against the overzealous piety of Alan's father. In Thackeray's novel, such rumors border on the prurient. The author seems to be leering and smirking in a way that Thackeray himself found so offensive in Sterne. At one point the editor of the Warrington papers rails at his fifty-eight-year-old maiden reader and the restraints she would put on his art, restraints comparable to the "tin draperies" on the statues at St. Peter's: "We have nothing for it but to submit. Society, the despot, has given his imperial decree" (p. 425). In his earlier works, in "A Vagabond Chapter" of *Vanity Fair* or the preface to *Pendennis*, Thackeray had found ways both to recognize and defeat his audience's prudery.[10] Here he submits. The "tin draperies" in which he swathes his subject become more and more ludicrous. The Lambert family, stick figures of virtue, are paraded on and off stage to demonstrate that a Georgian freedom of literary tastes is not inimical to the best ideals of Victorian family life. But the reader may wonder if this is so. The attempt to be simple and pure in *The Virginians* backfires. The editor of the Warrington papers conjures up salacious suspicions characteristic of Tom Eaves at his worst, and the evasions which Thackeray repeatedly emphasizes destroy all too often any trust between reader and narrator.

Thackeray's use of George Warrington as a narrator both explains and highlights this problem. Warrington shares the omniscient narrator's scruples about portraying sexual behavior, but he also has a valid reason for his reticence. He is not writing for his adult contemporaries or trying to present a narrative that will satisfy young readers as well as adults; he is actually writing for his children. Baroness Bernstein has told George some unsavory tales about his cousin Maria, "which, as this book lies open *virginibus puerisque*, to all the young people of the family, I shall not choose to record" (p. 783). The virgins to whom the general editor has deferred so often finally find literal embodiment in the virgins of the Warrington household. George's usual tolerance for this situation is amusing—"Papa is not going to scandalize his nursery with Old World gossip, nor bring a blush over our chaste bread-and-butter!" (p. 827)—but even this guise does not always eliminate

Thackeray's chafing at the restraints imposed by this nursery-school audience. Henry Esmond is a man who speaks to his grandsons as if they were men who could fully comprehend his desires and weaknesses. George would like to elicit such a response from his children, but he cannot allow himself his grandfather's candor.

Chapter 85 contains a very odd passage, added in manuscript, that emphasizes George's dilemma. He explains that he has become the squire of the Norfolk estate, that he has escaped poverty and the struggle to survive, but all is not well with him: "There came a period of my life, when having reached the summit of felicity I was quite tired of the prospect I had there: I yawned in Eden, and said, 'Is this all? . . . Only Eve, for ever sweet and tender, and figs for breakfast, dinner, supper, from week's end to week's end!' Shall I make my confessions? Hearken! Well, then, if I must make a clean breast of it." At this point there is a line of ellipses and the following note: "Here three pages are torn out of Sir George Warrington's MS. book, for which the Editor is sincerely sorry" (p. 905). When the manuscript does continue, the reader finds George wondering, in a general way, "when Mr. Random and Mr. Thomas Jones are married, is all over? . . . Are there no Lady Bellastons abroad? . . . The Sirens sang after Ulysses long after his marriage, and the suitors whispered in Penelope's ear, and he and she had many a weary day of doubt and care, and so have we all" (pp. 906–7). Clearly George has been confessing some sexual lapse or, at least, the fact that the sirens' song still appeals to him. Has he cut out these three pages, or are his wife or his daughters or son responsible for this censorship? Is the editor "sincerely sorry" for the loss of the material, or is he relieved that Warrington has done the bowdlerizing for him? Why does Thackeray allow George to start a confession if he knows that he must omit its substance? This situation would have been no problem for Henry Esmond; he would have said what he had to say or simply kept silent. This chapter cannot be considered a success. It says almost nothing about the actual events of George's life while it calls attention to the need for specific details. It is a far cry from the way in which Thackeray handles a similar problem in his presentation of Becky Sharp's Bohemian career.

Nor does the device of the Warrington manuscript allow Thackeray to avoid entirely the adversary roles of narrator and reader so promi-

nent in the editor's portion of the narrative. Like Dickens's more al-
lusive use of Dombey's animosity toward Florence, this hostility is
subsumed in the relationship between Sir George and his heir—"my
son the captain"—Miles Warrington. Miles becomes a fairly well-
developed character. He resembles his military uncle, Harry. He is a
man about town, and we learn that he freely spends what money his
aunt Hetty gives him in frequenting Pall Mall taverns, giving *petits
soupers*, and gambling. Some of the tensions apparent in the earlier
relationship of editor to reader reappear in the form of the conventional
distrust a father feels for his son; George tells Miles not to be too anxious to dethrone him and become the squire himself. George, like the
earlier editor, expects his reader to be bored. He knows that Miles does
not care to read his memoirs; he can be sure that Miles will destroy
unread all his parents' love letters because he finds the "perusal of
mss." so unpleasant (p. 829). Miles is a Chrystal Croftangry who never
learns to value his parent's narrative. At one point George tries to trick
Miles into reading his memoirs: "Why, this note-book lies publicly on
the little table at my corner of the fireside, and any one may read in it
who will take the trouble of lifting my spectacles off the cover: but
Miles never hath. I insert in the loose pages caricatures of Miles; jokes
against him: but he never knows nor heeds them" (p. 758). This passage is simply a more good-humored description of the "caricatures"
and "jokes against" the reader in which the editor has indulged. In
both cases the reader's response is disheartening. Only once does
Miles find one of these jokes, and he replies in kind, with a "rude picture" of his father.

Just as the characterization of George and Harry in *The Virginians*
serves to undercut the faith in his listeners that their grandfather demonstrates in *Henry Esmond*, so the characterization of Miles forces
George to admit that his audience is not all it could be. Even the
knowledge of the world that father and son share creates misunder-
standings. Sir George has been describing his misery when Theo's father refused to let him see her, and then he adds: "My son Miles, who,
for a wonder, has been reading in my ms., says, 'By Jove, sir, I didn't
know you and my mother were took in this kind of way. The year I
joined, I was hit very bad myself. An infernal little jilt that threw me
over for Sir Craven Oaks of our regiment. I thought I should have gone

crazy.' And he gives a melancholy whistle, and walks away" (p. 799). Unlike Beatrix and her reading of the *Spectator* paper in *Henry Esmond*, Miles has read the story and has misjudged the kind of love it describes. The analogizing processes of mid-century fiction have gone awry. Miles compares his mother to an "infernal little jilt" and his father's love for Theo, a love that has been described as a substantial reason for disobeying one's parents and risking poverty, to his own more superficial feelings. If Miles has not learned that a woman must be worth a great deal and that a man must love her in an uncommon way if they are to incur the pain of rebellion, then he has read the manuscript to no avail. Love, to him, is a temporary disease; his parents "were took in this kind of way."

The lesson that Miles provides is clear: Thackeray can allow Sir George to tell his story only if he also creates a character who invalidates the narrator's faith in the value of his endeavors. Miles is the model of the uncomprehending, obtuse, and uninterested audience that Thackeray postulates for the novel he himself writes. Disquieted by this self-doubt and mistrust, by his fear that his novel cannot serve the moral needs of readers whose imaginations he cannot engage in a fictional world, Thackeray is unable to achieve the moral and artistic integrity characteristic of his earlier novels. Every major point of failure in *The Virginians* can be traced back to his loss of faith in both himself and his readers. Nowhere in *The Virginians* does Thackeray demonstrate either the energy or the desire to create a new version of his earlier narrative techniques. Nowhere do we find the novel defined as the gossip's report or a dinner-table conversation, the witty and effective concepts that had analogized living and reading in *Vanity Fair* and *The Newcomes*. Nowhere is there the assumption of a friendly, even familial dialogue between narrator and reader like that found in *Henry Esmond*. The result of Thackeray's failure to develop such techniques is sad, but predictable. Little can be expected of the mid-century novel in which the narrator himself asks, "What is the good of telling the story?" (p. 186).

A year after finishing *The Virginians*, writing in one of his finest *Roundabout Papers*, Thackeray spoke of his desire to produce a "story which boys would relish for the next few dozen of centuries." He describes the effect of such a story in a way that recalls his earlier definition of the "confidential talk between writer and reader" (*Pendennis*, p. xxxv) and, more generally, the aims of the mid-century novel as he and Dickens and George Eliot describe them: "The boy-critic loves the story: grown up, he loves the author who wrote the story. Hence the kindly tie is established between writer and reader, and lasts pretty nearly for life." The model for this relation is "the kindly, the generous, the pure" Sir Walter Scott and Thackeray's own nostalgic memories of an "old duodecimo *Tales of My Landlord*" ("De Juventute," 17:431). Like Dickens striving to create an imaginative home to shelter both himself and his reader, like George Eliot postulating a more than familial intimacy between herself and her reader, Thackeray as late as 1860 still wanted to feel a sense of connection with his audience. His definition of that audience, however, had changed. Scott, whose work had suggested the plot of Thackeray's finest "middle-aged" novel, had finally become a pretext for juvenility. Much as Thackeray might long for an idealized version of his own youth, he could neither erase the experience that had created the tension and the ironic edge in his best work nor coordinate that experience with the image of the youthful audience which came to dominate his conception of the novelist's art. His editorial policy for the *Cornhill* and its effect on such a well-intentioned and unsuspecting contributor as Trollope reveal how limiting Scott's example had become. After a futile attempt to return to his old manner in *Philip*, an almost unreadable book, Thackeray again reverted to Scott and historical romance in *Denis Duval*. The result of that venture, of course, remains in doubt. Echoes of *The Bride of Lammermoor*, *Rob Roy*, and *The Antiquary* again predominate, and it is difficult to tell whether Thackeray would have succeeded in once again making Scott's materials his own.

There are other echoes of the end of Scott's career in the final novels that Thackeray wrote, and Thackeray was himself the first to notice the correspondence. Writing of his vain efforts to tie himself down to the task of *Denis Duval*, he spoke of the money he needed to insure his daughters' future comfort. "A man who lived at Abbotsford," he noted, had also "overhoused himself" (*Letters*, 4:291). Reading the portions of Scott's diary that Lockhart published in his memoirs, one cannot help but think of the last volume of the Thackeray letters. Although the magnitude of their difficulties varied substantially, the same complaints—the constant financial worries, the laments over age and illness, the fears that the next novel will fail, the anxiety to escape the writing of "idle" fictions—all these refrains sound again and again. Trying to nerve himself for the production of yet another novel, Scott would call for his cap and bells so that he could once more open his raree show.[11] Thackeray would lament the need to bake tarts for the public when he himself could stomach only bread and cheese. At the height of both their careers, such slighting references to their art would have been the prologue to novels written with enthusiasm, pleasure, and even conviction. But the task had turned stale, and good-humored self-mockery was no longer appropriate.

After Scott had come a generation of novelists, Thackeray among them, who chose to confront rather than evade the question of the dignity and use of the profession that the Great Unknown could never comfortably avow. After Thackeray would come George Eliot. As he was writing *The Virginians* and asking, "What is the good of telling the story?" she was beginning her career with her most self-consciously and rigorously articulated answers to that question. In one sense, George Eliot was the rightful heir to their tradition. Her adaptation of facets of their work, like Thackeray's use of Scott, conserved as it revitalized the craft they both found so distasteful at the end. She would take from Scott the germ of a story—from *The Surgeon's Daughter*, for instance, the plight of a doctor and his revolutionary method of treating fever in a provincial Scottish town called Middlemas—and see in it a complex social and moral dilemma. What she had learned from Thackeray and how she used his lessons would be evident in her first work of fiction, her *Scenes of Clerical Life*.

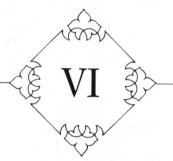

VI

Scenes of Clerical Life
The First Experiment

Speaking for his anonymous clerical friend, George Henry Lewes told Blackwood that her proposed "Sketches" depicting the "actual life of our country clergy" would accomplish "what has never yet been done in our Literature." Although Lewes acknowledged that Goldsmith and Austen had previously treated clerical experience in its *"human . . . not at all* in its *theological* aspect" (*Letters*, 2:269), the grandeur of his claim testifies to both George Eliot's intransigent belief in her own originality and the kind of response that her first work of fiction almost invariably received. To its contemporary readers the *Scenes of Clerical Life* (1858) seemed, in conception as in execution, unquestionably new, fresh, and remarkably "unliterary." The writer for the *Saturday Review* went so far as to say that her style "showed little or no family resemblances with that of any living author," and he elaborated on her "disregard of conventions" and of "circulating-library principles."[1] Such was exactly the impression that George Eliot strove to create. She wanted others to hear in her work the quality that Carlyle had always championed and that she had praised in Heine, "no echo, but a real voice" (*Essays*, p. 223). Even at the beginning of her career, her sense of independence and originality was as central to her artistic identity as Dickens's conviction of his dignity was to him. She insisted that she had none of the qualities of a popular novelist, even as she demanded from Blackwood any proof of popularity that he might be able to report. She repeatedly stressed her inability to pattern her work after any models, to follow any advice, or to "bend" to her readers' taste.

Yet for all the artistic autonomy and the self-assurance evident in the *Scenes*, these first tales continuously reveal George Eliot's affinity to her contemporary literary world, both to the popular novelists whose work she had come to know while writing her many essays on belles lettres for the *Westminster Review* and to the readership she now hoped to gain with the publication of her own fiction. The writing of the *Scenes* was, as Lewes stated, an "experiment" worth trying. It was, in fact, a process of testing a novice's creative capacities, first in conception, then in "dramatic presentation," dialogue, "fun," and pathos (*Letters*, 2:407–8). As the text of the *Scenes* frequently and self-consciously announces, the tales were also an experiment formulated to gauge the range and flexibility of the contemporary audience's interests. George Eliot's need for success in 1856 was quite fundamental. Both she and Lewes pursued new areas of literary work simply so that they could earn enough money to support themselves and Agnes Lewes's continually growing family. In her review essays she had generally focused on the narrative principles and practices which she judged inadequate; in the kind of fiction she chose to write, George Eliot would necessarily offer yet another evaluation of the literary achievements and standards of Victorian fiction. Her admiration for Jane Austen, her early and continued fondness for Scott would make these two novelists perhaps the most formidable models she would ever confront, but only much later in her career did she demonstrate the full extent of that debt. She was now in competition with more immediate practitioners of their art. Near the completion of this experiment in narration, George Eliot told one of her friends that, financial necessity notwithstanding, "writing is part of my religion, and I can write no word that is not prompted from within" (*Letters*, 2:377). To a greater degree than she was willing to admit, the composition of her *Scenes* was a way of testing what was "within" against both external influences and external judges.

By 1856 and 1857 there was no dearth of models for the would-be novelist to follow. What the contemporary critic David Masson called the "literary centralization of English life in London"[2] had been modified by pictures of provincial experience well before George Eliot wrote her *Scenes*. There were also models for the sympathetic treatment of clerical life. The gentle comedy of John Galt's *Annals of the Parish* (1821), for example, foretells the more expansive tolerance of mid-century fiction. Even though George Eliot had criticized *Ruth* (1853) because Elizabeth Gaskell, "misled by a love of sharp contrasts," had ignored the "half tints of real life" (*Letters*, 2:86), that novel depicts the stultifying effect of social conventions in a provincial town by focusing on the charity and refined conscience of the dissenting clergyman Benson. Even *The Warden* (1855), Trollope's first foray into the realm of Barchester's "clerico-political world," tempers the satiric denunciations characteristic of the journalist with a new laditudinarian charity toward the distinctly human fallibilities of its clerical characters. Although George Eliot does not seem to have read Trollope at this point in her career—and he was one of the very few novelists she would read later on—the concurrent publication of her *Scenes* and *Barchester Towers* is no small measure of the predominance of new conceptions of literary realism. But the run-of-the-mill fiction that the subeditor of the *Westminster Review* had to read, the fiction whose tendencies she lambasted so amusingly in her "Silly Novels by Lady Novelists" (October 1856), would prove such attempts at realism the rare exception rather than the rule. Freed from the burden of perusing such negligible works by her own writing of fiction, George Eliot chose to read with Lewes novels more in keeping with her own tastes. Her 1857 journal records their frequent nightly readings of Austen's fiction as well as novels by Hawthorne, Gaskell, Charlotte Brontë, and Thackeray, all authors whose works she had read with admiration earlier in the decade. Her reading of Gaskell's *Life of Charlotte Brontë* (1857) had a particularly strong impact. In 1856 George Eliot had referred to *Villette* (1853) as a novel "which we, at least, would rather read for the third time than most new novels for the first."[3] Not surprisingly, the *Scenes* contain unmistakable echoes of *Villette*; a passage at the end of chapter 5 in "Janet's Repentance" virtually encapsulates the metaphoric scheme of Brontë's novel. As early as 1851 George Eliot had called Brontë "perhaps the best" English novelist, a title that had by 1857 devolved on Thackeray (*Letters*, 1:355). It is appropriate, then, that the *Scenes* often recall *Shirley* (1849), the novel in which Charlotte Brontë had tried to imitate the Olympian stance of her own favorite author, Thackeray.

The reading that George Eliot did as she was writing the second and third scenes would have confirmed the intentions she had already embodied in "Amos Barton" during the previous fall. *Cranford* (1853) would prove that Gaskell, like George Eliot, was now loyal to the "half tints of real life." Although Hawthorne's tale of a wayward mother named Hester obviously impressed George Eliot, such material would have to wait until the writing of *Adam Bede.* Now she would treat only the materials that her principles of moral realism sanctioned. She would continue to write that "better book" which Hawthorne half-seriously apologizes for not having written because he cannot appreciate the "deeper import" of the "dull and commonplace" life he had encountered in his position at the custom-house. But even in 1850, when *The Scarlet Letter* was published, Hawthorne's definition of such literary innovations was not quite new. George Eliot's well-known justification of her treatment of unheroic characters ("Amos Barton," chap. 5) is remarkably similar to the intentions Charlotte Brontë announced in the first chapter of *Shirley*: "Something real, cool, and solid, lies before you; something unromantic as Monday morning, when all who have work wake with the consciousness that they must rise and betake themselves thereto."[4]

If George Eliot's sympathy with ordinary life was not quite as unique as she and Lewes thought, her insistence on her originality renders even more surprising her willingness to use the narrative techniques that had become by 1856 the conventions of a well-established and distinct tradition. In novels like *Villette, Shirley, Mary Barton, Cranford,* and *Ruth,* Brontë and Gaskell had demonstrated an interest in their readers often similar to the aims apparent in the mid-century work of Dickens and Thackeray. In the late 1850s George Eliot was fully prepared, if not compelled by her conception of the artist's moral role, to make the relation between the reader and the work the goal of her narrative form. Later on she would try to ignore the personal responses and the public reviews offered by her readers. But in the *Scenes* her manifest desire to establish a firm bond between teller and listener is earnest, even anxious.[5] In creating that bond she discovered what the novice could not be expected to know—her power to create characters capable of making their own appeals to the reader. After completing "Amos Barton," she finished an essay in which she attacked Edward Young's "grandiloquence," his desire to produce a "certain effect on his audience." The quality he lacked, according to George Eliot, was sincerity, "taking for a criterion the true qualities of the object described" (*Essays*, pp. 366–67). In the *Scenes* George Eliot tried to accommodate both of these procedures. In the process she discovered that her focus on her object, character, would produce the effect on the audience that she desired. If we trace the development of narrative technique in these three tales, if we examine the conventions that George Eliot employed, tested, rejected or accepted, we can watch her reach this conclusion. We can also watch as she marks out the thin line between derivation and innovation. At the beginning of her career, she would take advantage of the techniques that her contemporaries had developed to engage their readers' imaginations in the fictional life they portrayed, but she had to extend and modify those techniques if she were to make them her own.

First of all, any act of storytelling demanded a masculine pseudonym. The career of Currer Bell demonstrated the subterfuge necessary if a woman were to create a responsive, respectful relationship with her audience. That Lewes came to insist on this point could not be more ironic. When he had reviewed Charlotte Brontë's novels in the late 1840s, he had not understood the implications of her ambiguous pen name. The writer of *Shirley* was forced to explain, first politely and then rudely, that a woman who writes serious fiction wants to be judged "as an *author*, not as a woman."[6] George Eliot had recently made the same point in her essay "Silly Novels." Accordingly, the pseudonymous writer of the *Scenes* emphasizes his masculine qualities, and he does so in ways that recall Thackeray's male voices, Pendennis, or the gossip of *Vanity Fair*—certain female secrets, he tells us, are simply beyond his ken. Yet, more than Brontë, more than Carlyle or Thackeray, Marian Lewes, as she insisted on being called by her friends, needed a mask behind which she might freely develop a public authorial identity. Although she cited Scott as her model in the handling of her pseudonym, she did not follow his practice of admitting his identity as the Great Unknown to his friends whenever, in Lockhart's words, "any circumstance arose which rendered the withholding of direct confidence on the subject incompatible with perfect freedom of feeling on both sides."[7] Herbert Spencer and John Chapman could attest to Marian Lewes's need for "real concealment" and her refusal to imitate Scott's relative openness. Unlike the author of *Waverley*, she could not claim that she chose to remain anonymous because such was her humor. Intellectually and socially, Marian Lewes was cut off from any potential audience she might address. Associated with the radical *Westminster Review*, convinced of the falsity of conventional religion, stigmatized because of her illicit relation to Lewes, she could be only too aware of the profound differences between herself and her audience. Years before, she had said that she felt as if she lived in a "*walled-in* world" (*Letters*, 1 : 71). In some respects, she was even more effectively walled away from the rest of society in 1856 than she had been at Griff. Her fiction, whatever its other characteristics, would have to perform considerable acts of mediation between herself and her audience. She was quite literally inventing "George Eliot" so that she could speak, through him, to her reader.

Consequently, "George Eliot" emerges as more than a pseudonym; he is a persona, a mediating presence reminiscent of Pendennis, Thackeray's mask in *The Newcomes*, and Mary Smith, the narrator of Gaskell's *Cranford*. It is appropriate, although it would not be in the case of *Middlemarch*, for instance, to speak of the narrator of the *Scenes* and *Adam Bede* as "he" and his creator as "she," and in my discussions of her first two works I will take advantage of the distinction that Marian Lewes herself proposed. Like the fictional narrators created by Gaskell and Thackeray, George Eliot is part of the world he tells stories about and very distinctly at a distance from it.[8] He feels bound to the locations of his tales by his affectionate memories of them, but he refuses to be bound in by the social and intellectual limitations of their inhabitants. Similarly, Mary Smith resides in the market town near the village of Cranford, tells stories about the maiden ladies of the Jenkyns family to whom she might be distantly related, and often assumes a genially superior attitude toward their eccentric and homely customs. Although George Eliot has been a native of Shepperton, a past resident of Milby, he has clearly left the countryside for the urban world beyond it. In this sense, his situation is the reverse of Arthur Pendennis's; George Eliot is more sophisticated, more worldly than the society he describes. He may playfully talk about the "miserable town-bred reader" and demonstrate that, as a country-bred man, he knows the taste of fresh cream. Yet his depreciation of that "thinnish white fluid, delivered in infinitesimal pennyworths down area steps," his very knowledge of the way in which cream is delivered in the city, betrays his own town experience (1 : 10). His literary allusions and scientific terminology attest to the quality and range of his education; from his knowledge of medicine and his inquiring disposition, one might gather that he is a research physician. Unlike the narrators of *The Newcomes* and *Cranford*, he does not assume a pivotal role in the plot. Pendennis eventually changes the course of events by finding out Colonel Newcome's retreat at Grey Friars, and Mary Smith's search for Matty Jenkyns's brother constitutes the resolution of the plot. The narrator of the *Scenes* nevertheless reveals an increasingly personal involvement in the stories he tells. In "Amos Barton" he is the spectator; he has known the church where Barton preaches before Barton is installed as curate there. By the time he tells the tale of "Janet's Repentance," however, he has become a character, a young boy confirmed by the bishop on the day that Tryan is granted permission to deliver his evening lectures. At the end of the series, George Eliot has moved from recounting hearsay to reporting his own first-hand observation of events. The development is subtle, but effective. Each of the *Scenes* draws closer to the point at which the narrator can say that he knows the characters involved, as Thackeray's narrator does in chapter 62 of *Vanity Fair*. In a simultaneous and correlative development of narrative form, George Eliot creates increasingly effective and extensive imaginative bonds between the reader and such characters as Barton or Gilfil.

Even the first few pages of "Amos Barton" reveal this process at work. Although the initial description of Shepperton Church resembles a number of other openings in Victorian fiction, it attests to George Eliot's uniquely conscientious and comprehensive concern for the relation of narrator, reader, and character. Like the openings of both *Ruth* and *Shirley*, the passage treats the classically Victorian contrast between past and present. It resembles, in subject matter if not in tedium, the essayistic beginning of *Tom Brown's School Days* (1857), in which Hughes compares his own memories of coaching days to "these racing railroad times." George Eliot's first description of a novelistic setting may even look back to the opening of Scott's *Woodstock*, a passage in which another church is presented in terms of its former and its "improved" appearances. If so, the difference between the two openings only serves to emphasize the quality of combined omniscience and involvement that so often characterizes narrative voice in the Victorian novel. Scott introduces the parish church of Woodstock by noting that he himself has never seen it; even his "informant" may never have seen its interior. After this brief indication of his own lack of personal engagement in the tale, Scott's narrator goes on to tell the story. The purpose of the opening of "Amos Barton," however, is as much to introduce the narrator and his perspective as it is to describe the locale of the tale. The reader, in turn, is invited to participate in the development of the narrator's attitude toward the setting. In the process George Eliot neatly identifies the reader's experience of that development and the quality of the character's life.

"Amos Barton" begins with the mellow tones appropriate to the nostalgic personal essay often found in Thackeray's later works. The narrator first gives a present-tense account of how Shepperton Church looks now in the 1850s and then adds a past-tense account of how it looked twenty-five years before. Unlike the narrator of *Shirley*, George Eliot reserves his sarcasm for the present, not the past. Although the building is restored into a "symmetrical" and "resplendent" condition, the result of such changes is to render it as "smooth and innutrient as the summit of the Rev. Amos Barton's head, after ten years of baldness and supererogatory soap." The absurd clerical pun on *supererogatory* mocks the flux of theological fashions and disputes. The narrator then creates a straw man against whom he posits his own opinions of the changes in Shepperton Church: "Immense improvement! says the well-regulated mind, which unintermittingly rejoices in the New Police, the Tithe Commutation Act, the penny-post, and all guarantees of human advancement, and has no moments when conservative-reforming intellect takes a nap, while imagination does a little Toryism by the sly." Combining a pose of self-deprecation with considerable self-assurance, the narrator defines himself as the guilty proponent of Toryism; he admits to "an occasional tenderness for old abuses" and "dear, old, brown, crumbling, picturesque inefficiency" (1:3–4). As such language indicates, the narrator is ready to use all his descriptive skills to convince his reader that a nostalgic longing for the past is the only attitude one can adopt. He describes the old church less from the point of view of a man who has left the town where he spent his childhood than from the perspective of the child he was long before the restoration of the church took place. This approach combines the romantic appeal of both the attractions of memory and the child's propensity to see the world as a mysterious and fascinating spectacle. The shields of the Oldinports evoke a Gothic fantasy with their "inexhaustible possibilities of meaning in their blood-red hands, their death's-heads and cross-bones, their leopards' paws, and Maltese crosses" (1:5). Even the realm of the medieval knight comes alive in this passage. There is nothing "mechanical" or static about the past; it is replete with excitement, thrilling emotions, and "drama" (1:6).

Yet as soon as the narrator establishes the idea that reforms are to be deplored because they have obliterated this enchanting world, as soon as he cites the memories of his own past as a promise of the romantic and enticing realm to which the reader is about to escape, he lets the reader know that such opinions and expectations simply will not be validated by this particular story. In the fifth paragraph he says of Mr. Gilfil, the vicar in the old church in Shepperton, "I must not speak of him, or I might be tempted to tell the story of his life, which had its little romance. . . . At present I am concerned with quite another sort of clergyman—the Rev. Amos Barton" (1:7). The romance of the past holds out a temptation that must be resisted. By the fifth paragraph the narrator reveals that the contrast between the reforming intellect and a Tory imagination—in literary terms, the contrast between a Dickens and a Scott—does not so much propose a statement of two clearly opposed alternatives as it indicates the two poles between which his own loyalties oscillate. As soon as the narrator begins to speak of Amos Barton himself, he reveals his own reforming zeal; his outrage at the system of plural holdings which forces Barton and his large family to live on eighty pounds a year results in a passage of journalistic satire reminiscent of the attacks on the New Poor Law in *Oliver Twist*. The combination of loyalty to the past and disgust with the present is, of course, no contradiction. It underlies the temporal contrasts that would have been familiar to readers of Carlyle,

Tennyson, Ruskin, and Arnold. Yet George Eliot complicates the implications of this basic contrast because it embodies his character's difficulties as well as his own.

Barton's story takes place in neither the past of tender old abuses nor the present of sterile reform, but somewhere between the two. Barton is the curate at Shepperton "long after" Gilfil's death and after the initial innovations of Evangelicalism and the controversy over Catholic emancipation have made their mark. But, as the comments on pluralism imply, reform has not gone far enough to make Barton's life tolerable; indeed, like the orphaned Oliver, he finds himself a charity case, begging for more. In addition, Barton is at once the victim and the perpetrator of reform. He prefers meeting-house tunes and hymns to traditional psalms, he preaches extemporaneously on Sunday evenings, he has introduced religious tracts, and, worst of all, he is rebuilding the church. But Barton's incapacities render his reforms absurd as well as futile. One measure of his general incompetence is his tendency to rub his Low Church onion with High Church spices, thereby offending members of both parties when he might more profitably try to reconcile them. His own attempts at religious regeneration are self-defeating. His extemporaneous preaching is a failure; as one of the parishioners notes, "He rambles about, and doesn't stick to his text; and every now and then he flounders about like a sheep as has cast itself, and can't get on its legs again" (1:14). The irony of Barton's sponsorship of the church restoration is patent. He is enlarging a church which he can no longer fill with interested parishioners, and this monument to his zeal rises as his long-ignored wife sickens and dies. Barton clearly cannot come up to the standards that his own reforms demand of him. But such an evaluation of Barton's character is not allowed to undermine the reader's interest in him; rather, it is the basis of the linked analogies characteristic of the *Scenes*. The introductory passage has located the reader, like Barton, somewhere between the attractive past and the more clear-cut realities of the present. Because the introduction of Shepperton Church puts the reader through a course of adopting and altering his attitudes along with the narrator's, his imaginative participation becomes a way of identifying with the uncomfortably fluctuating and uncertain attitudes of the character.

As the opening of "Amos Barton" implies, the narrator's first function is to bridge the gap between the reader and the characters whose experiences are foreign to him. The quality of the narrative commentary in the *Scenes*, another technique central to the goals of the mid-century novel, suggests that such a connection is created well before each tale reaches its climax. The questions that the narrator first addresses to the reader emphasize the differences between reader and character. They resemble the kinds of questions that Mary Smith poses in *Cranford* ("Do you ever see cows dressed in grey flannel in London?"),[9] and they even support Masson's assumption that literature has somehow limited English life to the metropolis. But the more extended dialogues in which George Eliot engages the reader suggest that such geographical distinctions soon become irrelevant. In the fifth chapter of "Amos Barton" and the first chapter of "Mr. Gilfil's Love-Story," the narrator's addresses to his mock-reader, labeled Mrs. Farthingale or "my refined lady-reader," resemble Thackeray's addresses to the fifty-eight-year-old virgin reader of *The Virginians* or its Lector Benevolus. But the superficial similarity is misleading. These dialogues end successfully with the conclusion that the narrator has persuaded the reader to read on; Thackeray's end by assuming either that his listener is asleep or that the narrator has been forced to submit to the reader's stupidly conventional demands. Although Mrs. Farthingale is allowed to declare that Barton is "utterly uninteresting," the narrator is certain that there are other "readers who have begun to feel an interest in the Rev. Amos Barton and his wife" (1:68). Whatever his practice in *The Virginians*, however, Thackeray was the writer who had taught George Eliot the effectiveness of addressing such mock-readers when they can be used to debunk a false opinion or thwart a facile expectation. The narrator of "Amos Barton" avoids the hostility inherent in Thackeray's later practice by employing the confidence typical in his treatment of the mock-reader Jones in *Vanity Fair* or in Esmond's attitude toward his progeny. When the narrator of the *Scenes* does address the reader directly, he does so with considerable gentleness and fellow feeling.

Although such direct appeals to the reader of the *Scenes* never reach the sublime or denunciatory tones of Dickens's narrator in *Dombey and Son* or of Carlyle's voice in *The Latter-Day Pamphlets*, although they are never as discomforting or defeated as Thackeray's tones in *The Virginians*, George Eliot clearly discovered that—for her purposes, at least—such rhetoric was more grandiloquent than sincere. The dialogue between the narrator and the "critic" in chapter 10 of "Janet's Repentance" is briefer and more restrained than those in the earlier tales. Throughout this last scene the narrative commentary takes on the more assured and more subdued qualities of humane and reasoned discourse. The narrator's central appeal on behalf of Tryan is not an address to the reader, but an evaluation of Evangelical influence in Milby. In this passage the reader is not expected to argue with the narrator; George Eliot states his unconventional conclusions as if there were no reason to question them: "Yes, the movement was good" (2 : 164). Moreover, as George Eliot wrote the *Scenes*, she clearly moved from commentary based on the weaknesses that all men share— Thackeray's characteristic mode—to her own distinctive concern for the bonds forged by suffering, by the essential strength and generosity of human character, and by man's shared longings for a more ideal life. One of the earliest passages in "Amos Barton" is an echo of the kind of commentary to which Thackeray is so partial: "Let me be persuaded that my neighbour Jenkins considers me a blockhead, and I shall never shine in conversation with him any more. Let me discover that the lovely Phoebe thinks my squint intolerable, and I shall never be able to fix her blandly with my disengaged eye again" (1 : 21). Fictionalized models such as Jenkins and Phoebe, however, do not appear again in the *Scenes*. Often the narrator makes an unstated but implicit connection between character and reader, as he does when he attributes Dempster's one good mood to "those stirrings of the more kindly, healthy sap of human feeling, by which goodness tries to get the upper hand in us" (2 : 121). In "Janet's Repentance," this tendency toward reflective generalizations becomes more pronounced. Instead of addressing the reader directly, the narrator chooses to explain Janet's behavior in terms of what we all would do in the same situation. Through this kind of commentary, the author can render the character's inner life as she simultaneously identifies that life and the reader's own experiences.

The technique that George Eliot uses to make her most effective connections between reader, character, and narrator is also prominent in Dickens's mid-century art; and this fact, like the "climax of approba-

tion" reached in his appreciative response to the *Scenes*, testifies to
what George Eliot called his "finely-felt and finely expressed sympathy" with her work (*Letters*, 2:424). Just as Dickens identifies and
defines his narrative approach through analogies between it and characters like Florence Dombey and Little Dorrit, George Eliot creates a
bond between narrator and character by focusing attention on those
characters whose attitudes are most akin to his own. Moreover, the
characters singled out for such treatment in the *Scenes* assume more
and more prominent positions as the series unfolds. They are mediating presences within the stories themselves, and their actions become
more important in determining the events of the plot, as well as in establishing the reader's reaction to those events. In "Amos Barton" such
a figure is Cleves, a minor character; in the second tale it is Mr. Gilfil
himself (not, however, the young protégé of Sir Christopher, but the
aging vicar who exists in the frame of the story); finally, in "Janet's Repentance," this role is fulfilled by the Rev. Mr. Tryan, a character second in importance only to Janet Dempster. These clerical characters are
the narrator's representatives among the other characters.[10] Cleves is
the "true parish priest" (1:87). Though his role is minor, the action in
which he is involved is significant. At the Milby meeting, he counters
the false rumors about Barton, he is the one to comfort Amos with his
"life-recovering warmth" (1:113), and he presides over the burial of
Milly. The description of Cleves could easily be a self-portrait of the
narrator: "There is a great deal of humour and feeling playing in his
gray eyes, and about the corners of his roughly-cut mouth." Like the
narrator, he has "hereditary sympathies with the checkered life of the
people." Along with this understanding of the people, Cleves possesses
the education they lack; he is the "best Grecian" among the clergy surrounding Milby (1:87). In this respect he resembles the narrator, who
can both transcribe kitchen conversation and joke in Greek. Gilfil's
humor is similar to Cleves's, and the story of his meeting with the old
woman and her pet hog reveals both his warmth and his openness. He
clearly embodies the generous laditudinarianism of the pre-Evangel-
ical Church, as well as the narrator's more modern version of such
tolerance. Finally, as my earlier discussion of the tale suggests, the
analogy between the persona of George Eliot and Tryan is conceived
more clearly and expressed more forcefully than those in the two ear-

lier stories. At the end of chapter 10, the narrator counters the "birds-eye glance" that the critic would focus on Tryan by stating his equality with the clergyman: "But I am not poised at that lofty height. I am on the level and in the press with him." This claim for a brotherly relation to Tryan, a relation based on the "only true knowledge of our fellow-man . . . that which enables us to feel with him" (1:165–66), is itself the basis of their similarity. Both Tryan and George Eliot are capable of seeing the essential bond which their needs create between themselves and others. As Mrs. Pettifer notes, "What is so wonderful to me in Mr Tryan is the way he puts himself on the level with one, and talks to one like a brother" (2:178). The analogy is most evident, of course, when Tryan tells Janet the story of his past—and, again, Tryan's role illuminates the narrator's. The narrator tells his clerical stories because he feels, as Tryan does, the sympathy which is a "living again through our own past in a new form" (2:226). Because the narrator is connected to the events of these stories by the memory of his earlier years, his narration is literally a reliving of those times; because he now sees these events from an enlarged perspective, they assume the "new form" which sympathy creates. The reader, like Janet, is the beneficiary of this process.

These analogies between the persona of George Eliot and his clerical characters extend in two directions. While they suggest the reader's proper attitude toward the characters—like Cleves or Tryan, the reader should be both charitable and sympathetic—such analogies also describe the narrator's proper relation to the reader. As she had done in the case of the Evangelical preacher Cumming, George Eliot carefully evaluates the quality of the sermons preached by these clerics. Because she patterns the novelist's role after that of the parish priest, the novelist's words must live up to the standard of moral seriousness and responsibility that is set for a clergyman speaking to his parishioners. Neither Barton nor Tryan can live up to any such elevated criteria. Cleves, however, is a standard against which to judge them both. His priestly role, like Tryan's, is clearly modeled on that of Wordsworth's Pastor; he is described as "telling [his parishioners] stories, or reading some select passages from an agreeable book, and commenting on them" (1:87). Cleves, like the narrator, is a storyteller and commentator in one. Similarly, like the narrator, Gilfil knows that it is a "mere frustration of the purposes of language" to addresss a man in terms he cannot understand (1:137). In a sense, the sermons of these clerics explain why the narrator and the author who created him bother to tell stories at all. Through the simple and direct language of fiction, the speaker can avoid the abstractions of doctrine and theory. In her essay on Young, George Eliot had explained that "emotion links itself with particulars" (Essays, p. 371), and the reading habits of one of the characters in the Scenes illustrate the relationship between emotion and the novel's generic characteristics. Mrs. Linnet skips over the passages of doctrine and abstraction in the religious tracts she reads, seizing instead on the passages which refer to smallpox, ponies, or boots and shoes. Particularity must become the basis of art's moral role because it is so clearly the way in which to engage the reader's interest, even if the reader is more sophisticated than Mrs. Linnet.

The bond that links George Eliot's clerics and her narrator is, of course, the result of the narration, not its opening premise. Throughout the first half of "Janet's Repentance," Tryan would seem an unlikely candidate for an analogy with the narrator; he is fully the genteel Orlando of the white neck-cloth school of fiction that George Eliot had deplored in "Silly Novels." In later notes on the art of storytelling, she explained that "indirect ways of arriving at knowledge are always the most stirring" (Essays, p. 444), and throughout the Scenes she presents moral knowledge indirectly. She continually describes an event or situation as it might appear in the most foolish and frivolous of popular novels, and then reveals the falsity of such an explanation. Following the introductory satiric portrait of Milby as a dull and dingy manufacturing town preoccupied with false religion and medical quarrels, the narrator comments that, beneath this "dreary prose," there are examples of "purity, gentleness, and unselfishness" (2:65). This process of presenting one attitude or judgment and countering it with the awareness based on fellow feeling occurs not only in the depiction of Milby and Tryan, but throughout the Scenes. In "Amos Barton," the narrator presents Mr. Farquhar's gossip about the Countess and her "brother" before he straightens out the reader's misconceptions by telling him the Bridmain is indeed the Countess' half-brother. He lets the reader witness the clerical meeting at which Barton's supposedly scandalous behavior with the Countess is discussed before he deflates "that very evil interpretation" of very simple events (1:93). George Eliot's treatment of gossip suggests that in the *Scenes* we inhabit a simpler world than Thackeray's. Gossip becomes the only knowledge we have in *Vanity Fair* or *The Newcomes*; in "Amos Barton" it is authoritatively dismissed by the narrator's revelation of the "simple truth." The narrator of the *Scenes* needs to gain the reader's trust, and one way of doing that is simply to demonstrate how often and how thoroughly his opinion is to be trusted. The process of countering ignorant assumptions with enlightened explanation becomes more subtle as the *Scenes* progress, and the mistaken attitudes invalidated by the process become more sophisticated than the gossip of the Shepperton parishioners. By the time she wrote "Janet's Repentance," George Eliot was ready to confront and triumph over the abstract theories of the critic, the political economist, and the statistician. But, here again, the narrator lets the reader identify with such perspectives and then allows him to realize their inapplicability. Such indirection consistently encourages the reader to engage in the kind of moral "exercise" George Eliot had spoken of in "The Natural History of German Life." A year before she began her career as a novelist she noted, in the context of praising Carlyle, that "the most effective writer is not he who announces a particular discovery . . . but he who rouses in others the activities that must issue in discovery" (*Essays*, p. 213). The *Scenes* follow that prescription fully. The narrator does not announce his understanding of a character; he introduces himself to the reader, creates a bond between himself and his listener, and only then rouses the reader to the activities that must issue in the discovery of the character's appeal.

In the course of these tales, the reader is offered many occasions on which he discovers that the distinctions he has accepted are less clearcut, less significant than they have seemed—that, for all his shortcomings and in spite of his own "pigeon-hole" mentality, Barton is not a character to be dismissed or defined by some glib label that attaches to his beliefs. As each of the *Scenes* unfolds, the reader finds new and more fundamental grounds on which to identify his own condition with those of both the storyteller and his characters. Such is the case even in "Mr. Gilfil's Love-Story," the tale that apparently stands opposed to the principles set forth in the opening of "Amos Barton." Although the narrator seems to deny his own realistic doctrine by depicting the "antecedent romance" of Gilfil's life, to paint figures who might grace a canvas by Watteau or, more pertinently, who might appear in the drawing rooms of *Guy Mannering* or *Mansfield Park*, he is again engaging in purposeful indirection. Once the layers of civility and power have been stripped away by unexpected suffering, the courtly, dignified, and complacent Sir Christopher resembles no one more than Amos Barton, the poor, bald cleric with bad teeth. Indeed, both characters respond to their losses by finding substitutes in the next generation for the heir or the wife each has earlier taken for granted. Readers come to see that even Sir Christopher's complacency is a bond that permits them to identify themselves with this character. His own earlier imaginative participation in the aristocratic world of Cheverel has created the comforting assurance that the narrator of "Amos Barton" had promised and then withheld. Like Sir Christopher, the reader now discovers, through the agency of the unfolding story, that such fantasy is only a façade over the reality of feeling. In this sense, "Mr. Gilfil's Love-Story," though the weakest of the three scenes, foretells the more difficult problem that George Eliot sets for herself in *Adam Bede*. In both cases she deals with the paradox created by her realistic goals when she evokes what is conventionally artistic so that she can later invalidate its presuppositions. The evolution of attitudes in "Mr. Gilfil" also exemplifies her growing desire to present character from an interior rather than an exterior view; again we find her sharing an impulse with the author of *Little Dorrit* and *Great Expectations*. As George Eliot wrote "Mr. Gilfil's Love-Story," she told Blackwood, "I cannot stir a step aside from what I *feel* to be *true* in character" (*Letters*, 2:299). By the time she was writing "Janet's Repentance," she was becoming more interested in depicting what the character feels than in expressing what the narrator feels about the character.

This shifting of focus and intention is evident in George Eliot's use of one other narrative convention typical of mid-century fiction: narration in the present tense. In the decade since the publication of *Dombey and Son*, when Dickens had carefully explored its potential to identify the experience of reading and the lives of his characters, the device had become conventional in the most pejorative sense of that word. It often signals an author's dependence on an aura of melodramatic intensity and, even, his faked concern for his characters' fates. Although it rarely descends to this level in the *Scenes*, George Eliot is not above using present-tense narration to create rhetorical demands on the reader's attention. She uses this form of narration extensively on nearly a dozen occasions in "Amos Barton." In each instance the narrator draws a picture of the characters and uses the present tense to describe what "you," the reader, see there. The first chapter of the tale employs a technique that Brontë had borrowed from *Vanity Fair* for her "levitical" introductions in the first chapter of *Shirley*, and which Thackeray had later used more extensively in *The Newcomes*: "You and I will join the party," says the narrator to the reader (*Shirley*, p. 9). After introducing the characters, George Eliot presents their dialogue by locating the reader at the periphery of the gathering at Cross Farm: "And now that we are snug and warm with this little tea-party, while it is freezing with February bitterness outside, we will listen to what they are talking about" (1:12). In both *Shirley* and "Amos Barton," the rhetorical identification of reader and character, a technique which is both casual and graceful in Thackeray's best works, seems strained and slightly artificial. George Eliot may have realized this, and she discarded the device of making the reader "one of the party" while she retained present-tense narration to introduce Amos Barton, the paupers at the workhouse, the diners at Camp Villa, and the clerical meeting at Milby. For many chapters the story seems less a narration of one event that leads to another than a series of *tableaux vivants* in which the characters are allowed to speak. "Mr. Gilfil's Love-Story" opens in the same mode; the present tense describes the static poses of the figures on the lawn of Cheverel Manor. As the narrator notes, Lady Cheverel might have just stepped from the frame of the portrait Sir Joshua Reynolds has painted of her.

Yet the present tense comes to define not what the reader sees, but what the character perceives. It reveals "how dreary the moonlight is" when Tina's despair makes it appear as desolate as her future (1:220). In the most melodramatic passage of the tale, present-tense narration charts Tina's unfolding thoughts as she comes across Wybrow's body in the Rookery: "But what is that lying among the dank leaves on the path three yards before her? Good God! it is he" (1:280). At the beginning of "Janet's Repentance" in the passage describing Dempster's beating of his wife, George Eliot still uses the rhetorical questions and exclamatory phrases that recall the hysteria typical of a novel like *Ruth*, but by the end of the tale such techniques have disappeared. In the potentially melodramatic scene that occurs when Janet lies in bed waiting for her drunken husband and his predictably violent response to her earlier defiance of him, the narrator uses the simple language of the more conventional past tense to convey and analyze the character's thoughts: "What was he going to do to her?" (2:199). Again we can see George Eliot moving in the direction of *Adam Bede* and the concerns of that first novel. Her discovery of the effects of present-tense narration and her decision to modify her own adaptation of the technique remain, perhaps, the most revealing emblem of her relation to the mid-century tradition. She adopted one of its central conventions as long as it served her purposes and satisfied her desire to engage her reader's interest in the story; as soon as it had achieved that aim, an aim which she shared with the other earlier practitioners of this form, she had created the confidence she needed to reject the convention. The *Scenes of Clerical Life* are not unqualified successes—there are weak moments, failures of control, even occasional reversions to methods typical of the silly novels written by ladies—but they were a necessary and productive initiation into the practical demands and the possible achievements of narration. When George Eliot finished this series, she had developed not only the confidence to go on to the writing of a novel, but also what one reviewer praised as her "steadfast faith in the power of truth"[11]—the confidence that her characters could and would interest the reader without the support of the narrator's rhetorical appeals on their behalf.

The growth from caution to confidence is, of course, typical of the *Scenes* as a whole. The series struck its first readers as a "reminiscence of real life" because George Eliot was almost slavishly faithful to the facts of the clerical anecdotes she had heard in her youth. She responded quite literally to the request of Wordsworth's Solitary—"The mine of real life / Dig for us." With only the slight change of a few letters, the Rev. Bernard Gilpin Ebdell, vicar of Chilvers Coton, becomes the Rev. Maynard Gilfil of Milby.[12] In her next work George Eliot could afford to be more adventurous. She had tested both herself and her audience. Though the series did not sell as quickly as she would have wished, John Blackwood triumphantly announced, "Still the great point is attained, the reputation made, which will bring your next work an audience at once prepared to admire" (*Letters*, 2 : 462). Blackwood's judgment was, as usual, correct. The relative success of the *Scenes* gave George Eliot the freedom and determination to offer her readers the more challenging moral and imaginative experiences of *Adam Bede*.

The nature of that challenge is exemplified in a long passage from *The Virginians*, the first number of which George Eliot read and "groaned over" just after she finished "Janet's Repentance" (*Letters*, 2 : 401). Here, in one of his increasingly typical diatribes against his genre, Thackeray complains about the limitations imposed on the novelist by conventional conceptions of his proper material, and he echoes the comments made at the beginning of the decade by Hawthorne:

> The real business of life, I fancy, can form but little portion of the novelist's budget. . . . The main part of Ficulnus's life, for instance, is spent in selling sugar, spices, and cheese; of Causidicus's in poring over musty volumes of blackletter law; of Sartorius's in sitting, crosslegged, on a board after measuring gentlemen for coats and breeches. What can a story-teller say about the professional existence of these men? Would a real rustical history of hobnails and eighteenpence a day be endurable? . . . Law, stockbroking, polemical theology, linen-drapery, apothecary business, and the like, how can writers manage fully to develop these in their stories? All authors can do, is to depict men *out* of their business—in their passions, loves, laughters, amusements, hatreds, and what not. (pp. 603–4)

Although one senses that Thackeray here is as tired of life as he is of art (unlike Hawthorne, he could find no neutral ground between the Actual and the Imaginary where creation would be possible), the passage does highlight George Eliot's genuine originality. The *Scenes* had attempted to define the relation between a cleric's "passions, loves, laughters" and his "business" as a clergyman. But Thackeray's comment betrays a class prejudice that George Eliot had not yet confronted; her clergymen are, of course, gentlemen, not the workers who measure out cloth for a gentlemen's coat or the spices for his food. Other novelists had attempted to treat the "real business of life" in the working classes, but none of their works transcends what one reviewer called the "impassable barrier" between an educated man and a country carpenter as successfully as the "real rustical history" of *Adam*

Bede. Mary Barton, for instance, purports to depict "what the workman feels and thinks," but as soon as his thoughts and feelings become threatening—Chartist or Communist—the narrator announces that the working class is a Frankenstein. In a telling but common confusion of the scientist and his creature, Gaskell explains that the poor man is a "monster of many human qualities."[13] Here again generalities and aggregates inhibit the reader's sympathy with the particular and the individual.

In writing the "real rustical history" that Thackeray thought inconceivable, George Eliot would be less clearly dependent on the conventions of mid-century fiction that had formed and informed the narrative of her *Scenes*. In her only acknowledgment of that earlier debt, a debt which she admitted only after finishing *Adam Bede*, she told Elizabeth Gaskell that she had seen the "affinity" between their works, but she added two significant qualifications. She spoke specifically of *Cranford* and the "earlier chapters" of *Mary Barton*, where Gaskell has not yet drawn any egregious distinctions between the humane reader and the inhumanity of the character. Secondly, George Eliot conceded that she had been "conscious" of this similarity only when she was still a novice, only "while the question of my power was still undecided for me" (*Letters*, 3:198). Her power now no longer "undecided," she could combine the aims of her fellow-novelists and their tradition with her own unique conception of her proper object. To effect this accommodation, she would have to look beyond the models offered by Brontë, Gaskell, and Thackeray. When George Eliot describes Tryan's death by quoting Wordsworth's comment on Kilchurn Castle's "calm decay," she is offering the reader a promise of things to come.

Adam Bede

"The Art of Vision"

In lectures delivered in 1858 and published in 1859, David Masson ob-
served that the English novel had yet to conquer the province of
poetry. By poetry he meant not simply the lyrical potential of language,
but the "more massive and enduring," more elemental "phenomena
of the moral world"—"Birth, Life, Death; Labour, Sorrow, Love, Revenge." The timing of this remark could not be more appropriate.
In 1859 Meredith published *The Ordeal of Richard Feverel*, a self-
conscious attempt at a poetry of prose which universalizes a drama of
enduring love and sorrow. Yet another literary event that Masson himself mentions is an even more comprehensive response to the challenge he proposed: "At this moment readers are hailing the advent of a
new artist of the Real school, in the author of *Adam Bede*."[1] Standing
firmly in the mid-century tradition of the Victorian novel, *Adam Bede*
nonetheless strikes a distinctly new note, and it does so, paradoxically,
by returning to both an earlier poetic tradition and the elemental subjects that Masson enumerated. Although such a conceptual definition
of poetry recalls the dimensions and concerns of the world of *Dombey
and Son*—except, perhaps, that "Labour" is excluded from Dickens's
Märchen world—the rural simplicity of Hayslope and Stoniton, the
timelessness of the dilemmas and demands that their inhabitants face,
are all equally reminiscent of the moral landscapes found in the pastoral
tradition. In the *Scenes* George Eliot had treated stories of clergymen

whose lives had touched her own youth. In *Adam Bede*, however, she would return to the time of her father's youth. By choosing to tell what she called "My Aunt's Story," a tale of infanticide and confession, George Eliot would be ranging farther from her own experience than she had done even in the Cheverel Manor scenes of "Mr. Gilfil's Love-Story." Although she would need no help in re-creating the physical authenticity of a rural world, "full of the breath of cows and the scent of hay" (*Letters*, 2 : 387), the description of the child-murderer and her plight would place new demands on her inventive powers. In "The Natural History of German Life," she had denounced the "artistic mind, which looks for its subjects into literature instead of life" (*Essays*, p. 269), but the various facets of the Evans's past that she chose to explore now made such a procedure almost inevitable. As Theophrastus Such would say of his father, George Eliot could say of her father and aunt: they lived in the era of Wordsworth and Scott. When she decided to treat the crime of child-murder in relation to the life and values of the community in which it takes place, she would necessarily evoke the work of these two authors, specifically, "The Thorn" and *The Heart of Mid-Lothian*.[2]

Adam Bede is, in fact, the occasion on which George Eliot would define her allegiance to one or the other of these two writers, and, by doing so, establish the aims and methods of her art more clearly than she had in the *Scenes*. Scott, whom Lewes rightly called her "longest-venerated and best-loved Romancist" (*Letters*, 3 : 240), would always remain for her a repository of themes and incidents. Along with Thackeray, she developed the practice of adopting a subject from Scott and casting it in a more serious and challenging form. The deeds of Hetty Sorrel, like those of Beatrix Esmond, strain the limits of conventional morality as the behavior of Scott's more innocent Die Vernon and Effie Deans does not. The methods of Scott's art, however, were for George Eliot a less propitious example than they were for Thackeray. In writing *Adam Bede* she was reaching the conclusion that she articulated in 1861: "Dearly beloved Scott had the greatest combination of experience and faculty—yet even he never made the most of his treasures, at least in his *mode* of presentation" (*Letters*, 3 : 378). For mode of presentation, for narrative technique, George Eliot would ultimately look not to Scott, but to Wordsworth. Indeed, as she worked on this first novel, she and Lewes read his poetry "with fresh admiration for his beauties and tolerance for his faults" (*Letters*, 2:423). The novel itself is both the best witness to that admiration and an example of the difficulty of sustaining his methods in the mode of prose fiction. If in the *Scenes* George Eliot reconciled her sense of her unique artistic identity with the trends of the contemporary novel, in *Adam Bede* she enlarged the grounds of that accommodation to include as well the poetic tradition of the past.

Even the occasion on which Mary Ann Evans first heard her aunt describe the child-murderer reveals a Wordsworthian impulse. It was, for the mature woman who recollected it in her "History of Adam Bede," nothing less than a "spot of time": "The story, told by my aunt with great feeling, affected me deeply, and I never lost the impression of that afternoon and our talk together" (*Letters*, 2:502). That afternoon became an important emotional locus for George Eliot because her aunt was the one woman to whom she could reveal her "inward life," a secret domain "closely shut up from those usually round" her (*Letters*, 2:503); both the young Mary Ann Evans and the child-murderer had found in Aunt Samuel a comforter whose responsiveness invited confession. Like the Wordsworth of *The Prelude*, George Eliot "enshrines" the "spirit of the Past," but she does so by re-creating not the context of her own confession, but the events of the one she had heard at second hand. The mode of comparing past and present so characteristic of the *Scenes* is generally replaced—as it would be again in *The Mill on the Floss*—by the attempt to recapture the feeling of the past. Irwine, for instance, avoids any direct confrontation with the Methodists which would, in the manner of Barton or Tryan, necessitate a narrative concerned with change and its effects. Rather, the narrator wants us to savor the richness of an initial sensation. "Ah! I think I taste that whey now—with a flavour so delicate that one can hardly distinguish it from an odour" (1:327). As the epigraph of the novel implies, the narrative role of the Pastor in *The Excursion* and his story of Ellen provide one perspective on "My Aunt's Story." Yet the subject of *Adam Bede* clearly suggests that there is a more relevant Wordsworth text than either *The Excursion* or *The Prelude*. As soon as Arthur Donnithorne dismisses the *Lyrical Ballads* as "twaddling stuff" (1:94), we are alerted to their importance.

In poems like "The Complaint of a Forsaken Indian Woman," "The Idiot Boy," and "The Mad Mother," Wordsworth celebrates what he calls "maternal passion" (preface, 1800, p. 158) and what George Eliot describes at the end of *Adam Bede* as "that completest type of the life in another life which is the essence of real human love." But "The Thorn," of course, is George Eliot's central model. There Wordsworth celebrates maternal instincts as he examines the possibility that grief and madness may pervert them. His story is told by a "loquacious narrator" (advertisement, p. 4), presumably a sea captain who has settled in the village of "The Thorn" after his retirement. Like the Pastor in *The Excursion*, or Jedediah Cleishbotham in *The Heart of Mid-Lothian*, he tells the old story of love and betrayal. Martha Ray has been cast off by her lover; pregnant, alienated from the villagers by grief and shame, she has wandered on the mountainside. We do not know what has happened to her child: "There's no one that could ever tell" (l. 160). Whether the child is stillborn or murdered, either drowned or hanged by its own mother, is unknown. As is not the case in Effie Deans's story, here the death of the child is a certainty. The villagers believe that it has been buried beneath the thorn; there, twenty-two years later, the child's mother still wanders to mourn its death or perhaps her own guilt. The spot on the hillside, like the "naked pool" and the "blasted hawthorn" of Wordsworth's own memories in *The Prelude*, becomes a compelling if not obsessive emotional locus for both the narrator in "The Thorn" and the author of *Adam Bede*. Like the first of the *Lyrical Ballads*, *Adam Bede* is the story of sin, guilt, exile, and confession, yet it takes its form less from "The Ancient Mariner" than from the other "twaddling stuff" of the *Ballads*.

The impact of Wordsworth's poem on the novel is more imagistic than thematic. The scenes and figures of "The Thorn"—the muddy pond, the mossy grave, and the woman in a scarlet cloak—exert their power at both the beginning and climax of the action in *Adam Bede*. The association of the thorn-tree with suffering and, particularly, with child-murder is traditional.[3] Yet George Eliot invokes the image first in the drowning death of a drunken old man, Thias Bede. Lisbeth insists that her husband be buried beneath a thorn. In the dream which prompts this request, Lisbeth associates that location with childbirth: "Now she felt as if the greatest work of her life were to be done in seeing that Thias was buried decently before her—under the white thorn, where once, in a dream, she had thought she lay in the coffin, yet all the while saw the sunshine above, and smelt the white blossoms that were so thick upon the thorn the Sunday she went to be churched after Adam was born" (1:153). Lisbeth's dream of her own death is defined by a memory of the birth of her first son, an event that paradoxically involves both her own demise and her continued existence in this world. The implications of even this striking image might be overlooked if Adam's troubled dreams about his father's death did not make the same point. There Hetty, inexplicably and disturbingly, becomes an actor in the "scenes" related to Thias's drowning. She is "by the Willow Brook" (1:158)—an accomplice in Thias's death, perhaps— and she angers Adam's mother by invading their house. The logic of this dream is clear: Adam's marriage to Hetty will dispossess his parents; the ongoing life of the new generation will eventually entail their deaths. This harsh reality knows no class distinctions. Mrs. Irwine remembers Arthur's mother "flitting about," ghostlike, in "a white dress . . . like a shroud" on the day of her son's christening; she dies three months later and is buried with his christening dress (1:93). Like Dinah, Arthur is an orphan whose life has cost his mother's life. Although George Eliot's perspective on such matters is not Wordsworth's—his speaker tells us that Martha's love for her unborn child saves her from insanity—his images allow George Eliot to explore the questions of generation, the sexual jealousies and conflicting interests of contiguous generations that have concerned the writers of *Dombey and Son* and *Henry Esmond*.

Such jealousies and conflicts are, of course, opposed to the highest ideals of mid-century fiction. They threaten to disrupt if not deny both the community and its microcosmic embodiment, the family. The locus of such potential disorder is Hetty Sorrel. In *The Heart of Mid-Lothian*, Effie plays a similar role, and in her self-indulgence, her pretensions, her "little fund of self-conceit and obstinacy" (chap. 10, p. 96), Scott's character is certainly Hetty's kin. But Scott does not exploit the theme of the generational conflict that he treats so effectively and so often in novels like *Waverley*, *Rob Roy*, and *Redgauntlet*. It is easy to see why he would not place Effie in the light he casts on Darsie Latimer, for instance. For Scott the source of the discord between generations is financial or political, and not simply, as it is for George Eliot, emotional and physical. In her conception of this theme, George Eliot reveals a comparable independence from Wordsworth. What the poet suggests and seems to deny George Eliot makes explicit: Hetty's indomitable and "passionate love of life" (2 : 149), her instinctual self-preservation, will triumph only at the cost of her child's life. Yet, as George Eliot prepares to reveal the cause of Hetty's "hidden dread," she more frequently evokes the images of Martha Ray's story and her perpetual cry, "Oh misery! oh misery!" Beneath the natural beauty of the pastoral landscape is hidden grave human sorrow: "The sound of the gurgling brook, if you came close to one spot behind a small bush, would be mingled for your ear with a despairing human sob" (2 : 112). Dark ponds, like the one near which Martha sits, replace all the mirrors, real or fancied, in which Hetty has seen a flattering image of her own charm. Particularly in her second encounter with a pond, when her journey toward Stoniton has led her to the winter landscape of "The Thorn," Hetty acts out the flirtation with death-by-drowning that remains conjecture in Wordsworth's poem. In the rain and frost of February, Hetty comes closer to Martha's maddened state. Like Martha, who constantly returns to her child's grave, Hetty is found seated beneath the nut bush where she has buried her still-living child. Her hold on life is brilliantly and chillingly portrayed in the image of her sitting with "a big piece of bread on her lap" (2 : 222). Her earlier pink-and-white loveliness has been replaced by an ashen face above a scarlet cloak, but she has survived. As she later tells Dinah, "I wouldn't mind if they'd let me live" (2 : 243). George Eliot faces, with unflinching honesty, the potentially destructive energies that rise when the interests of one generation compete with those of the next, and her extensive embodiment of the theme in the households of the Bedes, Poysers, and Donnithornes suggests that such is almost always the case. The strength of the community must accommodate such conflicts if it is to progress, like the plot of *Adam Bede*, from funeral to harvest-home.

Whatever the thematic differences between "The Thorn" and *Adam Bede*, the problem that George Eliot faces in handling such material is essentially that of Wordsworth's sea captain: Martha Ray is, to both the speaker and the interlocutor who questions him, a mystery, an inscrutable figure in a landscape that bodies forth some ineffable significance. George Eliot examines various "mysteries" in *Adam Bede*—the inexplicable nature of sexual attraction, the mystery of "God's dealings," the unacknowledged agents of "our mental business" (1 : 259)—and she, like Wordsworth, suggests that superstition is the common response to such baffling questions. Yet Hetty is her greatest mystery. Less compulsively perhaps than the sea captain, the narrator of *Adam Bede* emphasizes our need to understand Hetty. While Wordsworth's narrator pleads ignorance, George Eliot's pleads for a comprehension that will embrace sympathy. She asks a good deal of both her art and her readers. The challenge that Hetty posed was, I think, greater and more profoundly personal than George Eliot at first realized. Sometimes, for instance in the pathetic appeals at the end of chapter 37, she betrays her uncertainty. Yet only a novelist who trusts her powers would choose child-murder, an uncompromisingly repulsive crime, to test her readers' acceptance of her perspectives.

In one sense Hetty's situation is stubbornly conventional; Thackeray would have thought her story too old to merit telling. But George Eliot takes advantage of this fact so that she can persuade the reader to see Hetty from a vantage that previous fiction could not provide. Scott's focus on Jeanie Deans rather than Effie, on the unattractive and genuinely dull embodiment of conscience rather than on her typically beautiful and predictably erring sister, is itself more daring than George Eliot's concern with a pretty dairymaid and the effects of her transgressions. For precisely this reason *The Heart of Mid-Lothian* is the only Scott novel in which George Eliot could find a pattern for her own genre painting. Moreover, she profits by Scott's insight when she balances her treatment of Hetty with an equal attention to Adam's Jeanie-like responses to Hetty's actions. Yet Scott solves the problem of the reader's relation to Effie simply by putting her offstage and out of sight throughout most of the novel, and George Eliot will not allow herself to practice such evasive tactics. Neither will she try to elicit the facile sympathy that is accorded the wronged innocent in Gaskell's *Ruth*. She insists on Hetty's complicity in her affair with Arthur, and she refuses to idealize motivations or exonerate guilt by conjuring up visions of the extremities which make Ruth's choice of sin seem almost admirable.

A passage from "The Natural History of German Life" suggests how George Eliot originally conceived the relations between her reader, Hetty, and the rural life of which she is a part. In an image that reappears in *Adam Bede*, she explains that the distance between an observer and the haymakers in a field allows him to see a "false object instead of the true one." Only when the observer "approach[es] nearer" can he see the "coarse" reality of this "smiling" scene. The "truth of rustic life" is particularly susceptible to the idealizing distortions that distance creates. And conventional art, she insists, is the mode most often responsible for such perceptual distortions (*Essays*, pp. 269–71). George Eliot concludes that the art which aspires to treat rustic life must reject the artistic traditions to which it might otherwise conform; it must eschew the idealization of a distanced view. Like the crude reality of an apparently charming pastoral landscape, the fact of Hetty's crime is the subject George Eliot must confront if she is not to present a "false object instead of the true one." Scott could be of no help in this regard. Twice in his diaries he recorded his infatuation with distance, the "magician" which transforms the "discordant" chant of peasant women into a "wild and sweet" song that he can enjoy.[4] The comment is a telling though unconscious revelation of Scott's typical narrative posture. George Eliot expends a good deal of energy in *Adam Bede* evaluating and then rejecting the techniques which distance Scott's peasant characters from his readers. Wordsworth's experiment in the imaginative relations between subject and object become, gradually but inevitably, the basis for George Eliot's unconventional perspective on Hetty and Hayslope. Distance is replaced by proximity, and the example of Scott is superseded by the practice of Wordsworth.

The relation between distance and a distorted view of Hetty is established in "The Game." Mrs. Irwine, who admits that she is able to see only "things at a distance" (1:412), is blind to the "striking resemblance" (1:415) between Hetty and Chad's Bess; she can see only Hetty's surface, the charm of her beauty. In Arthur's case, such a distance poses a clear moral danger, and George Eliot defines this danger in specifically artistic terms. Arthur is virtually quoting Scott's description of Effie's "Grecian-shaped head" and "Hebe countenance" (chap. 10, p. 94) when he tells Irwine that Hetty is a "perfect Hebe; and if I were an artist, I would paint her." Although Irwine replies, "I have no objection to your contemplating Hetty in an artistic light," he is wrong to think such contemplation will not "spoil her for a poor man's wife" (1:149). This conventional and oddly impersonal view of Hetty prevents Arthur from breaking off his relationship with her; it is as clear a violation of her integrity as rape would be. George Eliot must discover the artistic perspective on Hetty that will move beyond a superficial view without violating her reality. *Adam Bede* was originally conceived as the fourth tale in the *Scenes of Clerical Life*, but when George Eliot turned to the "large canvas" (*Letters*, 2:381) of a novel, she discovered that the "scenic" methods which allowed her to conceive of the novel itself as a "canvas" would have to be dismissed. Defining moral awareness in visual terms is a practice amost synonymous with mid-Victorian fiction: Thackeray wants to lift the veil from our eyes so that we can see our own faces in the mirror of his art, and Dickens conjures up his visions of past, present, and future to achieve the same end. In *Adam Bede*, however, George Eliot embodies the idea of moral life in a visual image so that she can transform vision into feeling; her reader is invited to feel as well as see the reality of her character's experience. When Dinah tries to confront Hetty with her potential trials in the "Two Bed-chambers," George Eliot outlines the pain involved in such a process. Although we assume that Dinah, "the higher nature," "commands a complete view" of Hetty, "the lower nature," the narrator tells us otherwise: "I think the higher nature has to learn this comprehension, as we learn the art of vision, by a good deal of hard experience, often with bruises and gashes incurred in taking things up by the wrong end, and fancying our space wider than it is" (1:240). Both Adam and Dinah, who represent the "higher" ethical and spiritual natures respectively, must confront with "hard experience" their physical counterpart, Hetty Sorrel. The reader must do the same. A "complete view" is possible only if one accepts the bruises which feeling with and for Hetty will necessarily entail.

The "art of vision" is, as George Eliot notes, a lesson learned only through experience, and she begins *Adam Bede* by offering her reader an aesthetic experience of the perceptual limitations he must eventually overcome. Throughout the first two volumes of the novel, the reader's vision of events is based on conventional artistic models. From the first paragraph, when the narrator poses as an Egyptian sorcerer whose magic will reveal "far-reaching visions of the past" (1 : 3), the reader is made aware of his distance from the world of Hayslope. Placed in the position of the spectator postulated at the beginning of Scott's *St. Ronan's Well,* he is asked literally to see this world as if it were a painted picture. If the two Irwine sisters are "inartistic figures crowding the canvas of life" (1 : 96), the life of the fictive world they inhabit is clearly a canvas created by the narrator's vision. In this "Eden-like peace and loveliness," Adam and Seth and the coffin they carry present a "strangely-mingled picture" (1 : 73). The Hall Farm, Bartle Massey's school, the dance at the Chase are only a few of the "scenes" offered for the reader's contemplation. In the first two volumes of *Adam Bede,* such pictures are often presented to the reader through the agency of a mediator;[5] the initial effect, unlike that in *The Newcomes* or *Little Dorrit,* is not liberation, but limitation. The reader, the "chance comer," sees the whole novel within the confines of the narrator's pool of ink. As he says in chapter 17, *Adam Bede* is not an "arbitrary picture"; it is the picture created for the reader's perception by the "mirror" of the narrator's mind (1 : 265). Yet there are perceptual limitations beyond those created by the narrator. The reader is introduced to Hall Farm through the powers of "imagination . . . a licensed trespasser," but he can only see what the frames of the dining room and kitchen windows reveal: "Put your face to one of the glass panes in the right-hand window: what do you see?" (1 : 103). Earlier the narrator uses the present-tense narration reminiscent of both *Shirley* and the *Scenes.* "We" enter the dining room at the Rectory and stand in the doorway, unable to see Irwine's face until he obliges us by turning around. In the second chapter, the mediator is human, and the reader sees and hears Dinah's sermon only as the stranger on horseback sees and hears it. The stranger remains undescribed; the reader views the scene through him as if he were performing the function of a windowpane. This particular technique, characteristic of novels by G. P. R. James as well as Scott and used by Mary Ann Evans in "Edward Neville," her abortive attempt at historical fiction, suggests that literary traditions set up a distance between the reader and the fictional world. Language itself, specifically the language of literature, becomes a buffer between the reader and the rural life of Hayslope.

Like Arthur, who thinks of himself as Eros "sipping the lips of Psyche" (1:204), the reader finds that his perception is filtered through classical references that are purposefully inappropriate. We are asked to see the woods where Arthur and Hetty meet as "just the sort of wood most haunted by the nymphs" (1:192), and the description again recalls Scott's rendering of Effie's "nymph-like form" (chap. 10, p. 96). Even biblical allusions create a distance between the reader and the fictive reality of the characters; Mrs. Poyser and Dinah "might have served a painter as an excellent suggestion for a Martha and Mary" (1:107). So much emphasis is placed on the typicality of the various characters that we may be lulled into a false complacency about their individuality.

Yet such a manner of perceiving the action and figures of *Adam Bede* is, at least at first, quite appropriate. It is the initial basis of the perceptual analogy that identifies character and reader, object and subject, in this novel. The characters themselves are as distanced from a direct engagement with their own present experience as the reader is. Their imaginations repeatedly work in terms of scenes and images rather than actions or sensations. In the first extended exposition of a character's thoughts, George Eliot comments that Adam's "mind seemed as passive as a spectator at a diorama: scenes of the sad past, and probably sad future, floating before him, and giving place one to the other in swift succession" (1:67). The same passivity and detachment characterize all the mental processes described in the first half of *Adam Bede*, whether they be Mrs. Poyser's or Mrs. Irwine's. The actual substance of Hetty's hopes is described as the "dim ill-defined pictures that her narrow bit of an imagination can make of the future; . . . of every picture she is the central figure in fine clothes" (1:230). Hetty has cast her life in the form of conventional romance just when it is about to reveal its all too conventional reality. With a similar irony, Arthur's "pictures" of the future are most fully developed when they are least likely to be realized. As he rides to the Chase after hearing the news of his grandfather's death and before hearing the news of Hetty's imprisonment, his imagination takes over: "These were Arthur's chief thoughts . . . which are only like the list of names telling you what are the scenes in a long, long panorama, full of colour, of detail, and of life" (2:228). These characters will later look back upon these scenes and pictures as the measure of their self-deception, but these static visual images, along with the narrator's emphasis on his role as a landscape painter or portraitist, create a rather strange impression: in a manner reminiscent of *The Newcomes*, the action of the novel seems to exist in a state of suspended animation.

In the first two volumes of the novel, the characters' insistence upon citing texts and authorities for their opinions corresponds to the narrator's concern with literary sources and literary tradition. As varied as their ideas may be, Adam's basically Carlylean work ethic, Dinah's semimystical Methodism, and Arthur's feudal definition of the squire's duties continually involve their proponents in debates and postures of self-justification. Breakfast at the rectory turns into a "moral discussion" on the irrevocable consequences of every action. The speeches and toasts at Arthur's birthday celebration turn into moral lessons that draw on his "exemplary" qualities. So much, George Eliot seems to say, for such earlier modes of moral narration. These discussions of the correct way to go about living have their comic counterparts in Joshua Rann's irritated attacks on nonconformist religion and Bartle Massey's acerbic railings against wedded bliss. In one sense, the action of the novel tests all these notions about life. Whether they turn out to be "maggots" or "megrims," as Mrs. Poyser often labels her niece's ideas, whether they are confirmed by events, all these opinions are supported by texts. The peasant wit of Mrs. Poyser's speech and Lisbeth's often vivid turn of phrase both suggest the role of communal folk wisdom in providing such consoling confirmations. More frequently, however, religious texts serve as a repository of supporting evidence. Dinah, of course, sees herself as the preacher of the "Word of Life," and her sermon resembles the speech of characters like Adam and Mrs. Poyser when she bases it on a Gospel text. Even her method of obtaining guidance by opening the Bible "at hazard" and reading the passage that presents itself is simply a more concrete example of each character's search for words that will have an authoritative force in his life.

Such discursive rather than dramatic impulses serve only to increase the often-noted slow pace of the action in *Adam Bede*.[6] The narrator is true to his pledge; we are offered "faithful pictures of a monotonous homely existence" (1 : 268). Because the reader's perception of these pictures is mimetically faithful to the characters' attention to the future rather than the present, the world of Hayslope and Broxton seems to exist more in potential than in actuality. Like Wordsworth's "Michael," the novel gathers energy through a gradual accumulation of detailed and minutely realized scenes. George Eliot devotes long stretches of the narrative to the description of habitual activities and normal workday patterns. Little actually happens in the first half of the novel. The first volume, containing sixteen chapters or an entire third of *Adam Bede*, consists of only one "event": Thias's death. That event occurs very much offstage, since it is an accomplished fact before the reader ever learns of it. In the second book Thias is buried, and the relationship between Hetty and Arthur develops unobtrusively. The third book is concerned with the events of only one day, the celebration of Arthur's majority. George Eliot refuses to exploit the dramatic—or melodramatic—potential of even these few occurrences. Larger ranges of time are dismissed as the time that passes between books, such as the four or more weeks between books 2 and 3 and the three weeks between books 3 and 4, not as the time encompassed by them. The first book covers four days; the second, two; the third, one; and until Arthur leaves Hayslope, the fourth book (to chap. 31) covers only four more days. With so few events to portray, the narrator has no need of Thackeray's redoublings or Dickens's often breathless tempo. The leisure of this part of the story, reminiscent of Scott's pace in *Ivanhoe* or *Guy Mannering*, evokes in the reader a false sense of security. Nothing dire can occur in a narrative that allows such expansion and such delay. By using this slow and unobtrusive exposition of events which are literally imperceptible in the case of Hetty's pregnancy, the narrative approximates the characters' sense of the gradual and almost unnoticed passing of their present moments.

The well-known excursus which constitutes chapter 17 of *Adam Bede* reveals George Eliot's desire to affirm this impression of leisure and detachment as she prepares to move beyond it. The narrator, like Mrs. Poyser, is allowed to "have his say out." The chapter resembles Scott's prefatory comments in the Waverley novels—the comic dialogues between the Great Unknown and his narrators in *The Fortunes of Nigel* or *Peveril of the Peak*—and its argument recalls Wordsworth's preface to the *Lyrical Ballads*. Yet, more in the manner of chapter 47 of *Dombey and Son* or of "How to Live Well on Nothing

A-Year" in *Vanity Fair*, the narrator offers his crucial commentary in
the middle of the story. Moreover, the "Story Pauses a Little" so that
he can reintroduce the reader to the fictional world after the break
created by the end of the first volume. The placement of this discursive chapter is yet another example of the immediacy of the concern
George Eliot expressed for her reader's responses at this point in her
career. John Blackwood had complained about her portrayal of Irwine:
"I wish for the sake of my Church of England friends he had more of
'the root of the matter in him.' However I hope he is to sublime as the
story goes on" (*Letters*, 2:445–46). Perhaps Blackwood was recalling
his earlier fears about Tryan, but no George Eliot character is likely "to
sublime" if his creator can prevent that outcome. Blackwood's misguided aesthetic standards therefore became the basis of the argument of chapter 17.

Significantly, in this chapter George Eliot moves from a dialogue
between the narrator and mock-reader, a technique that recalls the
Scenes and occasionally occurs in Scott's novels, to a dialogue between
character and narrator, a technique that harks back to similar narrative strategies in a number of the *Lyrical Ballads*. In the manner of
both Blackwood and Mrs. Farthingale in "Amos Barton," "one of my
readers" lodges the initial complaint about Irwine, and after the narrator's defense of that portrait, "my good friend" continues to act as the
proponent of idealism in literature. The narrator then sets out to refute
such callow demands. Like the voice of *Vanity Fair*, he instructs the
mock-reader. As a minister might instruct a parishioner seated in a
pew, he admonishes him: "Examine your words well, and you will find
that even when you have no motive to be false, it is a very hard thing to
say the exact truth" (1:268). The narrator provides a text for his lesson just as Seth or Dinah or Adam would. Because the novel is a picture, the "text" he appeals to is Dutch genre painting. He describes
several scenes typical of this school of painters; they are much more
"commonplace" than his own preceding pictures of Broxton Rectory or
Hall Farm. In a passage reminiscent of *Dombey and Son* as well as
Vanity Fair, he exhorts the reader and adopts the manner of the sermon: "But let us love that other beauty too, which lies in no secret of
proportion, but in the secret of deep human sympathy." Yet the narrator assumes this attitude of superiority so that he can dispense with it.

From the middle of the chapter to its conclusion, he no longer poses as the creator, the preacher, the measure of moral values. Rather, he becomes, like the mock-reader, a fallible man in need of moral guidance. Instead of saying, "I won't paint an angel," he says, supposedly to the "idealistic friend" who has just objected to Dutch paintings, "Paint us an angel, if you can . . . but do not impose on us any aesthetic rules which shall banish from the region of Art those old women scraping carrots."[7] His continued plea—"Therefore let Art always remind us" of "common coarse people" (1 : 270)—suggests that he, like the reader, needs such reminders. By talking about the moral effect that Dutch paintings have on him, the narrator has turned himself into the recipient rather than the source of art's moral benefits. To support his argument, the narrator now turns not to another artistic model, but to the character, Adam Bede, "to whom I talked of these matters in his old age" (1 : 272). He presents a dialogue he has had with Adam long after the action of the story has concluded, and here the character serves as the moral instructor. The narrator, in turn, plays the role of the mock-reader, the morally obtuse man who prompts further lessons by his insistently incorrect statements and questions.

This development recalls the frequent interchanges between narrator and character in the *Lyrical Ballads* or in a later poem like "Resolution and Independence," and it exemplifies George Eliot's rejection of Scott's methods and her acceptance of Wordsworth's. Although the questions posed by his often stubbornly uncomprehending narrators sometimes border on the comic, as Lewis Carroll's parody in "The White Knight's Tale" demonstrates, such dialogues are based on assumptions that George Eliot is quick to exploit. The conversation recorded in chapter 17, like that in chapter 62 of *Vanity Fair*, erases any distinction between the fictive status of narrator and character; if they can converse together, they must partake of the same reality. In a more serious fashion than is evident in Thackeray's sleight-of-hand, George Eliot locates the source of her story within the story itself. Yet the attitudes of her narrator are more akin to those of the speakers in "Michael" and "The Thorn" than to those of either Thackeray's young English gentleman or Scott's personas. Furthermore, by demonstrating his need to hear what Adam has to say, her narrator outlines the moral relation between himself and the story in which Adam is a principal actor. For Scott, on the contrary, such relations are themselves insignificant and even expendable, and in novels like *Ivanhoe* or *The Monastery* they serve as comic and irrelevant literary games. Chapter 17 also clarifies the narrator's role as mediator; he, like Pendennis and Mary Smith, asks the questions the reader would like to ask. Yet the choice of Adam rather than, say, Irwine as the spokesman proves that the Wordsworthian version of such mediation predominates. Like the narrators in "Old Man Travelling" or "We are Seven" or "Anecdote for Fathers," the narrator in *Adam Bede* is the gentlemanly but rather misguided interlocutor to whom the rural character offers the wisdom of experience. The "lower" nature reveals the folly of the "higher" nature by remaining true to the integrity of his simple beliefs. Such dialogues occur at least twice within the action of *Adam Bede*—Irwine questions Dinah about her preaching, and the stranger in chapter 2 asks Casson the landlord about the villagers—and even Casson's clearly limited perspective is given a patient hearing. It would not be unusual to find a character like Adam Bede in a Scott novel (Old Mortality, after all, is the source of Peter Pattieson's story about the Covenanters), but the characters comparable to Adam, Andrew Fairservice or Cuddie Headrigg or Caleb Balderstone, are the butt of comic relief, not, like Adam, the source of moral awareness. A comment from *The Bride of Lammermoor* marks the distance that class distinctions render inevitable in Scott: "Even the distresses, excuses, evasions, and shifts of Caleb afforded amusement to the young men" (chap. 8, p. 78). The heroic figure of Jeanie Deans is also portrayed from this perspective. The narrator's attitude—and therefore the reader's—approximates that of the Duke of Argyle. His admiration of Jeanie's integrity never erases his sense of his own superiority; indeed, her plight is a measure of his power and authority. It is not that class distinctions disappear in *Adam Bede*. They are a reality that cannot be avoided, but they have ceased to be the basis of moral distinctions.

Clearly, the most important development of chapter 17 is not the narrator's decision to step into the picture that he paints, but his readiness to bow out of the scene; like the ghosts of *A Christmas Carol*, he becomes almost silent so that the character can comment, in his own words, on the action. His modest self-effacement is the converse of Scott's impulse to offer the reader a literary and literate version of a lower-class character's stories. As Peter Pattieson says of Old Mortality, "I have been far from adopting either his style, his opinions, or even his facts" (chap. 1, p. 9). Instead of using as his "texts" Dutch genre painting or the pastoral tradition of classical literature, the narrator has accorded authoritative status to the "real" character's impressions and his quite Wordsworthian "real" language. Significantly, Adam himself dismisses both "texts" and "notions." Neither serves to clarify our understanding of human or divine mysteries: "It isn't notions sets people doing the right thing—it's feelings" (1:272); and chapter 17 allows Adam the opportunity to voice his feelings on a number of crucial questions. The narrator still insists upon the reader's distance from the fictive world. It is still a picture. He is still a mediator between the reader and the character, but he is beginning to approach the ideal which Wordsworth outlines in his 1802 addition to the preface to the *Lyrical Ballads*. It is the "wish of the Poet to bring his feelings near to those of the persons whose feelings he describes, nay, for short spaces of time perhaps, to let himself slip into an entire delusion, and even confound and identify his own feelings with theirs." Such sympathetic identification is at the source of George Eliot's conception of the moral imagination. Yet Wordsworth goes on to suggest why Adam is allowed to speak directly to the narrator and why the narrator quotes rather than paraphrases his words. According to Wordsworth, the poet's engagement with his subject teaches him that "no words, which his fancy or imagination can suggest, will be to be compared with those which are the emanations of reality and truth" (p. 166). The metamorphosis of the narrator's role in chapter 17 foretells the time in *Adam Bede* when such principles will define George Eliot's conception of an "art of vision" that is also an act of feeling.

Before the time comes, however, George Eliot seems to be proceeding by a definite narrative strategy. The narrative qualities of the novel—the slow unfolding of time, the sense of expectancy, the pictorial quality, and the emphasis on notions and texts—all seem to be moving toward a foreseeable end. Some expectations will be fulfilled, others disappointed; some ideas refuted, others confirmed; some texts dismissed, others verified. The reader is led to expect certain outcomes in the novel just as the characters hope for certain events in their lives. Yet "My Aunt's Story" demands that George Eliot introduce into this fictional world a disruption so radical that it essentially transforms the way in which the characters conceive of their lives and the reader's established relationship to the narrative. According to the time scheme of *Adam Bede*, the literally "obscene" beginning of Hetty's sexual relationship with Arthur occurs between the third and fourth books, at the halfway point in the novel. Hetty's pregnancy is developing in its slow, unnoticed course until it cannot be ignored. Her decision to leave Hayslope is the first overt rupture in the apparently impassive world of *Adam Bede*. The world which we have been encouraged to see as both Edenic and picturesque now reveals its essential reality, as the equilibrium of existence is disturbed and replaced by useless activity. The present, formerly dominated by the potentiality of the imagined future, becomes a painfully experienced moment of active suffering, suffering augmented by the memory of irrevocable loss. Pictures, scenes, attitudes of expectancy, all become journeys. Texts and words are obliterated by sensations. Slowly unfolding time turns into repetitive cycles. Moreover, the reader's distance from a character is dissolved by George Eliot's demands for active participation, and all these developments strengthen the perceptual analogy that identifies the characters' lives and the reader's experience of them.

Preparations for this radical transformation have occurred throughout the first two volumes. When Dinah sits at her bedchamber window and contemplates the evening landscape, her thoughts reveal the futility of imagining "pictures" of the future. The view from her window is a "mere scene" when compared to the realities of "life's journey." She suggests the pathos of Hetty's presence in that scene when she thinks of her as "a child hugging its toys in the beginning of a long toilsome journey" (1 : 234–36). At the beginning of volume 3, the four main characters all undertake such journeys. Hetty's "Journey in Hope" to Windsor is actually a pilgrimage of disillusionment. She arrives at Windsor only to find that Arthur has gone to Ireland; she confronts the "borders of a new wilderness where no goal lay before her" (2 : 135). The goals of her "Journey in Despair" are equally elusive. When she does reach the pool she has been seeking, "it was as if the thing were come in spite of herself, instead of being the object of her search" (2 : 146). Later, when she tries to find another pool, she finds only a hole beneath the nut bush. When she tries to return to the baby she has abandoned, she finds that it has disappeared. In "The Quest," Adam undertakes a search also characterized by elusive goals and wasted motion. Although he sets out with complete confidence that he will find Hetty at Snowfield, he learns that she has never been there. Like the locale of "The Thorn," the "barer and barer" landscape (2:158) that he finds in Snowfield is the physical equivalent of the "hard, inevitable reality" (2:167) he must confront. His "long, long journey" (2:162) only leads to the point of departure; after two days wasted in "almost useless" inquiries, he returns home. In three separate places, George Eliot establishes the point that Dinah has been on a trip to Leeds the entire time that Hetty is away from Hayslope. This journey would be unremarkable if it were not for another point that George Eliot continually emphasizes. Dinah has gone to an unknown destination. It is doubtful that she can be reached by letter. Like Hetty's, her journey is a kind of exile, one which places her beyond normal human contact. In returning from Liverpool, Arthur, like both Hetty and Adam, begins a journey in hope and ends in despair. When he reaches the Chase, Irwine's letter informs him that his hoped-for goal, his inheritance of the squire's role, has been replaced by the proof of the one "ugly fault" in his life (2:231). The end of his trip turns into the beginning of another journey, this time to Stoniton. From chapter 36 to chapter 44, all the main characters are "poor wanderers," ancient mariners set on their way by a crime against community.

The dispersion of these characters on their journeys involves a substantial quickening of narrative pace. Although Hetty's journeys are "wearily long" (2:130) and marked by difficulty, the actual narration is rapid. Seven days pass in one chapter, "Journey in Hope." The movements of the characters are carefully calculated to correspond to each other, but different chapters cover the same time period, so that time repeats and doubles back on itself. Adam's journey (chap. 38) takes place at the same time as the events treated in chapters 36 and 37. "Arthur's Return" narrates the action that corresponds in time to that recorded from chapter 30 to chapter 43. The trial scenes and Hetty's confession to Dinah contain within them narrations of events from Hetty's night in the hovel to her arrest. Like the images of circularity in

Little Dorrit, these temporal repetitions suggest that each character's "objectless wandering" (2:153) exists within a larger framework of purposeless, recurrent action.

Irwine views Hetty's arrest as a "terrible illumination which the present sheds back upon the past" (2:180). The new light cast by this event transforms vision into sensation. Here again the quality of the characters' perceptions is a touchstone for the reader's. Hetty's only conception of the future is now expressed, not by a picture of herself in a fine dress or by her image in a mirror, but by a physical reaction to the present. The "beginning of hardship is like the first taste of bitter food . . . if there is nothing else to satisfy our hunger, we take another bite and find it possible to go on" (2:127). The transformation of image into sensory response is prefigured earlier, when Hetty reads the letter in which Arthur advises her to "try to forget everything." "When she looked up from [this letter] there was the reflection of a blanched face in the old dim glass—a white marble face with rounded childish forms, but with something sadder than a child's pain in it. Hetty did not see the face—she saw nothing—she only felt that she was cold and sick and trembling" (2:65–66). Although such frightening physical reactions disappear once Hetty decides to marry Adam, they are a warning of the condition that will eventually prevail. After her arrest Hetty experiences only regret for the past and pain in the present, not hope for the future. Her past exists as both a scene—"that place in the wood" (2:251)—and a sensation, the hallucinatory sound of her baby's cry. Like the sea captain in "The Thorn," Hetty is obsessed by a place and a cry. Her relationship to her child is expressed as a sensation: as the albatross weighs down the Ancient Mariner, so the child is "a heavy weight hanging round [her] neck" (2:249). Adam also reacts to the present as if it were a physical force: "The reality—the hard, inevitable reality—of his troubles pressed upon him with a new weight" (2:167). Adam's reactions to events exemplify the kind of stasis that lies at the end of the pointless journeys the characters undertake, and his sensory responses are shared by Irwine, Arthur, and the Poysers, as well as by Hetty. For the child-murderer herself, such stasis is literally a prison cell. As Hetty journeys toward that point of immobility, George Eliot asks the reader not to see her as a modern

Hebe or nymph, but to feel with and for a woman whose mental limitation and concrete physical reality are themselves the form of her
suffering.

Earlier in the novel, George Eliot devotes considerable time to conveying Hetty's thoughts to the reader, but the mode of their presentation usually demonstrates his distance from Hetty. When describing
her hopes, the narrator comments, "Hetty had never read a novel; if
she had ever seen one, I think the words would have been too hard for
her." Novels, obviously, are not phenomena unknown to the reader.
Even less could Hetty understand the simile that the narrator uses to
describe her situation: "It was as if she had been wooed by a river-god"
(1:202). But when George Eliot comes to narrate Hetty's experiences
from the moment she leaves Hayslope until the moment of her arrest,
she presents those actions in Hetty's own terms. As Barbara Hardy has
noted, George Eliot here develops a "dramatic method which presents
the character in its nakedness,"[8] and the term *nakedness* quite accurately describes Hetty's status as an elemental figure, a fact as natural
and immediate as the rural landscape itself. The reader is submerged
in a narration of physical realities which recognize no intellectual or
class distinctions. Here George Eliot has discovered the emotive and
poetic potential of her language; the psychological subtlety of her images and their sometimes uncanny, almost visionary power clearly announce the future author of *Middlemarch* and *Daniel Deronda*. All the
earlier conventional comments on the dangers of a pretty face are
swept away in the narrator's response to the authenticity and integrity
of a character and her trials. The vitality of the prose in these chapters
invites the reader's imaginative participation. He is almost caught up
by the movement of the style: "When she got off this coach, she began
to walk again, and take cheap rides in carts, and get cheap meals,
going on and on without distinct purpose, yet strangely, by some fascination, taking the way she had come" (2:143–44). The intensity of
these passages recalls Dickens's description of Sikes's flight in *Oliver
Twist*, and it demands a similarly visceral response: "The horror of this
cold, and darkness, and solitude—out of all human reach—became
greater every long minute: it was almost as if she were dead already,
and knew that she was dead, and longed to get back to life again"

(2 : 147–48). The reader is invited to participate in Hetty's experience because the rhythms and the simplicity of the language used to describe it are themselves mimetic of her fear and desperation.

Ultimately the narrative is reduced to the barest essentials when Hetty speaks directly to Dinah; a mediator no longer stands between Hetty's experience and the reader's grasp of it. George Eliot's handling of the exposition of the period from the night Hetty tries to drown herself to her arrest emphasizes this narrative development. The account of Hetty's journey breaks off after chapter 37; from chapter 38 through chapter 42, the reader's attention is directed toward Adam, Irwine, and Arthur. The narrative of the trial moves from Bartle Massey's account of the proceedings (chap. 42) to Adam's and therefore to the reader's actual attendance at the trial (chap. 43). Similarly, the narrative moves from the accounts of the trial witnesses, Sarah Stone and John Olding, to Hetty's account of herself in her confession to Dinah. This first-person narrative completes the two "Journey" chapter accounts. The novel moves from observation of Hetty, including that offered by the narrator, from the detached viewpoint of those "who told Hetty Sorrel's story by their firesides in their old age" (2 : 216), to her subjective revelation of what she felt and did.

The effect of this process is wholly to invalidate any conventional response to Hetty and her actions. As she is reduced to the level of her physical reality—no more a responsible moral agent than a child or an animal—the reader is invited to see her plight primarily in its physical terms. Because he can be persuaded to feel what Hetty feels, he is asked, as Dinah and Adam are asked, to accept such physicality as part of his own human nature. An earlier account of a child-murder, co-authored by Dickens and published in *Household Words* (10 May 1851), suggests just how radical and how successful George Eliot's approach is. A woman named Maria Clarke has killed her child by burying it alive. To guarantee that we will feel a full measure of moral repulsion when told of this crime, the journalists use the same technique that George Eliot would later employ to achieve a quite dissimilar effect:

She took a spade, and going into a meadow,—but let her own confession tell the tale. "I took the spade—went into the meadow—dug a hole—and laid my child in." She appears, in the first instance, to have deluded herself, as to the legal consequences she incurred, with some half-delirious sophistry about not directly murdering the child, but only getting rid of it out of the way. "I then covered the child over with earth." But the child screams, and then all other human feeling vanishes in terror for herself. "To stifle its screams," says she, "I stamped upon the sod. *When the child was covered up with the earth, I heard it cry!*" Can anything ever yet recorded of crime, exceed this?[9]

The case bears a remarkable resemblance to Hetty's, yet the effect of Maria Clarke's confession is only to increase the reader's sense of moral distance, the "wide space" between himself and the speaker. George Eliot does not avoid the horror of the event she depicts; her readers are not asked to ignore the crime so that they can excuse the criminal. Rather, they are encouraged to experience with her the "bruises and gashes" which her actions cause.

At this point George Eliot's imaginative sympathy for Hetty has gone as far as, perhaps farther than, she herself intended. She has fulfilled completely the Wordsworthian prescription that the poet "slip into an entire delusion, . . . even confound and identify his own feelings" with those of the character he portrays. As George Eliot so accurately noted in her "History of 'Adam Bede,'" "the scene in the prison [was] of course the climax towards which I worked" (*Letters*, 2:503). The conclusions that such a climax would have suggested are, at best, disturbing. The novel depends extensively on moral concepts and texts, but the action of volume 3 suggests a radical questioning of all texts and notions. After Hetty's arrest and confession, Adam's belief in the sustaining value of work becomes meaningless. All Arthur's talk about a "man's plain duty" takes on the most biting of ironies. Life has become a series of journeys to elusive goals; all activity implies a return to one's starting point. Just as journeys prolong themselves and seem to usurp the will of the traveler, so actions begin to tyrannize over the actor. At the end of this process lies stasis—not rest, but a dehumanizing existence as a statue, a "stone." Such a climax would have conveyed the Wordsworthian sense in which "Suffering is permanent, obscure and dark, / And shares the nature of infinity" (*The Borderers*, ll. 1543–44).

Yet, instead of ending on this note, acting rather on Lewes's advice, George Eliot decided to conclude the novel with the reconciliations and reconstitutions that characterize *The Heart of Mid-Lothian*. Like

Jeanie Deans, Arthur arrives in the nick of time with Hetty's reprieve. Like Effie, Hetty is given a second chance. Community, once threatened by the Poysers' plans to leave Hayslope, is reestablished. Adam and Dinah marry and establish a home that accommodates three generations of characters, just as Jeanie and Butler find a new and better home on Argyle's island of Roseneath. The last ten chapters of *Adam Bede* reverse the direction that the action has so precipitously taken as well as all its previous implications. Earlier the narrator has impressed upon the reader the idea that Arthur and Hetty's actions are, like Adam and Eve's, irrevocable. The fortunate results of the Christian Fall depend on a dimension of spiritual reality that is no longer available to George Eliot as a source of consolation. Yet it is consolation that she wants for her readers, her characters, and herself. The novel has tended toward a demonstration of Adam's statement that "there's a sort of wrong that can never be made up for" (2:379). By manipulating Hetty's fate, both Arthur and his creator are given the sense that they can erase the consequences of events they have initiated. By choosing to end the novel in a way that she did not originally envision, George Eliot casts doubt on the very perspectives that she has so carefully developed.

Late in *Adam Bede* the narrator proposes the imaginative equivalent of the evolutionary claim that progress once made cannot be negated: "The growth of higher feeling within us is like the growth of faculty, bringing with it a sense of added strength: we can no more wish to return to a narrower sympathy, than a painter or a musician can wish to return to his cruder manner, or a philosopher to his less complete formula" (2:365). At the end of *Adam Bede*, however, George Eliot returns to both the "narrower sympathy" and the "cruder manner" of the first two volumes. Scott's mode of distanced observation now replaces the Wordsworthian ideal of imaginative identification. Action is again presented to the reader through a mediator. When Arthur rides up with Hetty's reprieve, the scene is first described from the point of view of the onlookers: "It was a sight that some people remembered better even than their own sorrows—the sight in that grey clear morning, when the fatal cart with the two young women in it was descried by the waiting watching multitude" (2:262). The conventional melodrama of this conventional romance scene is emphasized by the artificiality of a phrase like "fatal cart" and by George Eliot's use of the present tense when Arthur rides up, "his eyes . . . glazed by madness" (2:263). Yet the narrator draws back even farther from this picture. The wedding of Adam and Dinah is a sight that not even he sees directly; speaking of the other characters, he says, "I envy them all the sight they had when the marriage was fairly ended and Adam led Dinah out of church" (2:371). The narrator also distances himself from the characters. He pretends, with obvious coyness, not to know what Dinah feels about Adam. His attitude toward the characters at the harvest supper is generally one of ironic condescension, and his commentary ceases to have a vital connection to the life of the novel. His often quoted description of Old Leisure is very much beside the point. The kind of life that the country gentleman Old Leisure enjoys corresponds not at all to the lives of Adam, Irwine, or even old Squire Donnithorne.

The artistic uncertainty evident in *Adam Bede* resides, therefore, in its ending, in its reversion to narrative methods with which it has earlier dispensed, not, as recent critical accounts would suggest, in George Eliot's conception of the novel as a whole. There is perhaps a quite personal as well as aesthetic explanation for this situation. In achieving an "art of vision" that rejects the conventions of art, in identifying her character with her persona, George Eliot probably did not realize that both the character's reality and her own identification with it would become as overpowering as they evidently are. Instead of punishing Hetty for her beauty, as some readers too easily assume that George Eliot has done,[10] she chose Hetty as the character for whom she would demand the reader's closest attention and most wide-ranging sympathy. Yet one can see why George Eliot would wish to re-treat from such a perspective. The *style indirect libre* of Hetty's journeys and the direct address of her confession are stunning imaginative and emotional achievements. But it is one thing to identify with an Amos Barton or an Edgar Tryan and quite another to "confound" one's sense of self with that of a Hetty Sorrel. For a woman actually involved in an illicit relationship, such identification would be both a natural and an undesirable outcome. Perhaps like Conrad, who dreaded the total absorption that his imaginative life required of him, George Eliot sensed the danger that Hetty would usurp her narrative identity. If an equilibrium were to be achieved and such consequences averted, Hetty would have to be set once again at a distance. That, I think, is precisely why she is treated so cursorily after she has made her confession. The death of this "poor wanderer" is merely a fleeting shadow in the otherwise "dazzling" picture of legitimate love that dominates the epilogue. Yet the scene in the prison and its power remain unchanged by the narrative compromises that follow. Hetty's confession is one of those rare experiences that Adam describes to the narrator in chapter 17. It is a time "when feelings come into you like a rushing mighty wind, as the Scripture says, and part your life in two a'most, so as you look back on yourself as if you was somebody else" (1 : 274). The reader who has followed George Eliot's progression from the detached observation of Hetty to intimate contact can never see her or the fictive world of which she is a part with quite the same eyes. The narrator asks that the reader be as changed as Scrooge and Janet are by their experiences.

By granting Hetty the place occupied by character in the linked circle of analogous bonds, George Eliot makes those bonds both more powerful and more threatening than they are in the work of either Dickens or Thackeray. In *Adam Bede* the reader's representative within the world of the novel, the figure comparable to Arthur Clennam or Janet Dempster, is Adam. Like Janet in his self-righteousness and hardness of heart, Adam must confront and accept the unflattering reflection Hetty's actions cast on his facile assumptions about our capacities for violence and destruction. When he stands by Hetty during her trial, the reader is asked to take the same stand. Similarly, the narrator's analogue, like Florence Dombey or Little Dorrit or Edgar Tryan, is Dinah. She elicits the confession from Hetty; she, like the narrator of chapter 17, lets the character have "her say out." Yet the bond that eventually unites these analogues in the earlier works—the spiritual fellowship of Janet and Tryan, the wedding of Little Dorrit and Clennam—becomes in *Adam Bede* a marital bond which joins Adam and Dinah only to exclude Hetty and Seth Bede and Arthur Donnithorne as well. The circle is both completed and segmented by the same event. Moreover, the ties that link narrator and reader in chapter 17 equate living and reading as effectively as either the narrator's tale-telling role in chapter 62 of *Vanity Fair* or Thackeray's request that the reader join the dinner guests in *The Newcomes*. But Hetty's confession threatens to collapse that equation into simple identification. While she speaks, narrative mediation is no longer necessary or possible. To maintain this approach would, of course, involve the narrator's disappearance. In moving from the methods of Scott to those of Wordsworth, George Eliot was moving toward the modern novel. Yet if Hetty's halting, inarticulate confession is a step in the direction of Molly Bloom's night thoughts, George Eliot, unlike Joyce, is not ready to let her authorial presence be, "like the God of the creation, . . . refined out of existence."

Whatever its more disturbing implications, however, the scene in the prison is, for both its creator and its reader, an exceptionally demanding exercise in the moral imagination. In drawing on Hetty's "real language," George Eliot requires of her readers "that attention to what is apart from themselves, which may be called the raw material of moral sentiment" (*Essays*, p. 270). Such attention may indeed impress with the weight of pain. By basing the goals of her first novel in the mid-century ideal of imaginative sympathy, George Eliot discovered not only the irrefutable claims of character but also an "art of vision" that attempts to be more animate than artistic and more tactile than visionary.

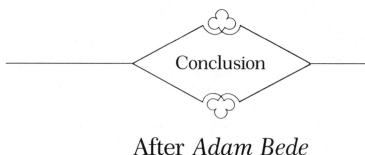

Conclusion

After *Adam Bede*
Severing Relations

My last words about Jim shall be few. I affirm he had achieved greatness; but the thing would be dwarfed in the telling, or rather in the hearing. Frankly, it is not my words that I mistrust but your minds.
— Marlow in *Lord Jim* (1900)

Adam Bede is by no means the last word on the bonds of narration. Its publication in 1859 does not mark the end of their usefulness as a goal nor is it the final demonstration of the possibility or the difficulty of their achievement. In *Great Expectations* (1860–61) the alignment of the narrator's, reader's, and character's vision is the given of Dickens's narrative approach, and one might argue that this, his most successful attempt to coordinate the complexities of psychological, social, and moral life, results from his use of a first-person narrator telling his own tale. Four years after the death of Thackeray in 1863, Trollope published his *Last Chronicle of Barset*. There the experiential equation of the characters' lives and the reader's aesthetic experience rests on the same ties of gossip, rumor, and scandal that had sustained a similar analogy in *Vanity Fair*. Yet, as Ian Gregor has pointed out, *Adam Bede* is both an "end and a beginning"; it marks a "notable change in the art of fiction."[1] Gregor's comment pertains to a shift in focus from public to private; but, as my concluding remarks on *Adam Bede* have already suggested, his assessment equally describes the passing away of mid-century ideals. *Great Expectations*, like *Adam Bede*, reveals such antithetical impulses. Dickens's use of autobiographical form in this novel, unlike its partial use in *Bleak House*, implies that character alone is a sufficient vehicle of narrative meaning. The omniscience which, in Dickens's hands, had been a form of mediation, is here a perspective hovering unexpressed beyond the actual narration. In many ways the relationship of Pip and Estella recalls the imaginative import of the marriage of Little Dorrit and Clennam. Here, however, we do not know whether Pip will embrace the woman who, like Esmond's Beatrix, has embodied the escape and fulfillment promised by romance. The tentative nature of the novel's conclusion suggests that the author's relation to his fictive world has now become more indirect, the significant imaginative relations more oblique. Even a brief look at George Eliot's major fiction will confirm this impression.

In *Adam Bede*, when Irwine claims that "men's lives are as thoroughly blended with each other as the air they breathe" (2:205), he recalls the metaphor of physical relation invoked in chapter 47 of *Dombey and Son*. In *Middlemarch* George Eliot returns to Teufelsdröckh's "organic filaments" to make the same point, but now she insists that one's "sense of connection with a manifold pregnant existence [has] to be kept up painfully as an inward vision" (p. 189). The wisdom and composure exhibited by the narrator invite the reader to develop his capacity for such vision, and George Eliot's use of the metaphor of the web itself provides the analogies that had characterized mid-century fiction. The narrator is a spinner at work on "this particular web," a more refined and reliable version of the gossip Mrs. Taft, "who was always counting stitches and gather[ing] her information in misleading fragments caught between the rows of her knitting, [and who] had got it into her head that Mr Lydgate was a natural son of Bulstrode's" (pp. 96, 182). Once again, gossip is the tie that unites the interests of reader, character, and narrator. This thread is extended to include Dorothea and Rosamond, the characters who determine the fates of the men with whom they live, when they are compared to Ariadne—though Rosamond is condescendingly labeled an Ariadne of the "charming stage" variety (p. 207). These linked analogies generate new connections as the reader, with Dorothea, is invited to inhabit at least temporarily the labyrinthine corridors of both Casaubon's house and his mind.

Yet that sojourn is soon judged to be a "moral imprisonment" which it is a mercy to escape, and the bonds that might unite the agents of narration in *Middlemarch* are less complete, less lasting than those of *Adam Bede*. The figure of a circle is no longer an appropriate spatial image for the temporal narrative process. Similarly, no character can fulfill the role of Janet Dempster and mediate between an individual and the community. Dorothea's attempts to reconcile Lydgate and the Middlemarchers are signally unsuccessful. Bulstrode does not even come within the compass of her concern. In the crucial confrontation between Will Ladislaw and Bulstrode in chapter 61, the narrator specifically states that "no third person listening could have thoroughly understood" the feelings of the participants (p. 432). The "third person" who does understand is, of course, the narrator, but to achieve such knowledge or to communicate it, the narrator must go beyond what the two characters can know of each other. In many ways *Middlemarch* is the epitome of the *via media* of Victorian fiction, but already the goal of a "keen vision, and a feeling for all ordinary life," the mid-century ideal on which the circle of analogous bonds depends, is ultimately unapproachable. It is a Palingenesia which no narrative bridge can reach; it stands on "the other side of silence." *Middlemarch* unwillingly sketches this conclusion, but nowhere are its implications more evident than in George Eliot's last novel, *Daniel Deronda* (1876).

Like Dorothea, Deronda stands for the values of the moral imagination that George Eliot continues to cherish. At the same time, his characterization more clearly illuminates their potential dangers. He is described in terms that recall George Eliot's definitions of her vocation as a novelist: "Persons attracted him . . . in proportion to the possibility of his defending them, of rescuing them, telling upon their lives with some sort of redeeming influence" (2:71). George Eliot once said that "young men" are "just the class I care most to influence" (*Letters*, 4:397), and Deronda seems to be a young man brought up on the novels she wrote. Yet she does not create in Deronda the ideal argument for her values. The other characters in the novel may consider Deronda a deity, but by doing so, they reveal their own desperate need for a personalized and familiar source of authority, not George Eliot's faith in Deronda's ability to fulfill that role. His "too reflective and diffusive sympathy" threatens to become so inclusive that it will negate "moral force" (2:132). As Hans Meyrick points out, Deronda would take an antediluvian point of view before he would do injustice to a megatherium. The terminology here is significant. Like Hardy's Jude Fawley, Deronda is an anachronism. In Jude's case, the values of the mid-century novelist, translated to a *fin de siècle* atmosphere, have become more than potential disabilities; they are the burdens of consciousness to which the character must submit. Jude's sympathy with life's victims, whether they be a flock of hungry birds or a supposedly pregnant pig farmer's daughter, transforms him into their victim. Deronda, of course, escapes such a fate—in his world it is still possible to marry the right woman—but his weaknesses and dilemmas obviously foretell the plight of individuals like Jude or Conrad's Lord Jim, characters for whom imagination itself is an incapacitating limitation which offers no compensatory advantages.

Deronda is, metaphorically if not actually, the last in the long line of increasingly secular clerics who epitomize the aims of George Eliot's fiction. Throughout the novel he tries to be for others what Tryan has been for Janet Dempster. He succeeds most obviously in the case of Mirah Cohen, and she is less in need of moral guidance than almost any other character in the novel. Deronda's mother dismisses as nonsense his claims that his imagination allows him to participate in her suffering. Her telling of her own story effectively silences this would-be comforter. Deronda's effect on Gwendolen Harleth is more complicated, but no more conclusively satisfying. She turns to him as to a "priest," but more often than not, he has no story, no words, which could help her as Tryan's have helped Janet:

Words seemed to have no more rescue in them than if he had been beholding a vessel in peril of wreck—the poor ship with its many-lived anguish beaten by the inescapable storm. How could he grasp the long-growing process of this young creature's wretchedness? how arrest and change it with a sentence? He was afraid of his own voice. The words that rushed into his mind seemed in their feebleness nothing better than despair made audible, or than that insensibility to another's hardship which applies precept to soothe pain. He felt himself holding a crowd of words imprisoned within his lips, as if the letting them escape would be a violation of awe before the mysteries of our human lot. (3:99–100)

When Deronda does finally speak to Gwendolen, his words merely "widen his spiritual distance from her" and render "more difficult" her own attempts at confession (3 : 229). Although she eventually tells him that her life will be "better" because she has known him, her halting words merely highlight the inconclusiveness of the novel's ending. In "Janet's Repentance," the narrator could turn to Janet as the living monument of Tryan's function and, by implication, as proof of the novelist's effectiveness. In *Daniel Deronda*, that statuesque form has turned into an image of Gwendolen's sad face.

In treating the sexual potential of the relationship between Deronda and Gwendolen, George Eliot presents her most straightforward recognition of the forces that often come in conflict with even the most earnest of moral intentions. Like the depiction of Pip and Estella in *Great Expectations*, this relationship, posited but even more clearly denied, is a metaphor of its creator's increasingly difficult art. George Eliot's relation to Deronda approaches the kind of covert identification and even more covert judgment that characterizes Joyce's relation to Stephen Dedalus and Lawrence's relation to either Paul Morel or Birkin. Perhaps for this reason, narrative voice in *Daniel Deronda* is more reticent than it is in her earlier fiction, less willing to articulate the values of the sympathetic imagination and the community. Though the narrator does not relinquish omniscience, the task of conveying such values is here, as it is in *Great Expectations*, the burden that character must bear. Despite the doubts it casts on the ultimate power of sympathy, *Middlemarch* ends with an affirmation, indeed a celebration of Dorothea's effect on others. The ending of *Daniel Deronda*, however, is more equivocal. Deronda and Mirah go off to search for a community that may not exist; that the Middle East has less substantial reality for the reader than the urban world into which Dorothea disappears is a comment on George Eliot's uncertainty. In novels like *Vanity Fair* and *Little Dorrit* and even *Middlemarch*, the Victorian novelist developed to a consummate degree a form which qualifies the traditional happy ending and makes it resonate with complex implications. Affirmation is balanced by the recognition of difficulty; hope is set against the realization that it may be inappropriate. But *Daniel Deronda* tips the balance toward negation. The narrator concludes not with his own words, but with a quotation from *Samson Agonistes*; it is as if his speech, like Deronda's, might be a "violation of awe." Storytelling as a source of relations and mediations is no longer the powerful force it has been.

Though *Daniel Deronda* is perhaps at least psychologically and stylistically George Eliot's greatest achievement and the farthest reach of her art, most readers would agree that she has gone beyond the bonds connecting reader, narrator, and character that have, even up to this point, been crucial to the imaginative and moral success of her fiction.

The reasons for this development are obvious. Again, as in the earlier establishment of mid-century ideals and goals, they depend on the conjunction of internal and external impulses. George Eliot's maturity—the years of deepening insight and more limited capacity for affirmation—coincided with social factors that undermined the relation between novelist and public, the source and object of the mid-century faith in the bonds wrought by imagination. Although George Eliot had feared that *Adam Bede* was "too unflattering to dominant fashions ever to be very popular" (*Letters*, 3:191), its immediate and almost faddish success proved her wrong. To have one's novel quoted in Parliament and cherished by Victoria herself is no negligible measure of one's ability to accommodate private vision and public taste. Yet in writing *Romola* (1862–63), George Eliot would produce a work almost as certain to alienate its audience as Thackeray's *Virginians*. Now she would say, more pointedly and more accurately than she had said of the *Scenes* and *Adam Bede*, that she was writing for an elite:

Of necessity, the book is addressed to fewer readers than my previous works, and I myself have never expected—I might rather say *intended*—that the book should be as "popular" in the same sense as the others. If one is to have freedom to write out of one's own varying unfolding self, and not be a machine always grinding out the same material or spinning the same sort of web, one cannot always write for the same public. (*Letters*, 4:49)

Here we must take into account the amount of self-protection and self-defense prevalent in all George Eliot's comments on her work. She would have been delighted by an enthusiastic and widespread appreciation of *Romola*, and she was disappointed when it did not materialize. But her apparent superiority to the general public, proclaimed in the name of artistic integrity and freedom, is as much a sign of the times as Thackeray's conversion to moral responsibility had been in 1847. The divorce between novelist and general public was soon to become an accomplished fact. As George Eliot lamented later in the decade, her novels were not the ones displayed in railway bookstalls, and the mass of travelers would not buy and read them if they were. The assertion that art and popularity are mutually exclusive would become a commonplace in the careers of Meredith and Hardy. The man who earned a living as a publisher's reader would thank God that he had never written a word to please the public. In the 1870s the young Dorsetshire architect who was forced to choose between drafting buildings and writing novels thought that the latter, not the former, was a trivial "trade" that would imprison him in the superficiality of manners and the futility of social climbing. Neither Meredith nor Hardy was a very acute judge of his artistic self or his reading public, but their often similar confusions, their perpetual misjudgments, the irregularities of their art, and the multiple ironies of their relations with their contemporary audience all stem from the dilemma of the late Victorian novelist, whose traditional aims found no responsive reception from a community of common readers.

The genre which in 1850 had been a form capable of breaking down social, intellectual, and aesthetic distinctions served in the last three decades of the century as the basis for creating new ones. A constantly expanding reading public, the result of compulsory education acts, divided the merely literate popular audience from the more highly educated critical reader. The effect of such trends is well known. One audience demanded escapist fiction comparable to that of the 1830s; another required examples of accomplished art. Only drastic measures could accommodate the two groups. As Hardy said of one of his last novels, it had to be "finished, mutilated, and restored"—mutilated for family magazines, restored for volume publication[2]—if it was to conform to two sets of standards. Both Trollope's *The Way We Live Now* (1874–75) and Gissing's *New Grub Street* (1891) testify to the divorce between art and morality that occurs when novels become nothing more than commodities offered for sale; as the serious novelist is alienated from the marketplace, "literary charlatans" like Lady Carbury practice a trade that knows too well the difference between scruples and success. Simultaneously, as the popular readership widened, the meaning of the word *moral* became narrower and more limiting. By the 1880s the definition which threatened and finally undermined Thackeray's work had become generally accepted. The morality of any given novel depended simply on how its author treated sexuality, and a conventionally "moral" novel was one in which the fact of sex did not appear. In the 1850s the term had been a comprehensive expression of all one's dealings with other people, but a concept which had justified realism and candor now became the argument for a blind and sometimes prurient pose of ignorance. Though Hardy could defiantly label Tess a "pure woman" and get away with the claim (the novel, indeed, was one of his most popular), from the 1860s through the 1880s such daring was risky as well as unusual. No less significant was the emergence of novelists even more obsessively concerned with social status than Dickens or Scott had ever been. The grandson of a tailor and the son of a charity child would have little to do with a popular form that could not raise them above the common herd. If the writing of novels could not attain that goal, then they would turn to poetry, the time-honored genre of the socially and aesthetically elite.

More than any other author, Meredith tried to make fiction a form of exclusion, and *The Egoist* (1879), more than any of his other novels, serves that end. In its prelude the narrator engages in a dialogue, not with his reader, but with the Comic Spirit. In the process he dismisses all the grounds on which the mid-century novel had rested. Realism is an attribute of watchmakers, and persuasion is irrelevant: "We have no dust of the struggling outer world . . . to make the correctness of the representation convincing." In the long run the narrative itself moderates these claims. Clara Middleton must stoop to the dust and mire of the railway station if she is to conquer her own fears and the dominance of Willoughby's egoism. Still, Meredith's break with the common reader could not be more complete. The perverse and almost impenetrable concatenation of his metaphors, elliptical allusions, and high-flown theorizing stand in his preface as a No Trespassing sign to warn off any but the most intrepid reader. Speaking of the Book of Earth, the narrator notes that the sight of its complexity and length "staggers the heart, ages the very heart of us at a view."[3] His preface has nearly the same effect. Thirty years before, Dickens had won the astonished admiration of an illiterate charwoman who had listened as her landlord read each monthly number of *Dombey and Son*. To such an audience Meredith's masterpiece would have offered fewer delights. Serious fiction had become inaccessible to the common reader, and Meredith dearly relished his role in that development.

Although the divorce between artist and audience was a gradual process—Meredith's crotchety and sniping complaints were only the most vocal note in an ongoing argument—fiction written as early as the 1860s moved further than one might expect from mid-century conceptions of form and audience. The sensation novel which captured the imagination of the popular audience did not ignore morality, but in a curious fashion it returned to the kind of moral disengagement that had characterized Scott's fiction. In a novel like Wilkie Collins's *Woman in White* (1859–60), morality is a set of basic and unquestioned assumptions (one should not, for instance, try to do away with one's wife) and those assumptions never interfere with other, more engaging sources of narrative interest. The signposts are clear and simple. The woman, after all, is dressed in white, and the reader can enjoy, without any dangerous or distracting uncertainties, the charming ambiguities of the villain, Count Fosco. Collins's apparently complex, interconnected narratives are imaginatively unchallenging; the reader knows that without much effort on his part the mystery will inevitably reveal itself. As Hardy said of *Desperate Remedies* (1871), his first published novel and his own attempt to appeal to popular tastes, the sensation novel involves "mystery, entanglement, surprise, and moral obliquity." It is oblique in two senses: while being at times titillatingly suspect in its treatment of crimes and criminals, its concerns with moral life are indirect at best.

Yet it is no small tribute to the vitality of the mid-century tradition that it would appear in a new but recognizable form in twentieth-century fiction. In novels like *The Good Soldier* or *Absalom, Absalom!*, it serves, not as the source of affirmation, but as the vehicle of ironic implications or as the measure of defeated intentions. Conrad's turn-of-the-century fiction actually draws on the earlier tradition of narrative as it recapitulates its decline. In the tale "Youth," Marlow, like the earlier personas Pendennis and the "George Eliot" of the *Scenes*, assumes that the telling of his tale strengthens "the strong bond of the sea" which identifies him with his listeners. He is, in this case, correct. His listeners nod assent as he finishes his tale. Furthermore, the temporal distance which seems to separate him from the younger self he describes merely underscores the unchanging "romance of illusions" which both he and his audience find endlessly attractive. In *Heart of Darkness* and *Lord Jim*, Marlow again mediates between character and "reader," between Kurtz and those who hear his story, between Jim and the indolent cigar-smoking audience on the verandah. As Conrad's citation of Novalis reveals, forging connections between speaker and listener is as profoundly his goal as it has been Dickens's or George Eliot's. But, as Carlyle says of the "ironic man," "division, not union is . . . his procedure." In *Heart of Darkness* the distinctions between the speaker and his subject, between the subject and the audience, are both wider and less comfortingly distant than they might be. "You can't understand," Marlow tells his auditors, but the real fear is that they can understand, that they can recognize in themselves the hollowness at the heart which Kurtz exemplifies. The lie that Marlow tells the Intended is as necessary as any fiction that Little Dorrit maintains, but it embodies, even in the sanctity of its civilizing virtue, "a taint of death, a flavor of mortality." Similarly, Tuan Jim is "one of us," and his relation to those who witness or recall his failures is of quite personal relevance; to Marlow he seems, in fact, "my very young brother." Again Jim's common humanity is the source of fear and incomprehensibility. "We ought to know," Marlow protests, but "who knows?" Those convinced of the analogies which identify them with Jim may, like Brierly, decide that such potential for dishonor is reason enough to put an end to life.

Like Latimer in "The Lifted Veil," Marlow is another Ancient Mariner, burdened with someone else's crime, a crime that is somehow hauntingly his own. Unlike Latimer, however, he never finds the Wedding Guest who can respond adequately to his need for confession. Marlow's compulsive sense of identification with Jim not only blurs moral judgments, it also apparently bores his listeners. Only one of the men on the verandah is interested in Jim, and he is clearly a skeptic when it comes to the question of Jim's greatness. Like George Warrington appealing to his crass son in *The Virginians*, Marlow mistrusts the minds he addresses. Faulkner would take the process one step further. In *Absalom, Absalom!* he turns the relations that had constituted the moral life of the Victorian novel into a nightmare vision of obsession. As they sit in their room at Cambridge, Quentin Compson and his listener Shreve become the characters they resurrect, Henry Sutpen and Charles Bon. The once creative bonds of analogous experience have become a measure of neurosis and inexpiable guilt. Extreme as this development may seem, the frightening potential of Victorian conceptions of narration had been evident, if not pervasive, even at mid-century, as Thackeray's depiction of reading under the Sword of Damocles suggests, Lockwood's willingness to draw a child's arm across a jagged glass testifies to the disturbing power of identifications. The realm of Wuthering Heights, both as locale and as novel, exerts a spell that its mediating narrator cannot resist. Lockwood, Emily Brontë seems to say, is for better or worse, like Becky Sharp or Merdle or Hetty Sorrel, "one of us."

Long before modern novelists like Conrad or Faulkner exploited the ironic capacities of the mid-century tradition, the aesthetic on which it was originally based had become so outmoded and commonplace as to seem genuinely nonexistent. Yet its influence survived. By 1884 when James wrote his famous essay "The Art of Fiction," his immediate predecessors were all safely in their graves, and he was free to offer a condescending evaluation of their work: "There was a comfortable, good-humoured feeling abroad that a novel is a novel, as a pudding is a pudding, and that our only business with it could be to swallow it." Their work was *naïf*; it had "no air of having a theory, a conviction, a consciousness of itself behind it—of being the expression of an artistic faith, the result of choice and comparison."[4] Just before writing this essay, James had finished "The Author of Beltraffio." There Mark Ambient—a far cry from the morally responsible and domestically content authors like Copperfield and Pendennis—defines the "perfection" of form as the only true "holy grail." Yet in both essay and tale, the Victorian conception of fiction exerted its appeal as well as its influence. James's emphasis on the need for conviction and artistic faith, the attenuated strain of Evangelical earnestness in his critical vocabulary, is itself a vestige of mid-century attitudes toward art. Later, in *The Ambassadors*, his own comprehensive as well as moving treatment of the relationship between morality and art, he would again pay tribute to such conventional considerations. Life's inescapable moral claims, the lesson of the mid-century novel, is the lesson that Strether learns when he stands by the river and watches Chad and Madame de Vionnet drift into the Lambinet painting that his imagination has composed from the rural French landscape. Just as George Eliot's Dutch

genre painting in *Adam Bede* yields to emotion that bears down with
the weight of sensation, Strether's complacent sense of aesthetic distance disappears in a cold chill of recognition. As he ultimately admits,
art and morality interpenetrate in every picture that the mind creates.

Even Hardy, near the self-imposed end of his career as a novelist,
would bear witness to the force of the mid-century tradition. In some
respects his attitudes and those of his predecessors seem irreconcilable. His comments on *Tess of the d'Urbervilles* bespeak the increasingly limited aims that the late Victorian novelist was willing to propose in his public statements about his art: "A novel is an impression,

"Gaunt House," chapter 47, *Vanity Fair*

not an argument," and the novelist is a "mere tale-teller who writes down how the things of the world strike him, without any ulterior intentions whatever." The novelist at mid-century had had ulterior motives, and his novels were, if not arguments, then at least friendly interchanges with a reader whose imagination he attempted to engage in the life of a fictive world. At mid-century, narrative had been a way of asking that the reader assent to the substantiality and accuracy of the novelist's "impressions." Hardy is ready to surrender and deny those earlier ideals, but he is not content with the insecure position in which his solipsistic definitions of the novel have placed him. Speaking of "the responsive spirit in which *Tess of the d'Urbervilles* has been received," he expresses his surprise at the success of the novel, surprise greater even than that which Thackeray recorded in his preface to *Pendennis*. Echoing a famous phrase from *Vanity Fair*, Hardy betrays his own attraction to the novelist's mediating, social role: "For this responsiveness I cannot refrain from expressing my thanks; and my regret is that, in a world where one so often hungers in vain for friendship, where even not to be wilfully misunderstood is felt as a kindness, I shall never meet in person these appreciative readers, male and female, and shake them by the hand."[5] Hardy's quaintly nostalgic tone is appropriate. It was with the hope for precisely such a gratifying and sustaining responsiveness that Dickens and Thackeray and George Eliot began their work fifty years before. The difference between his narrative techniques and theirs is ultimately the difference between a defensive disdain for the art of the novel and a quietly confident belief in its potential. For them the "sense of an audience"[6] was an assumption that justified lavish outlays of creative energy; for Hardy it was both a frustration and an inevitable limitation. Although these Victorian novelists knew quite well that they could not transmute print and paper into the warmth of a handshake, although the goal of uniting themselves and their readers and their characters remained in some instances as distant as the "other side of silence," an imaginative communion based on such narrative relations and transformations was the home they strove to establish in a world where even friendship might seem too much to ask.

Notes

Chapter I ◇ The Bonds of Reading

1. John Forster, *The Life of Charles Dickens*, ed. J. W. T. Ley (New York: Doubleday, Doran, 1928), p. 721. Hereafter cited in the text.

2. John Holloway treats this insistence on the reader's need to "open his eyes" as characteristically Victorian; see *The Victorian Sage: Studies in Argument* (London: Macmillan, 1953), pp. 9–10. For two considerations of Carlyle's relation to Victorian fiction, see George Levine, "*Sartor Resartus* and the Balance of Fiction," in *The Boundaries of Fiction: Carlyle, Macaulay, Newman* (Princeton: Princeton University Press, 1968), chap. 1; and Kathleen Tillotson, *Novels of the Eighteen-Forties* (Oxford: Clarendon, 1954), pp. 150–56.

3. For an interesting, though sometimes exaggerated account of the role of Evangelicalism in the development of early Victorian attitudes toward fiction and its influence on Dickens's career, see Samuel Pickering, Jr., *The Moral Tradition in English Fiction, 1785–1850* (Hanover: University Press of New England, 1976).

4. Thomas A. Noble contends that it is Tryan's "presence rather than his words" that comforts Janet, *George Eliot's "Scenes of Clerical Life"* (New Haven: Yale University Press, 1965), p. 78, but Tryan's ministering presence has no effect on her until he tells his story.

5. *An Autobiography*, ed. Frederick Page, Oxford Trollope, Crown Edition (London: Oxford University Press, 1950), p. 146, my emphasis.

6. Robert Lee Wolff, *Gains and Losses: Novels of Faith and Doubt in Victorian England* (New York and London: John Murray, 1977), p. 149.

7. J. Hillis Miller, *The Form of Victorian Fiction: Thackeray, Dickens, Trollope, George Eliot, Meredith, and Hardy* (Notre Dame: University of Notre Dame Press, 1968), p. 11.

8. For other perspectives on the significance of "The Lifted Veil," see Gillian Beer, "Myth and the Single Consciousness: *Middlemarch* and *The Lifted Veil*," in *This Particular Web: Essays on "Middlemarch*," ed. Ian Adam (Toronto: University of Toronto Press, 1975), pp. 91–115; Ruby V. Redinger, *George Eliot: The Emergent Self* (New York: Knopf, 1975), pp. 400–5; and Sandra M. Gilbert and Susan Gubar, *The Madwoman in the Attic: The Woman Writer and*

the Nineteenth-Century Literary Imagination (New Haven: Yale University Press, 1979), chap. 13.

9. "Chapman's Diary for 1851," in Gordon S. Haight, *George Eliot and John Chapman* (New Haven: Yale University Press, 1940), p. 179.

10. Anne Mozley, *Bentley's Quarterly Review* 1 (July 1859), rpt. in David Carroll, ed., *George Eliot: The Critical Heritage* (New York: Barnes and Noble, 1971), p. 88.

11. The sincerity of Thackeray's commitment to the moral responsibility of authorship is still a widely debated question, and it has reappeared recently in Jack P. Rawlins's *Thackeray's Novels: A Fiction That is True* (Berkeley: University of California Press, 1974) and in John Carey's *Thackeray: Prodigal Genius* (London: Faber and Faber, 1977). Gordon N. Ray first argued for the genuine sincerity of Thackeray's avowals in *"Vanity Fair:* One Version of the Novelist's Responsibility," *Essays by Divers Hands* 25(1950):87–101. Although Geoffrey Tillotson has disputed this case and clarified some of Thackeray's attitudes toward fiction in *Thackeray the Novelist* (Cambridge; Cambridge University Press, 1954), pp. 216–20, Ray's basic argument deserves acceptance.

12. The image of the clown appeared in additions to the manuscript of *Vanity Fair* only after Thackeray knew that Bradbury and Evans, the proprietors of *Punch*, were to be the novel's publishers. On its title page the serial is even identified as "Published at the Punch Office." Needless to say, *Dombey and Son*, also published at the same time by Bradbury and Evans, bears no such designation. It seems clear that *Vanity Fair* is another product of what Gordon N. Ray calls the "'Punch' connexion," *Thackeray: The Uses of Adversity* (New York: McGraw-Hill, 1955), chap. 13. Robert A. Colby has recently treated the thematic and iconographic connections between *Punch* and *Vanity Fair* in *Thackeray's Canvass of Humanity: An Author and His Public* (Columbus: Ohio State University Press, 1979), pp. 231–37. For a detailed account of the complicated publishing history of *Vanity Fair*, see Edgar F. Harden, *The Emergence of Thackeray's Serial Fiction* (Athens: University of Georgia Press, 1979), chaps. 2 and 3.

13. For an account of the mid-Victorian interest in history, see Carl Dawson, *Victorian Noon: English Literature in 1850* (Baltimore: Johns Hopkins University Press, 1979), pp. 230–32.

14. *Thackeray*, English Men of Letters (New York: Harper, n.d.), p. 198. Alexander Welsh discusses the Victorian "religion of the hearth" in *The City of Dickens* (Oxford: Clarendon, 1971), chap. 9.

15. The "Scrooge problem" has been concisely reviewed in Elliot L. Gilbert's essay, "The Ceremony of Innocence: Charles Dickens' *A Christmas Carol*," *PMLA* 90(1975):22–31. The most famous statement of disbelief is Edmund Wilson's "The Two Scrooges," in *The Wound and the Bow: Seven Stud-*

ies in Literature (New York: Oxford University Press, 1947), p. 64. Gilbert claims that Dickens's interests in the *Carol* are "metaphysical" rather than moral or psychological, but Harry Stone's treatment of the fairy-tale elements in the story offers additional proof that it is fundamentally a moral tale, *Dickens and the Invisible World: Fairy Tales, Fantasy, and Novel-Making* (Bloomington: Indiana University Press, 1979), pp. 119–26.

16. "Art and Belles Lettres," *Westminster Review* 65(1856):626.

17. The various roles of the narrator in *Vanity Fair* have been treated frequently: Ann Y. Wilkinson, "The Tomeavesian Way of Knowing the World: Technique and Meaning in *Vanity Fair*," *ELH* 32(1965):370–87; Juliet McMaster, *Thackeray: The Major Novels* (Toronto: University of Toronto Press, 1971), pp. 1–49; and Wolfgang Iser, *The Implied Reader: Patterns of Communication in Prose Fiction from Bunyan to Beckett* (Baltimore: Johns Hopkins University Press, 1974), pp. 104–6. My own approach differs from theirs in stressing the narrator's coherent development from one role to another. Peter K. Garrett offers yet another perspective on this aspect of *Vanity Fair* in *The Victorian Multiplot Novel: Studies in Dialogical Form* (New Haven: Yale University Press, 1980), pp. 104–27.

18. John A. Lester, "Thackeray's Narrative Technique," *PMLA* 69(1954): 392–409.

19. *Letters of Thomas Carlyle to John Stuart Mill, John Sterling and Robert Browning*, ed. Alexander Carlyle (New York: Frederick A. Stokes, 1923), p. 284.

Chapter II ◇ *Dombey and Son*

1. In one of the best treatments of the novel, Steven Marcus finds Dickens's attempts at affirmation "less impressive" and convincing than his depiction of the "unredeemable" world of Dombey, *Dickens: From Pickwick to Dombey* (New York: Basic Books, 1965), p. 338. F. R. Leavis notes, "The book is not a whole conceived in any unified or unifying imagination," *Dickens: The Novelist* (London: Chatto and Windus, 1970), p. 12. In an attempt to follow the implications of the social themes of the novel, John Lucas concludes in a tone of frustration that the happy ending involves a "plain faking of the issues," "Dickens and *Dombey and Son*: Past and Present Imperfect," in *Tradition and Tolerance in Nineteenth-Century Fiction*, ed. David Howard et al. (New York: Barnes and Noble, 1967), p. 131. For accounts of Dickens's original sketch of the novel see Forster's *Life*, bk. 6, chap. 2; and John Butt and Kathleen Tillotson, *Dickens at Work* (London: Methuen, 1957), chap. 5.

2. It is not my intention to examine Carlyle's influence on *Dombey and Son*; for this issue, see Michael Goldberg, *Carlyle and Dickens* (Athens: University

of Georgia Press, 1972); and William Oddie, *Dickens and Carlyle: The Question of Influence* (London: Centenary Press, 1972). Though it is not possible to prove that Dickens read *Sartor Resartus* before 1853 (Oddie, p. 2), he had certainly read much of Carlyle's work, and the many echoes of *Sartor* even in *Dombey* suggest the complicated nature of their relationship. Blimber and his school recall the descriptions of Teufelsdröckh's classical education. Perhaps even Cousin Feenix, the man who witnesses Edith's marriage by putting "his noble name into a wrong place, and énrols himself as having been born, that morning" (p. 427), has some witty relation to the World-Phoenix. Conversely, other echoes suggest that Dickens's response to Carlyle was not quite the passive acceptance that is usually noted. In Mrs. Skewton's lament over the departed past, one can hear a snickering parody of *Past and Present*: "We have no Faith left, positively. . . . We have no Faith in the dear old Barons, who were the most delightful creatures—or in the dear old Priests, who were the most warlike of men" (p. 375). Yet Dickens seems to have accepted more numerous and more varied qualities from Carlyle than has been realized. Both Oddie (p. 29) and Goldberg (p. 178) state that in questions of religion and belief, Dicken's owes no debt to Carlyle. Perhaps because they emphasize Dickens's acceptance of Carlyle's analysis of what is wrong with society, they find it difficult to perceive the affirmative concepts that the two men shared at least in the early parts of both their careers.

3. "The Number Plans," appendix B, Clarendon edition, p. 835. Hereafter cited in the text as "Plans."

4. Tillotson, *Novels of the Eighteen-Forties*, p. 172. See also A. E. Dyson, *The Inimitable Dickens: A Reading of the Novels* (London: Macmillan, 1970), p. 111.

5. G. B. Tennyson, *Sartor Called Resartus* (Princeton: Princeton University Press, 1965), p. 190.

6. Butt and Tillotson, *Dickens at Work*, p. 93; Horsman, introduction, Clarendon edition, p. xviii.

7. See Michael Steig, "*Dombey and Son* and the Railway Panic of 1845," *Dickensian* 67 (1971):145–48; and Humphry House, *The Dickens World*, 2d. ed. (London: Oxford, 1942), p. 139; Dombey is less "full" of this topical subject than either critic suggests. For a summary of various interpretations of the railroad, see Susan R. Horton, *Interpreting Interpreting: Interpreting Dickens's Dombey* (Baltimore: Johns Hopkins University Press, 1979), pp. 31–36.

8. This passage is often treated as an example of Dickens's incompetence or immaturity. See, for instance, George Gissing, *The Immortal Dickens* (London: Cecil Palmer, 1925), pp. 147–48; House, *The Dickens World*, pp. 192–93. In his introduction to the Penguin edition (Harmondsworth, 1970), how-

ever, Raymond Williams finds this passage a proof of "a new dimension of social consciousness" (p. 20).

9. See George Rosen, "Disease, Debility, and Death," in *The Victorian City*, ed. H. J. Dyos and Michael Wolff, 2 vols. (London and Boston: Routledge and Kegan Paul, 1973), 2:625–67. My work on *Dombey and Son* has been greatly aided by this fine anthology of essays.

10. "The Health of Towns," *Punch* 13 (July 1847):33.

11. Dickens certainly would have known and agreed with Douglas Jerrold's Q-editorials in *Punch*, one of the first of which actually quotes Sir Peter's comment on the "morbid humanity" of the poor, 1(1841):210. These attacks reappeared as a popular *Punch* subject again in 1845, and in April of 1847 there appeared another article on "Peter the Putter-Down," which was illustrated if not actually written by Thackeray, 12(1847):173. This unfortunate alderman would later infuriate Dickens by declaring in 1850 that Jacob's Island of *Oliver Twist* was a negligible fiction.

12. Although essays in the second volume of *The Victorian City*, by E. D. H. Johnson, G. Robert Stange, and George Levine all describe the reluctance with which Victorian artists and writers confronted the "modern" subject of the city, the fact of the city—if not detailed descriptions which record either its appeal or its wretchedness—is a touchstone of social vision throughout Victorian prose. See also Philip Collins, "Dickens and London," in *The Victorian City*, 2:537–57, for various analogues and perspectives on the sermon of chapter 47.

13. One medical inspector called the overcrowded conditions of the slums "a very baptism into infamy" (quoted in Rosen, "Disease, Debility, and Death," 2:613). Gertrude Himmelfarb discusses Mayhew's preface to the first volume of *London Labour and the London Poor* and Thackeray's 1850 *Punch* review of Mayhew's first sketches, published in the *Morning Chronicle*; she speculates on Thackeray's possible influence on Mayhew, but both texts so clearly recall chapter 47 of *Dombey* and the first chapter of *Past and Present* that they may have had a common source. See "The Culture of Poverty," in *The Victorian City*, 2:714–15.

14. Quoted by John W. Dodds, *The Age of Paradox* (New York: Rinehart, 1952), p. 364.

15. Marcus, *Dickens from Pickwick to Dombey*, p. 338.

16. See Alexander Welsh's illuminating treatment of Florence, *The City of Dickens*, pp. 180–95.

17. "*Dealings with the Firm of Dombey and Son*: Firmness *versus* Wetness," in *Dickens and the Twentieth Century*, ed. John Gross and Gabriel Pearson (Toronto: University of Toronto Press, 1962), p. 131.

18. Marcus, *Dickens from Pickwick to Dombey*, pp. 283–92.

Chapter III ◇ *Little Dorrit*

1. Trollope, *Autobiography*, appendix 1, pp. 370–71; for his 1867 speech, see Fielding's edition of Dickens's *Speeches*, p. 374. Dickens, "Curious Misprint in the Edinburgh Review," *Household Words* no. 386 (15 August 1857): 146. Dickens applies the same ironic description to the Barnacles and the Circumlocution Office in the preface to the 1857 edition (p. lix). Modern readers have adopted traditional and simplistic attitudes toward the question of truth or falsehood as it applies to the fiction of *Little Dorrit*. James R. Kincaid assumes that Dickens takes a negative attitude toward the "lying" implicit in any creative activity: "In this black world, the work of the creative imagination is likely to be seen simply as lying," *Dickens and the Rhetoric of Laughter* (Oxford: Clarendon Press, 1971), p. 198. As John Holloway sees it, the final chapters of the novel present "an end to surfaces for good and all," and the "life of surface and sham" is "set aside" for a "new and valid" life of reality, "Introduction," *Little Dorrit* (Harmondsworth: Penguin, 1967), pp. 26–29. Dickens's treatment of this question is, however, considerably more complex than such statements suggest.

2. John Holloway provides a helpful guide to Flora's use of literary sources in his notes to the Penguin edition of *Little Dorrit*.

3. "The Number Plans," appendix B, Clarendon edition, p. 827. Hereafter cited in the text as "Plans."

4. Trilling, "Introduction," *Little Dorrit*, Oxford Illustrated Dickens, p. xvi. Leavis, "Dickens and Blake: 'Little Dorrit,'" in *Dickens: The Novelist*, p. 226. See also Avrom Fleishman, "Master and Servant in *Little Dorrit*," in *Fiction and the Ways of Knowing* (Austin and London: University of Texas Press, 1978), pp. 69–70; and Edwin B. Barrett, "*Little Dorrit* and the Disease of Modern Life," *Nineteenth-Century Fiction* 25(1970):214.

5. Barbara Hardy uses this fairy tale as an example of the stories that Dickens's characters frequently create, *Tellers and Listeners: The Narrative Imagination* (London: Athlone Press, 1975), pp. 171–73. Hardy analyzes the psychological implications of the relationship between listener and teller that this story creates, although she concludes: "Little Dorrit comes very close to her creator but it would be a mistake to identify Dickens with any one of his many story-tellers" (p. 173).

6. Fitzjames Stephen called the plot "singularly cumbrous and confused," "The License of Modern Novelists," *Edinburgh Review* 215 (July 1857): 126. Jerome Meckier finds it "neither extremely clear nor overly convincing," "Dickens's *Little Dorrit*: Sundry Curious Variations on the Same Tune," *Dickens Studies* 3(1967):56. K. J. Fielding complains that it "contains far too many mysteries" and then attempts to ignore the fact that Dickens "fell down

on the plot," *Charles Dickens: A Critical Introduction* (London: Longmans, 1958), pp. 145, 148. In an article on the political implications of the novel, however, William Myers dissents from this conventional judgment, but to do so, he must isolate and dismiss its "deliberate mystery element," "The Radicalism of *Little Dorrit*," *Literature and Politics in the Nineteenth Century*, ed. John Lucas (London: Methuen, 1971), pp. 77–78.

7. Myers, "Radicalism of *Little Dorrit*," p. 77.

8. J. Hillis Miller, *Charles Dickens: The World of His Novels* (Cambridge: Harvard University Press, 1958), p. 234.

9. House, *Dickens World*, p. 27.

10. The "deconstructive" tendencies of such an observation have been explored by Alistair M. Duckworth, "*Little Dorrit* and the Question of Closure," *Nineteenth-Century Fiction* 33(1978):110–30; and Dianne F. Sadoff, "Storytelling and the Figure of the Father in *Little Dorrit*," *PMLA* 95(1980):234–45. Dickens stands, I think, one step short of this abyss.

Chapter IV ◇ *The Newcomes*

1. *Letters of Carlyle to Mill, Sterling and Browning*, p. 74.

2. McMaster, *Thackeray: The Major Novels*, p. 155. Robert A. Colby provides an illuminating comparison of Thackeray's treatment of this theme to its prominence in popular literature of the 1850s in *Thackeray's Canvass of Humanity*, chap. 11.

3. As Juliet McMaster notes, "Pen as narrator watches Clive going through the same agonies and perplexities . . . that he had himself suffered. . . . Yet he can only record Clive's progress, not assist it," *Thackeray: The Major Novels*, p. 167.

4. In the 1856 edition of *Barry Lyndon* in his *Miscellanies*, Thackeray deleted the editorial machinery that included Fitz-Boodle and his footnotes. Geoffrey Tillotson comments, "Why Thackeray expunged most of the authorial commentary from the second edition . . . I do not know," *Thackeray the Novelist*, p. 215. Robert L. Morris suggests that Thackeray "by the middle 1850's was no longer exercised over the public's insistence on a moral worked in or tacked onto a story," appendix A, *The Memoirs of Barry Lyndon, Esq.* (Lincoln: University of Nebraska Press, 1962), p. 336. When one considers the preponderance of moral commentary in Thackeray's later work, this solution seems unlikely. Perhaps he realized that the popularity of *Vanity Fair* and its successors, in which his moral concerns are made very clear, rendered unnecessary Fitz-Boodle's attempt to explain that *Barry Lyndon* is a "moral" novel.

5. Both Barbara Hardy and Juliet McMaster discuss this framework. Hardy claims that it "forces an awareness of the difference between fables and real

life" and "proffers the most uncomfortable reminder of all, that of the reader's preference for escape and comfort in fiction," *The Exposure of Luxury: Radical Themes in Thackeray* (Pittsburgh: University of Pittsburgh Press, 1972), p. 169. Juliet McMaster states that the "overture" and epilogue "set the whole novel in an ironic framework"; "the world of the Newcomes is *not* fable-land, any more than it is fairyland," *Thackeray: The Major Novels*, pp. 169–72. Peter K. Garrett offers a reading that mediates between these two poles in *The Victorian Multiplot Novel*, pp. 130–34.

6. George Saintsbury, *A Consideration of Thackeray* (London: Oxford, 1931), p. 212. Thackeray had adapted this technique from the earlier silver-fork fiction which he deplored. See his review of Disraeli's *Coningsby* (13 May 1844): "There is something *naïf* in this credulity on both sides: in these cheap Barmecide entertainments, to which author and reader are content to sit down," rpt. in *William Makepeace Thackeray: Contributions to the 'Morning Chronicle,'* ed. Gordon N. Ray (Urbana: University of Illinois Press, 1955), p. 40.

7. *Quarterly Review* 194 (September 1855): 377–78. Barbara Hardy makes a similar observation about a specific aspect of *Vanity Fair* when she explains "the realistic effects of the self-conscious reference": "Thackeray insists on the illusion, the art, the performance, the drama, the novel, but in such a way . . . that brings the novel very close indeed to life," *The Exposure of Luxury*, p. 58.

Chapter V ◇ *Henry Esmond* and *The Virginians*

1. *Examiner* (22 July 1848); rpt. in *Thackeray: The Critical Heritage*, ed. Geoffrey Tillotson and Donald Hawes (London: Routledge and Kegan Paul, 1968), p. 54.

2. Whitwell Elwin, *Some Eighteenth-Century Men of Letters* (London: John Murray, 1902), 1 : 156–57. Thackeray discussed this "American continuation" as early as 1852. See a letter quoted by Gordon N. Ray, *Thackeray: The Age of Wisdom* (New York: McGraw-Hill, 1958), p. 193.

3. In his analysis of *The Virginians*, J. A. Sutherland suggests three reasons for the novel's breakdown: "(1) structural diffusion and confusion, (2) undue deference to American sensibilities and (3) moral insipidity," *Thackeray at Work* (London: Athlone Press, 1974), p. 90. The last of these reasons, to which he gives only cursory attention, is an important aspect of my contention that Thackeray has lost his faith in the moral value of his work. John Carey also treats this problem in *Thackeray: Prodigal Genius* (chap. 7), but he locates the "disastrous decency" (p. 150) which undermined Thackeray's work much too early in his career.

4. This reading of the thematic interests in *The Virginians* is consistent

with Barbara Hardy's discussion of his approach to social criticism in her study, *The Exposure of Luxury*. Although she does not discuss this particular novel in these terms, the material offered in her introduction (pp. 11–21) is applicable here. Robert A. Colby treats the relation between international and domestic rebellions in *Thackeray's Canvass of Humanity* (pp. 402–5, 414–17).

5. Sutherland, *Thackeray at Work*, pp. 66–68.

6. For Scott's response to Satchells, see J. G. Lockhart, *Memoirs of Sir Walter Scott*, 10 vols. (Edinburgh: A. and C. Black, 1869), 1:88–90. For the plan which preceded *The Fortunes of Nigel*, see ibid., 6:407–8. In 1856 Thackeray recorded reading Lockhart's work on Scott "all day," and his tone suggests that he might have read it when it was originally published in 1837 and 1839 (*Letters*, 3:634).

7. For treatments of the sexual complications of these relationships, see John Hagan, "'Bankruptcy of His Heart': The Unfulfilled Life of Henry Esmond," *Nineteenth-Century Fiction* 27(1972):293–316; and Sylvia Manning, "Incest and the Structure of *Henry Esmond*," *Nineteenth-Century Fiction* 34(1979):194–213.

8. McMaster, *Thackeray: The Major Novels*, p. 124.

9. Tillotson, *Novels of the Eighteen-Forties*, p. 54.

10. Edgar F. Harden offers an interesting example of the subtlety with which Thackeray handled this problem in *The Newcomes*; after cancelling his original attack on the "squeamish reader," he added a passage which makes the same point about moral failings without alienating the reader. See *The Emergence of Thackeray's Serial Fiction*, pp. 91–95.

11. Lockhart, *Memoirs of Sir Walter Scott*, 9:9–10.

Chapter VI ◇ *Scenes of Clerical Life*

1. "A New Novelist," unsigned review, *Saturday Review* 5 (29 May 1858): 566. Thomas A. Noble's *George Eliot's "Scenes of Clerical Life"* opens with a comprehensive estimate of the unconventional aspects of these tales. He cites George Eliot's use of "perfectly ordinary people and scenes," her interest in the "conflict of moral qualities," and her "sympathetic presentation of characters . . . who if admitted at all into other books would have been comic figures" (p. 25). Conversely, Sybil Oldfield and Derek Oldfield point to the conventionality of the *Scenes*, though they are too ready to suggest that every contemporary convention that appears in these tales is an "inorganic element." See "'Scenes of Clerical Life': The Diagram and the Picture," in *Critical Essays on George Eliot*, ed. Barbara Hardy (New York: Barnes and Noble, 1970), p. 14.

2. David Masson, *British Novelists and Their Styles* (Cambridge and London: Macmillan, 1859), p. 220.

3. "Belles Lettres," *Westminster Review* 65(1856):301.

4. Ed. Herbert Rosengarten and Margaret Smith, Clarendon Edition (Oxford: Clarendon, 1979), p. 7.

5. The existence of such a "community of values" between narrator and reader is a point of contention between J. Hillis Miller and Karl Kroeber. Kroeber tries to refute Miller's argument for such a community of values as it is set forth in *The Form of Victorian Fiction*. He states specifically that George Eliot's fiction depends on the "subversion of an original illusion of community between author and reader," *Styles in Fictional Structure* (Princeton: Princeton University Press, 1971), p. 50. Kroeber, however, ignores the fact that George Eliot often reacts against the mock-reader's false attitudes in order to establish a new set of values that both she and the reader can share.

6. *The Brontës: Their Lives, Friendships and Correspondence*, ed. Thomas J. Wise and J. Alexander Symington (Oxford: Shakespeare Head, 1933), 3:68.

7. Lockhart, *Memoirs of Sir Walter Scott*, 4:403.

8. Barbara Hardy calls this technique the "voice of personal knowledge and recollection" and notes that "the story is told as the thing remembered, not the thing invented," *The Novels of George Eliot* (London: Athlone, 1959), pp. 156–57. Henry Auster credits the "use of the reminiscing narrator" with George Eliot's ability to combine attitudes of "detachment" and "involvement," *Local Habitations: Regionalism in the Early Novels of George Eliot* (Cambridge: Harvard University Press, 1970), p. 91.

9. Elizabeth Gaskell, *Cranford*, Knutsford Edition (London: John Murray, 1920), 2:6.

10. See David Lodge's introduction to the *Scenes* (Harmondsworth: Penguin, 1973), pp. 7–32, for an excellent discussion of the way "orthodox religion is allowed to serve as a metaphorical vehicle for humanistic values without itself being called radically into question" (p. 8). The use of clerical characters as "doubles" for the narrator confirms this point.

11. *Saturday Review* 5 (29 May 1858): 566.

12. Unsigned review, *Atlantic Monthly* 1 (May 1858): 892. See Gordon S. Haight's account of the sources of the *Scenes* in *George Eliot: A Biography* (New York: Oxford, 1968), p. 221.

13. "*Adam Bede*," unsigned review, *Saturday Review* 7 (26 February 1859): 250. *Mary Barton*, Knutsford Edition, 1: 24, 196.

Chapter VII ◇ *Adam Bede*

1. Masson, *British Novelists and Their Styles*, pp. 305, 260.

2. The relation between Wordsworth's poetry and *Adam Bede* has been canvassed on numerous occasions; for example, see U. C. Knoepflmacher, *George Eliot's Early Novels: The Limits of Realism* (Berkeley: University of California Press, 1968), chap. 4; and Jay Clayton, "Visionary Power and Narrative Form: Wordsworth and *Adam Bede*," *ELH* 46(1979):645–72. My approach differs from theirs in its focus on questions of narrative technique.

3. See Mary Jacobus, *Tradition and Experiment in Wordsworth's Lyrical Ballads (1798)* (Oxford: Clarendon, 1976), pp. 241–43.

4. Quoted by Lockhart, *Memoirs of Sir Walter Scott*, 8:323; 4:307–8.

5. Hugh Witemeyer's treatment of *Adam Bede* in *George Eliot and the Visual Arts* (New Haven: Yale University Press, 1979) proves that she had visual as well as literary models for her "scenic" rendering of action in this novel. He notes specifically, "The convention of the Gilpinesque tourist-guide may help to account for the anonymous observer who opens so many of George Eliot's stories" (p. 130).

6. Dorothy Van Ghent, "On *Adam Bede*," in *The English Novel* (New York: Rinehart, 1953), pp. 173–75; and Ian Gregor, "The Two Worlds of 'Adam Bede,'" in *The Moral and the Story* (London: Faber and Faber, 1962), p. 17. Both Van Ghent and Gregor suggest that this leisurely pace sets up a distinction between the reader's sense of his own "modern" experience and a simpler, rural world; I would reply that this distinction is created so that it may be effectively invalidated.

7. George Henry Lewes uses strikingly similar rhetorical ploys in a passage of his contemporaneous essay "Realism in Art: Recent German Fiction," *Westminster Review* 70(1858):493. This fact would support W. J. Harvey's contention that in chapter 17 of *Adam Bede* "we have crossed, probably without realizing it, the vague boundary between the fictional microcosm of the characters and the macrocosm of George Eliot and the real world," *The Art of George Eliot* (London: Chatto and Windus, 1961), p. 71.

8. Hardy, *The Novels of George Eliot*, pp. 177–79.

9. Dickens with R. H. Horne, "Cain in the Fields" (10 May 1851), in *Charles Dickens's Uncollected Writings from 'Household Words,' 1850–1859*, ed. Harry Stone (Bloomington: Indiana University Press, 1968), 1:280–81.

10. For treatments of the flaw in George Eliot's conception of the novel, see Gregor, "Two Worlds," pp. 13–15; Miller, *The Form of Victorian Fiction*, p. 80; and U. C. Knoepflmacher, *George Eliot's Early Novels*, p. 117. Knoepflmacher also offers a good instance of the confusion Hetty sometimes causes. Although he realizes that Hetty has a central role in the novel—like Martha Ray in "The

Thorn," she serves an "exemplary" function in the moral growth of both Arthur and Adam—he claims that George Eliot's work is undercut by her "disproportionate castigation" of Hetty as well as her "pretended pity" for her; see *Early Novels*, pp. 95, 117, 119. Gregor notes that, in turning from Hayslope to Stonyshire, George Eliot turns from "visual contemplation to imaginative participation," but he later claims that *Adam Bede* consistently demands a "contemplative response" (pp. 19, 31). W. J. Harvey reaches the same conclusion: "The fictional microcosm . . . is a world surely designed for our contemplation, not for our imaginative participation," *The Art of George Eliot*, p. 79. The case of Hetty Sorrel would suggest otherwise.

Conclusion

1. Gregor, "Two Worlds," pp. 30–32.

2. Florence Emily Hardy, *The Later Years of Thomas Hardy, 1892–1928* (New York: Macmillan, 1930), pt. 1, chap. 3.

3. Sir Lawrence Jones spoke of this preface as one of the "dishes too tough for the Common Reader," and he claimed that he had planned as an undergraduate at Oxford to translate the novel into English (quoted by Lionel Stevenson, introduction, *The Egoist* [Boston: Houghton Mifflin, 1958], p. v). Similarly, James noted that his copy of *Middlemarch* contained "a dozen passages marked 'obscure'" because of the "echo of Messrs. Darwin and Huxley," "*Middlemarch*," *The Galaxy* (March 1873), rpt. in *The Future of the Novel*, ed. Leon Edel (New York: Vintage, 1956), p. 89.

4. "The Art of Fiction," *Partial Portraits* (London: Macmillan, 1888), p. 376.

5. "Preface to the Fifth and Later Editions," 1892. Wayne C. Booth has recently suggested that we resuscitate the concept of the author as the reader's friend, in "'The Way I Loved George Eliot': Friendship with Books as a Neglected Critical Metaphor," *Kenyon Review*, n.s. 2(1980):4–27. His argument has a distinctly Victorian ring to it, particularly when he states that we should concentrate our ethical criticism on the "qualities of experience sought or achieved by authors and readers *during the time* of reading or listening" (p. 5).

6. Virginia Woolf uses this phrase to characterize Victorian fiction; she speculates that the "sense of an audience" is linked to a novelist's excitement about and engagement in character; see *The Letters of Virginia Woolf*, ed. Nigel Nicolson and Joanne Trautmann (New York: Harcourt Brace Jovanovich, 1979), 5:334–35.

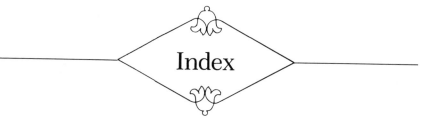

Index